PIERRE-JOSEPH PROUDHON

STUDIES IN THE LIBERTARIAN
AND UTOPIAN TRADITION

Pierre - Joseph
PROUDHON

His Life and Work

GEORGE WOODCOCK

SCHOCKEN BOOKS • NEW YORK

First published 1956
First SCHOCKEN PAPERBACK edition 1972
Copyright © 1972 by Schocken Books Inc.
Library of Congress Catalog Card No. 72-80045
Manufactured in the United States of America

CONTENTS

	ACKNOWLEDGEMENTS	ix
Part I.	THE HILLS OF THE JURA	1
II.	THE CRITIC OF PROPERTY	36
III.	THE MAN OF AFFAIRS	71
IV.	THE VOICE OF THE PEOPLE	115
V.	THE PRISONER	150
VI.	THE PALADIN OF JUSTICE	181
VII.	THE EXILE	219
VIII.	THE STRICKEN YEARS	245
IX.	EPILOGUE	270
	BIBLIOGRAPHY	281
	BIBLIOGRAPHICAL SUPPLEMENT TO THE 1972 EDITION	287
	INDEX	289

Pierre-Joseph Proudhon and his Children
by Gustave Courbet
Painting in the Petit Palais, Paris

PIERRE-JOSEPH PROUDHON

ACKNOWLEDGEMENTS

The completion of this book would have been immeasurably more difficult had it not been for the encouragement and financial assistance given me by the John Simon Guggenheim Foundation of New York, who granted me a Fellowship in 1951 for the purpose of studying Proudhon and his times. I am also greatly indebted to Mlle Suzanne Henneguy and Mme E. Fauré-Fremiet, the granddaughters of Proudhon, for allowing me to inspect Proudhon's manuscript diaries and other documents in their possession and for the time and patience they devoted to answering my queries. Among the French students of Proudhon and of the movements influenced by him, M. l'Abbé Pierre Haubtmann, M. Alexandre Marc and M. André Prudhommeaux were particularly generous with their advice, while Mr Arthur Lehning drew my attention to material on Proudhon in the collections of the International Institute for Social History. Finally, throughout the preparation of this book my wife rendered invaluable assistance in research, in typing and, above all, in helpful criticism.

Vancouver, 1955.   G. W.

ILLUSTRATIONS

PIERRE-JOSEPH PROUDHON AND HIS CHILDREN BY
GUSTAVE COURBET. PAINTING IN THE PETIT PALAIS,
PARIS   *Frontispiece*

PORTRAIT OF PIERRE-JOSEPH PROUDHON BY GUSTAVE
COURBET. DRAWING, MUSÉE DE MONTPELLIER   *page* 96

Part One

THE HILLS OF THE JURA

I

THE old city of Besançon, whose streets of grey stone houses have changed little since the early days of the last century, lies snugly held within a large U-shaped bend of the River Doubs. Over the bridge at the base of the U is the seventeenth-century suburb of Battant. It has always been a quarter of working people. Now its grimy, scaling houses are inhabited mostly by workers in the watch and artificial silk factories, but in the early nineteenth century it was peopled, according to the local historian Lucien Febvre, 'by vine-growers, workmen and industrious, honest and caustic petty landowners.' In this half-rural faubourg, at 37 Rue du Petit Battant, Pierre-Joseph Proudhon was born on the 15th February, 1809.

His parents, who had married early in the preceding year, were both of Franc-Comtois peasant stock. Claude-François Proudhon came from the mountain village of Chasnans, close to the Swiss frontier, and his wife, Catherine Simonin, from Cordiron, a hamlet on the Ognon, whose valley runs parallel with that of the Doubs. Thus, in after years, Pierre-Joseph was able to boast of his 'rustic blood'; 'I am pure Jurassic limestone,' he declared.

The Proudhons, in fact, were peasants gradually becoming absorbed into the urban middle class. Already in this assimilative process, the family had divided into two branches, 'right' and 'left.' The leading Proudhon of the respectable 'right' was François-Victor, Professor of Law at Dijon, and another of the same line, Jean-Baptiste, served after the fall of Robespierre as a member of the Directory for the Doubs. The 'left' branch remained for the most part peasants, artisans and small traders, with a tendency to rebellion and obstinacy, and François-Victor once remarked of them: 'There was a touch of bad blood among the Proudhons and it has passed to that side.' It was a judgment made without ill will and, as Pierre-Joseph later remarked, 'out of pure impatience,' nor was it resented by the 'left' Proudhons, in whose everlasting litigation their distinguished cousin 'never refused service or advice.'

Most prominent among the 'left' Proudhons was Melchior, a cousin of Pierre-Joseph, 'remarkable . . . for the great firmness of his character', who abandoned holy orders in 1789 to become a leader of the Revolution in Besançon. He presided over the local Jacobin Club, was imprisoned after the Terror, and figured as a leading Freemason at a time when that movement was still equated in the popular mind with revolutionary and secularist ideas.

Pierre-Joseph often boasted of the courage, pride and rebelliousness of his father's family, but it was in his maternal ancestors that he took the greater pride. His grandfather, Jean-Claude Simonin, who bore the nickname of 'Tournesi' for his service during the Hanoverian war in the regiment of Tournay, was celebrated among his neighbours 'for his audacity in resisting the pretensions of the landlords . . . and for his struggles with their foresters.' Tournesi mortally wounded one of these foresters in a quarrel over firewood; the victim expired repentant of his oppressions of the poor, recognising 'the instrument of celestial vengeance in the hand of Tournesi.' Tournesi himself died, no less abruptly, through a fall on an icy road during the winter of 1789, when he was going around preaching rebellion to his neighbours. 'I place him on a level with the men of Plutarch,' said Proudhon in a flight of romantic zeal.

A distant cousin of Pierre-Joseph assured Gustave Courbet that the Proudhons laboured under a papal curse that made all their affairs end in failure; whenever this old man was in Besançon,

he would search through the city archives for a clue to the supposed malediction. The curse doubtless existed only in his
eccentric imagination, but it is true that the 'left' Proudhons were
characterised by an unusual lack of practical success. Claude-
François, Pierre-Joseph's father, was typical, for, though he was
extremely hard-working and conscientious, he remained poor
until his death.

His amiable ineffectualness was partly balanced by his wife's
strength of character. To her son she was 'a proud peasant . . .
free, busy and uncrushed by life', and Charles Weiss, the Besançon
writer, described her as a woman of 'heroic' character. She had
been a cook, and brought into her household an industry which
helped to tide over the many crises of family life. Like her father,
she was a republican, and transmitted to her eldest son not only
this characteristic of the redoubtable Tournesi, but also much of
his appearance, for Pierre-Joseph grew to resemble the old soldier
both in his combative character and also in 'my brow, my eyes,
my free laughter and my broad chest.'

Pierre-Joseph's admiration for his mother was lifelong. 'To
her,' he said many years afterwards, 'I owe everything.' She seems
to have been the most important personal influence in his early
life, and his attachment to her had a great effect even on his
mature thought. He remembered her strength of character and
integrity of principle, her capacity for hard work and self-sacrifice.
He remembered also how these characteristics were combined
with a simple piety, with an absence of any desire to mingle in
the affairs of men, with an unquestioning peasant acceptance
of woman's position as manager of the household. It was according to whether they reflected these qualities that he was always
inclined to judge the women he met; few passed this severe
test.

At the time of his marriage, Claude-François Proudhon (he was
then twenty-nine and his wife five years older) was not entirely
propertyless, since he owned his house and clung to it in the
deepest adversity, but if he possessed any land it was not sufficient
for independence, since he was obliged to work as a brewer and a
cooper.

His five children—all boys—were born between 1809 and 1816.
The third and fourth died in early childhood, but the second,
Jean-Etienne, born in 1811, and the youngest, Charles, born in

1816, were both attached to Pierre-Joseph by bonds of close affection. The first impression he recounts of his childhood is a vividly recollected jealousy at the birth of Jean-Etienne, a feeling which soon passed so completely that later he was able to say, 'I never loved anyone so much as my brother.' Jean-Etienne, indeed, seems to have resembled him more, in the independence of his character, than the rather weak and dependent Charles.

The second event that Proudhon remembered clearly from his childhood was the siege of Besançon during the latter end of the Napoleonic wars; it was at this period that Claude-François decided to abandon his employment and set up on his own as a brewer and tavern-keeper. He conducted his business on principles whose very excellence robbed him of financial success. Forty years afterwards his son was to remark, 'since the day he ceased his brewing I have never drunk such good beer,' and Claude-François not only gave good quality, but also sold his beer almost at cost price. When his friends exhorted him to sell at the market price, he would reply mildly: 'Not at all. So much for my costs, so much for my work—that is my price!'

Pierre-Joseph, at eight years old, was intrigued by this problem of principles as, serving beer in the family tavern, he watched his father's methods working out to the detriment of the family. 'I realised perfectly the loyalty and the regularity in the paternal method, but I also saw to no less a degree the risk it involved. My conscience approved of the one; my feelings for our security pushed me towards the other. It was an enigma.' It was also the boy's first introduction to those contradictions inherent in social and economic relationships which played a most significant part in his later thought.

In 1817 occurred the great famine in Eastern France, due partly to crop failures and partly to the economic aftermath of the Napoleonic wars. The Proudhons, having no surplus to pay extravagant prices, went hungry like most of their neighbours, and Pierre-Joseph would go into the fields with his parents to gather ears of unripe rye so that they could make some substitute for bread. But it was not merely the general scarcity that afflicted the family, for by the following year Claude-François' experiment in tavern management on the basis of unadulterated morality had ended in bankruptcy. There remained one recourse for the penniless family. Catherine Proudhon's mother retained Tournesi's farm near Burgille, barely twenty kilometres from Besançon, and there they retired to live off the land.

At Burgille, Pierre-Joseph began his working life, herding the cows, doing chores in the house and around the holding. It was often an arduous life for a young child, yet in later times Proudhon looked back on those years of roaming the limestone crags and deep valleys of the Jura with a haunting nostalgia.

'What pleasure in those days to roll in the high grass, which I would have liked to browse like my cattle!' he rhapsodised fifty years later. 'To run with naked feet on the smooth paths and along the hedgerows! To sink into the fresh, deep soil as I hoed the green maize! And often, in the hot June mornings, I would throw off my clothes and bathe in the dew that drenched the turf. . . . I could hardly distinguish "me" from the "non-me." "Me"—it was all I could touch with my hand, all I could embrace in my vision, all that seemed good for some purpose; "non-me" was all that could hurt or resist me. The idea of my personality was confounded in my mind with that of my well-being, and I had no anxiety to search above for unextended and immaterial substance.'

Perhaps there is an idyllic exaggeration in these thoughts on a childhood seen through the prism of twenty years of urban frustrations. Yet the fact remains that Proudhon never ceased to gain pleasure from returning to the fields and mountains of the Jura, and there is a moving simplicity in the way he talks of the frugality in which his family lived:

'In my father's house, we breakfasted on maize porridge; at mid-day we ate potatoes; in the evening bacon soup, and that every day of the week. And despite the economists who praise the English diet, we, with that vegetarian feeding, were fat and strong. Do you know why? Because we breathed the air of our fields and lived from the produce of our own cultivation.'

2

During these years Proudhon had little education except what he learnt through this pagan contact with nature—an existence which, he confessed, led him to believe in nymphs and fairies until he was already a grown youth.

His mother was his earliest teacher, and he remembered learning to spell at the age of three when he was still in petticoats. But, though he learnt to read well, the only books he had encountered up to his tenth year were 'the Gospels and the Four Aymon Brothers,' and a few provincial almanacs, fitting companions for his naïve rustic beliefs.

But Catherine Proudhon was anxious that her eldest son should have an education that would give him something better than the insecurity of rural artisanship, and in 1820, when the family was once again in Besançon, she set about seeking his admittance into the city's college. Through the influence of his father's former employer, he was granted a bursary, and his parents were saved the fee of 120 francs a year which they certainly could not have afforded to pay; the mere fact that their son could not work for his keep was as much of a hardship as they could support.

Poverty, indeed, created many difficulties in Pierre-Joseph's school life. He had neither hat nor shoes; he would go bareheaded to school and take off his sabots before entering a room for fear their clatter might disturb his class-mates. 'I was habitually in need of the most necessary books; I made all my studies of Latin without a dictionary; after having translated whatever my memory provided, I left blank the words which were unknown to me, and filled in the spaces at the school door. I suffered a hundred punishments for having forgotten my books; it was because I had none.'

Above all, there were the humiliations which any youth, particularly one of 'most irritable self-esteem,' as Proudhon described himself, will inevitably encounter under such conditions. He learnt in a hard way the truth of the local proverb: 'It is not a crime to be poor, it is worse.' Most of the students were children of the local burgesses, and, smarting under the real and imagined slights of his wealthier comrades, Pierre-Joseph developed a brusque exterior which armoured his timidity and concealed the real warmth of his nature. He soon gained the repute of being surly and misanthropic, yet with some of his fellow students he formed friendships that were to be lifelong.

The initial transition from the freedom of the fields to the restrictions of a priestly education was not easy, and Pierre-Joseph experienced a sense of mental exile when the world of nature was replaced by that of 'narratives and themes.' But he had a natural linguistic sense and soon became an adept Latinist. Nor did he restrict his studies to school hours or to the set subjects. Besançon then possessed an excellent public library, and there Pierre-Joseph would read regularly. His zeal soon aroused the interest of Charles Weiss, the librarian, who had watched him reading assiduously from eight or ten books at a time, and one day remarked: 'But what do you want to do with so many books, my little friend?' Pierre-Joseph, whom experience had made defiantly independent, scowled at his questioner, and replied surlily: 'What has that to do with you?' Weiss accepted the rebuff in silence, but from that time he took a close interest in the boy's progress.

It was during his fourth year at school that Pierre-Joseph began to doubt the religious dogmas which his teachers attempted to inculcate. His upbringing had not been irreligious, for Claude-François and his wife had the simple faith, without supererogation, of the ordinary Comtois peasant, and Catherine regularly led her children in prayer. As for Pierre-Joseph, he experienced as a child an almost instinctive acceptance of God. 'Seized since childhood with that great idea,' he declared, 'I felt it overflowing within me and dominating all my faculties.'

Yet even as a boy he had little use for the overt acts of religious ritual. He talked of his first Communion as having been forced upon him, and regretted not having shown the courage of a friend who appeared at the altar rail holding boldly before him a copy of d'Holbach's heretical *Système de la Nature*. 'I have always had little taste for the works of the devout life,' he declared. 'To confess, take Communion, kiss the crucifix, attend the washing of feet—all that was displeasing to me.'

During the Legitimist Restoration there were great efforts at religious revivals in the French provinces; in 1825 a Mission was preached in Besançon, and the excessive manifestations of pietism had a wholly adverse effect on Pierre-Joseph, who was then in his sixteenth year.

Yet, while there is no doubt that such scenes had a profound influence on the thoughts of this resentful youth, it seems unlikely that this would have been so strong if his intellectual experiences had not acted as a fulcrum by which the revulsion against excessive piety could work on his deeper religious feelings.

One of the prizes he received at the end of his fourth year was Fénélon's *Démonstration de l'Existence de Dieu*, an essay in Christian apologetics which has long passed out of circulation. 'This book,' he said thirteen years later, 'seemed suddenly to open

7

my intelligence and illuminate my thought.' But the illumination was not of a kind Fénélon had intended; the theologian's 'tottering physics' sapped rather than strengthened Pierre-Joseph's original faith, and, in trying to refute the sceptics, revealed unorthodox beliefs which proved irresistibly fascinating. 'When I learnt . . . that there were atheists, men who denied God and explained everything by a combination of atoms, or, as said La Place, by matter and movement, I fell into an extraordinary reverie. I wanted to hear these men defend their own thesis, to read them, as I had read Fénélon.' But, though shaken, Proudhon's faith was by no means destroyed, and it would be some years before the ineffectual logic of the Archbishop of Cambrai bore its full fruit of scepticism.

Economic difficulties continued to pursue the Proudhon family throughout Pierre-Joseph's school years. At this period Claude-François appears to have been in possession of land in the neighbourhood of Besançon, in addition to the house in Battant. But the life of the petty proprietor in the early nineteenth century was often as precarious and as unrewarding as that of the landless labourer; Claude-François had still to supplement agriculture by coopering, and during his holidays Pierre-Joseph would go into the woods to cut branches for the hoops on his father's barrels. But the family's unremitting efforts were frustrated by a succession of sicknesses and other misfortunes. The crowning blow to their hopes was given by Claude-François' obstinate passion for litigation, and on the very day when Pierre-Joseph was about to receive the laurel wreath of graduation, his father was risking the family's whole future in a last desperate lawsuit. It was a day the son remembered with bitterness and humiliation.

'I went with a very sad heart to that solemnity where everyone else seemed to smile . . . while my family was at the court, awaiting the decision. I shall remember it always. The Rector asked if I would like to be presented by some relative or friend who would see me crowned by his hand. "I have nobody, Monsieur le Recteur," answered. "Very well," he said, "I will both crown and embrace you." Never have I felt more moved. But I found my family in consternation, my mother in tears; our case was lost. That evening we all supped on bread and water.'

Instead of going on to take the *baccalauréat* for which he was studying, Pierre-Joseph had to start work in order to help his parents in their misfortune. 'Now you should know your trade,' his father said to him. 'At eighteen I was earning my bread, and I had not enjoyed such a long apprenticeship.' Proudhon agreed and forthwith abandoned his studies. As one reads between the scanty lines of his reminiscences, it seems to have been a reluctant decision, for, despite the humiliations he had suffered at school, he appears to have been devoted to his life there, with its glimpses of a different, more spacious and more exciting world than the grinding care in his father's house.

3

Pierre-Joseph had seen too much of his father's difficulties to follow his example by becoming a farmer or a rural craftsman. He liked agriculture, and, had Claude-François been a substantial proprietor, he would have preferred to work on his land and succeed him in ownership. 'Perhaps if there had been a good rural credit institution I should have remained all my life a peasant and a conservative,' he remarked many years afterwards. But the little land they had was now lost in the foreclosure of mortgages, and Proudhon became instead an urban artisan and a rebel.

The trade he chose was printing; towards the end of 1827 he became an apprentice in the house of Bellevaux, in his own suburb of Battant, and at Easter the following year he transferred to the Besançon press operated by the family of his school friend, Antoine Gauthier. Here he was first a compositor and later a proof reader. He learnt quickly and took a pride in the complexity of his work. 'I still remember with delight,' he wrote, 'the great day when my composing stick became for me the symbol and instrument of my freedom.'

Besides, he enjoyed the comradely atmosphere of the workshop. At school he had been made to feel an intruder in a middle-class preserve; among the printers he found men of his own class, who had undergone or at least understood the hardships he himself had experienced, and who accepted him as an equal. From some of them, in whom their occupation had developed an intellectual curiosity uncommon among the artisan class, he gained mental stimulation, and, with the talent for friendship which he retained throughout his life, he was soon on the best of terms with most of his companions. A quarter of a century afterwards,

9

when he had long left his native city, he still claimed with pride that more than a dozen of his old workmates were among his friends; the rest were dead. One of the survivors, Milliet, who later became the editor of a Burgundian newspaper, remembered Proudhon as an 'excellent boy, always passing his hand through his hair, and going from time to time to the desks of the correctors to ask them about their occupation of gleaning errors and to raise questions concerning history or the events of the day.'

There were times, indeed, when Pierre-Joseph found the labour of the printing works more onerous than he could endure. 'The day was ten hours long,' he remembered. 'In that period I had sometimes to read in galley eight sheets of theological and devotional works, an excessive task to which I owe my shortsightedness. Poisoned by bad air, by metallic vapours, by human breath, my mind dulled by insipid reading, I found nothing more urgent than to go out of the town in order to shake off that infection. . . To find the purest air I would scale the high hills that border the valley of the Doubs, and I did not fail, whenever there was a storm, to treat myself to the spectacle. Crouching in a hole in the rocks, I loved to look into the face of flashing Jupiter, without either defying or fearing him. . . I told myself that the lightning and the thunder, the winds, the clouds and the rain, were all one with me.'

It is possible that these lines, written in 1858 at a time when Proudhon was most opposed to organised religion, tended to exaggerate his adolescent leaning towards pantheism. Nevertheless, his first years as a printer do appear to be marked by a double crisis, which he may well have seen symbolised and reflected in the conflict of the elements. For what seems to have been the only occasion in his life, he experienced intense romantic love, and at the same time he underwent a renewal of religious fervour that extended over two or three years, and ended in final disillusionment with Catholic orthodoxy.

Nothing is known about his first love beyond the references he himself makes, and these are inexplicit. 'I know today,' he was to write in his diary for 1846,[1] 'what at twenty made my spirit so full, so loving, so enraptured: what made women seem to me so

---

[1] Proudhon's diaries, which are in the possession of his descendants and are yet unpublished, begin in 1843, and their eleven volumes cover, with varying fullness, the whole period up to his death in 1865.

angelic, so divine; what in my dreams of love (wherein faith in God, in the immortal soul, in religious practice, mingled and combined with faith in infinite love) made my religion so precious to me. . . . I was Christian because I was in love, in love because I was Christian—I mean religious.'

That his love was incompletely fulfilled seems evident, for in *De la Justice* (1858) he insists that the experience actually prolonged his sexual innocence, while in *Les Contradictions Economiques*, written, like the diary note, in 1846, he rhapsodises: 'What a memory for a man's heart in after years, to have been in his green youth the guardian, the companion, the participant of the virginity of a young girl.' Finally, there are some reflections in a letter of 1841 which, though expressed generally, clearly have reference to his own past experience. 'I always console myself with the reflection . . . that the first loves which, in chaste souls, leave such deep traces, have often the merit of preparing a more solid happiness for a second attachment. In general, my dear friend, young lovers do not know how to be happy in their love and to get the most out of it; they adore each other in a silly way, but their spirits have more vivacity and fire than true warmth; often they do not know each other or realise each other's true value. In other words, the art and knowledge of reciprocation are lacking in their passion.'

These are the only glimpses we have of this youthful relationship. It is possible that a half-arrogant gaucherie, bred of childhood humiliation, may have been at least partly responsible for its failure to endure, or that Proudhon's poverty may have prevented him from making the offer of an early marriage which the girl perhaps expected. Perhaps also his mother's influence played some part, for he tells us that when she saw him 'troubled by the dreams of youth,' she counselled caution, saying: 'Never speak of love to a girl, even when you propose to marry her.' But these are conjectures, and we must leave this misty relationship, to tell what happened to the religious upsurge that accompanied it.

In Proudhon's day Besançon was an important religious centre in Eastern France; its seminaries were celebrated by Stendhal in *Le Rouge et le Noir*, and there existed among its priests a tradition of scholarship which made them copious producers of devotional literature. The printing presses were therefore devoted largely to religious treatises, and thus Proudhon was introduced to many theological subtleties of which, in the more direct faith of his youth, he had been unaware. 'Soon I believed myself called upon to become an apologist for Christianity, and I set myself to read the books of its enemies and its defenders. Need I tell you the result? In the ardent furnace of controversy, often exciting myself with fancies, and hearing only my private thoughts, I saw my cherished beliefs gradually fade away; I professed successively all the heresies condemned by the Church . . . until in the end, from sheer exhaustion, I halted at the last and most irrational of all; I became a socinian.'

Ironically, it was still the defenders of the faith who drove him away from it, and a work by the radical Abbé Lamennais (*De l'Indifférence en Matière de Religion*), loaned to him by a well-meaning cleric who did not suspect what furies of doubt he was feeding, brought the final collapse of Pierre-Joseph's religious fervour. 'As happens always in a desperate case, that apology was the last blow that overthrew the edifice already so strongly shaken by the controversies . . . which at that time formed my habitual reading.'

Nevertheless, despite this breach with orthodox Christianity, Proudhon's interest in religion did not disappear. He never under-estimated the part belief plays in human lives, its importance in the evolution of society, or the enduring value of many of its insights into moral truth, and it remained an important subject of his study and thought even in his most bitter periods of anti-Catholicism.

4

By 1829 social questions were beginning to rival religion for a place in Proudhon's thoughts, and the chance encounters of his trade served to strengthen these interests. He had been consciously a republican since 1827, but, though he never disputed the necessity of the July Revolution of 1830 (and even idealised the half-starving workers who fought that month at the Parisian barricades), he looked with bitter cynicism on those citizens of Besançon who before had been violently Royalist and now hurried to overthrow Charles X.

There is no evidence that he himself took any part in the July rising, and the outstanding radical influence that can be detected in his life at this time was social rather than political. During 1829 a customer of Gauthier was Charles Fourier, the founder of the idea of phalansterian communities, who brought into the printing house his masterpiece, *Le Nouveau Monde Industriel et Sociétaire*, one of the most curious combinations of insight and eccentricity, of sound social reasoning and chiliastic fantasy, ever to be published. Proudhon, who had now qualified as a corrector, supervised the printing of the book, and had several opportunities of talking with Fourier.

He was not impressed by the physical aspects of the man, for later he recollected: 'I knew Fourier. He had a medium-sized head, wide shoulders and chest, a nervous carriage, narrow brow, mediocre cranium; a certain air of enthusiasm which spread over his face gave him the look of an ecstatic dilettante. Nothing in him proclaimed the man of genius, any more than it did the charlatan.'

Fourier's ideas, however, made a great impression on a mind which up to now had been nourished on the arid diet of theological casuistry, and Proudhon encountered with astonished fascination the bold conceptions that rose like shining buildings out of the chaotic fantasy of Fourier's lonely and speculative mind. 'For six whole weeks,' he said, 'I was the captive of this bizarre genius.' It was not long before his natural common sense revolted against Fourier's absurdities, but the latter's serialist theory (to which I shall return in greater detail), and even some of his minor suggestions, had a lasting effect on Proudhon's philosophical and social beliefs.

A more immediately productive meeting in the same year was his encounter with Gustave Fallot, a young Huguenot scholar from Montbéliard. By this time Proudhon had already begun to attract the attention of the Bisontin intellectuals; he was emerging from the surly misanthropy of his schooldays and, though he was never a spontaneously effective talker and remained stiff and reserved on first acquaintance, his conversation was intelligent and illuminated by an enthusiastic longing for knowledge. Charles Weiss had remained interested in his progress since the day of their brusque encounter in the Besançon library; Pérennès, the secretary of the Besançon Academy, had been one of his teachers in 1827. His circle of acquaintances gradually widened, and it was about this time that he began lifelong friendships with

Jean-Pierre Pauthier, the sinologist, who was already preparing his book on Taoism, and with Olympe Micaud, a young Comtois poet.

Proudhon valued friendship and knew how to practise it. 'I spit on the gods and on men, and I believe only in study and friendship,' he declared, and there is a significant difference between the pleasure with which he always pronounced the word '*amitié*' and the disgust with which he often spoke of '*amour*'. Throughout his life the acquiring and keeping of friends remained one of his talents, but none of his other friendships was to have the same almost romantic intensity as his relationship with Fallot. Fallot's family, well-to-do industrialists, disapproved of his desire to follow an intellectual vocation, and he had therefore severed his connection with them and come to Besançon to study in frugal independence. In order to live, he prepared a Latin edition of the *Lives of the Saints*. It was printed by Gauthier, and one day Fallot was surprised to see some improvements in his Latin text which showed that a student of the language had been at work on the proofs. He asked the printer who had made the corrections. 'One of our workmen,' was the answer, and Fallot, astonished to hear of an artisan who was also an excellent Latinist, immediately made Proudhon's acquaintance.

Fallot was two years older than Proudhon, and his upbringing had been far more comfortable, but they had in common an extraordinary passion for languages and a voracity for miscellaneous erudition. Through his work as a printer Proudhon had already performed the considerable feat of teaching himself Hebrew and was becoming interested in etymology, and Fallot encouraged him in pursuing this branch of learning. But he also widened his friend's perspective in a more general way, since he was the first intellectual Proudhon had yet known whose mind was not bound by the prejudices of Catholic dogma. Fallot had that omnivorous curiosity which so often characterises French Protestants (Gide was an outstanding example in our own age). 'I would like to be an eye,' was his most self-revelatory phrase, but he might have added to the eye an ear to embrace his craze for words.

During the evenings they spent together in Fallot's gloomy, smoke-filled room, Proudhon began to emerge from his twilit world of theological controversies and to absorb the great

French literature of the seventeenth and eighteenth centuries, Montaigne, Rabelais, Rousseau, Voltaire, Diderot, and to understand the methods of philosophical thought. Fallot's restraining influence was eminently beneficial to the impetuous, idea-intoxicated Proudhon. 'Hold your mind long on the same subject,' urged the older man. 'Become permeated with a science, whatever it may be, or with a book or an author. . . .' It was excellent and timely advice, and there is no doubt that through Fallot's influence Proudhon began the difficult process of disciplining his thought that preceded his first appearance as an author. He was never a systematic thinker in the strict sense, but in all his works there is a strong organic pattern, which arose from the combination of his natural dynamism with the method and premeditation he acquired from Fallot.

The political disturbances of 1830 troubled the fortunes of the two friends, and temporarily parted them. Fallot went to Paris in search of employment, while Proudhon began to suffer from the prevalent depression in the printing trade. In September, 1830, he received his certificate book as a journeyman compositor, but after that followed an interval of unemployment and poverty, until he was reduced to selling his college prizes—the only library he owned. He left Besançon and even went outside the printing trade to find work, and early in 1831 he tried his hand as a teacher in the college of Gray, a small town north-west of Besançon. Whether from discontent or unsuitableness for a pedagogic employment, he stayed there only from Shrove Tuesday until the middle of Lent, and then decided to try his fortune abroad. On Good Friday he set out on foot through the Jura into Switzerland, where he found employment in Neufchâtel and stayed for half a year, an unhappy exile during which he conceived an active dislike of the Swiss. In November he returned to Besançon and to printing.

Such a migrant existence gave Proudhon neither the time nor the means to continue his studies, but he might have become resigned to this had it not been for the exhortations of Fallot, who had conceived the highest opinion of his friend's abilities. 'Here is my prediction,' he assured him in an extraordinary letter written at the end of 1831. 'You, Proudhon, will inevitably, despite yourself and by the fact of your destiny, be a writer, an author. You will be a philosopher; you will be one of the lights of the epoch, and your name will have its place in the annals of the nineteenth century. . . . Such will be your fate! Act as you like, compose lines in a printing house, teach brats, vegetate in some deep retreat, seek out obscure and isolated villages—it is all the same to me; you will not be able to escape your destiny. . . . I await you in Paris, philosophising, platonising; you will come here whether you like it or not.'

These were high promises indeed, but that there was no insincerity in the zeal that provoked them is shown by the fact that Fallot immediately set out to find means of providing his protégé with the facilities for studying and writing. The Academy of Besançon administered a fund, left by the critic Jean-Baptiste Suard, for a bursary to be given every three years to some young man of outstanding promise from the Franche-Comté. At first Fallot thought of Proudhon as a candidate, but it seemed unlikely that a manual worker lacking in scholastic background would gain the suffrage of the academicians; Fallot therefore hit on the idea of applying for the pension himself, calculating that, with a hundred francs a month already assured him, he would have enough to share with Proudhon, if only the latter could be persuaded to come to Paris.

Fallot had no trouble in securing the Suard Pension, and his main difficulty lay in persuading Proudhon to accept his offer of help. M. Daniel Halévy has suggested that Proudhon, having learnt a trade of which he was still proud, was reluctant to abandon it and take a step which would isolate him from the people among whom he had been born and reared. However, it seems likely that, while these considerations doubtless existed, they were not the sole or even the principal reasons for Proudhon's attitude. It must be remembered that the field of learning in which Fallot moved with familiarity and confidence was still to him a new and relatively unexplored terrain, and, at this time, he probably found it difficult to believe that he, a simple and self-educated worker, could be successful in philosophy. Failure would mean a fruitless interruption in his chosen occupation; worse than that, it might make him unable to help his family.

Fallot, however, was extremely persistent in propelling Proudhon towards a decision. He recruited the persuasive powers of their common friends, Micaud and Weiss, and continued his tireless epistolary bombardment. 'The will, the will, Proudhon! it is a lever whose power you do not know,' he exhorted his undecided friend. 'Decide, make an end to it; if you wish to leave the printing house, if you can get away from Besançon, if you want to reach your objective in the shortest way, here it is: come to Paris —I have a bed to give you, I have a revenue of 1,500 livres to share with you and six months will not pass, after your arrival, before I shall have succeeded in getting you an occupation by which you can live.'

This offer broke down Proudhon's resistance. 'I flew to his appeal.' In more prosaic terms, he walked to Paris and was there before the end of March. Fallot's welcome was as generous as his word; 'I entered his house,' said Proudhon, 'like the house of my father.'

Proudhon now settled down to familiarise himself with the Latin Quarter, where Fallot lived in the Rue Mazarin. Paris in those days, before Haussmann had set to work on his vast programme of reconstruction, was still the city of narrow mediaeval streets which had seen the Revolution; indeed, the district Proudhon frequented was virtually unaffected by the changes during the Empire, and the visitor who walks in it today still traverses the narrow carriage-ways, and passes between the high shabby houses which Proudhon saw when he first arrived there, less than two years after the July Revolution of 1830.

In some respects metropolitan life disquieted and disgusted this uncompromising young provincial. Fallot introduced him to his scholarly friends and to the savants who gathered at the house of his uncle, the pastor Cuvier, but Proudhon was awkward and suspicious among these professional intellectuals, and he preferred to continue his studies alone. Besides, the city was under the shadow of a cholera epidemic which gave life an unusually sombre aspect, and on Maundy Thursday Proudhon wrote a letter to his parents in which the discontent he felt with his circumstances appears clearly beneath the attempt to reassure their querulous anxiety. It is the first letter we have from his hand, and one of the few strictly contemporary documents of his life at this period, when the revolutionary prophet was just beginning to stir under the rough surface of the self-taught artisan with a mania for words.

'My dear Parents,

The water of Paris does not trouble me; it is more agreeable than that of Besançon, because it is fully filtered and saturated with oxygen, which acts as a further preservative against cholera. For the rest, do not be anxious; at its worst, in Paris, the disease does not kill even one man in three hundred; that is not a bad gamble. Paris is infected with chlorine and camphor. For the present, I do nothing but read and write in our room, read and write in the libraries. It is a little annoying for you, I admit; it is not all I had led you to expect; but in everything one must always begin at the beginning. Besides, this should not last as much as six months. If at the end of that time we see that I am good for nothing, I shall become a compositor and corrector once again, which I can always do whenever I wish. I shall get away with the slight humiliation of hearing myself called an author who has failed, for I am at present placed between these alternatives—to work at becoming an author, or to die of hunger, or to become a printer once again. The last hardly tempts me, the second even less; for lack of anything better, I am left with the first choice; what would I not do to avert death and the cholera? I am indifferently pleased with Paris, and Fallot's intention, as well as mine, is to leave it as early as we can; Besançon calls us, one as much as the other.

> I embrace you, my dear Parents,
> Your son, P. J. Proudhon.'

The two friends did not succeed in departing together for Besançon, since Fallot was stricken by cholera, and Proudhon became his nurse.

Fallot did not die, but his illness depleted both his funds and his ability to earn more. In these circumstances it was impossible for Proudhon to continue accepting his generosity, and he began to tramp through Paris from one printing house to the next, seeking 'a few lines to compose, a few galleys to read.' He had no success, and in the end reconciled himself to the necessity of touring the provinces and of leaving Fallot to convalesce as best he could.

Fallot remained in Paris, gaining eventually some little success in the scholastic world. Though he and Proudhon continued to correspond, they never met again, and Fallot died in 1836. Their common life in Paris seems to have taken the ardour out of their friendship, and Fallot's later letters lack the enthusiasm of discovery that was evident in the high days of 1831 and 1832, while, in maturing, Proudhon himself grew away from the influence of his early mentor. Nevertheless, a great deal of feeling remained, and when Proudhon heard of Fallot's death, he told Weiss: 'I felt that half of my life and spirit had been cut off from me: I found myself alone in the world. I do not doubt that Fallot leaves friends who regret him as much as I; I did not drop a tear, for I never weep, but since that time I have probably not passed four hours together without his memory, like a fixed idea, a true monomania, occupying my thoughts.'

And one might add that, despite the apparent failure of the expedition to Paris, it transformed Proudhon's whole attitude towards his future. Had it not taken place, he might have been content to remain a working printer; but once he had been propelled into accepting a new object in his life, there was no turning, and however often in the next few years he might appear to be resuming the old craftsman's life, he had accepted decisively the notion that his destiny lay outside the doors of the workshop, away from the lead vapours and the inane devotional texts and the thudding presses, and out in the free space of the public arena. All this was doubtless latent in him, but it was Fallot's influence that brought it to the surface and it was Fallot who first revealed the breadth of that community of thought and learning to which the young printer henceforward belonged by right.

5

'With fifty francs in my pocket, a pack on my back, and my notebooks on philosophy for provisions, I directed my steps towards the South of France.' Proudhon in fact became a companion of the *'tour de France,'* one of the journeymen who wandered from town to town, taking employment where they could find it, living precariously, but gaining in experience more than they lost in cash.

He tramped down the Rhône valley to Lyons, where he found a few weeks of work, and then on to Marseilles. By the time he reached Toulon, his resources were reduced to three and a half francs. There was no work to be found, and, inspired by the example of the unemployed workers who had just raised the barricades in Paris with a demand for work, he decided to make his own individual 'appeal to authority.' He went into the office of the mayor of Toulon and, producing his passport, formally demanded assistance in obtaining work.

'The person I addressed was a little, chubby, plump, self-satisfied man, with gold-rimmed spectacles, who certainly did not seem prepared for such a demand . . . He was M. Guieu, nicknamed Tripette. "Sir," he said to me as he hopped about in his armchair, "your demand is unprecedented, and you misinterpret your passport. It means that, if you are attacked or robbed, authority will undertake your defence; that is all!" '

Proudhon argued that these were rights which applied to everybody, and that the protection mentioned in a passport must be something more. Thereupon, Tripette offered him fifteen cents a league to pay his way home; Proudhon proudly rejected this offer as alms, and then decided that the man might be better than the functionary—for Tripette had a 'Christian face.' 'Since your office does not allow you to do justice to my request,' he said, 'give me your advice. If need be, I can make myself useful elsewhere than in a printing shop, and I despise nothing. What do you advise me?' 'To go away,' snapped Tripette, impatient at such a persistent stickler for rights.

'I sized up this personage,' Proudhon records. 'The blood of old Tournesi rose to my head. "Very well, Mr. Mayor," I said to him through clenched teeth, "I promise to remember this audience." '
And remember it he did, long and bitterly; twenty-six years later, in *De la Justice*, he told the story in every detail.

It was a stage in a revolutionary's education, but if this incident taught Proudhon the negative aspect of authority, he was soon to learn its positive malignance as well. He found work for a while in Draguignan, and here he heard that Jean-Etienne, the brother he loved more than anyone else in the world, had been unlucky in the draw for military service. Had the Proudhons been wealthy they might have bought a substitute; as it was, Jean-Etienne had no choice, and, with his potentialities for earning lost, Pierre-Joseph would have to return to help his parents. He condoled with his mother, 'for you in particular have most need of consolation in these sad circumstances,' but he also indulged in an outburst of bitterness in which he seemed to interpret his brother's misfortune as a blow directed by fate against himself. 'How destiny pursues me with its animosity! It seems as if the fatality that follows me attaches itself to all whom I approach . . . I sometimes go into transports of rage which are frightening and laughable at the same time; I do not know what to do with myself. I

call upon my black angel and defy him; I long either to be overcome or to destroy him!'

In this condition of acute depression, he returned to Besançon
and began to seek new employment. It was offered immediately
by Just Muiron, the disciple of Fourier, who invited him to
direct the Bisontin paper *L'Impartial*. It was a flattering offer,
but Proudhon was still too unsure of himself to accept light-
heartedly.

' For two years,' he told Muiron, 'I have run up and down the
world, studying, questioning the little people with whom I find
myself most related by my social condition; having hardly the
time to read, even less to write, hastily arranging the ideas that
occur to me through the observation and comparison of so many
subjects; I completely lack the talent to write and talk imagina-
tively on all kinds of subjects, a quality essential to a journalist.'

Muiron persisted, and in reasoning with Proudhon seems to
have suggested that the latter might be willing to disguise his own
personal opinions while editing *L'Impartial*. This drew from
Proudhon a characteristic defence of bold writing. ' Why should
L'Impartial not be a republican journal—in its own manner, of
course? . . . Why should we not profess publicly an absolute
pyrrhonism towards all ministers, past, present and future? Why
should we not invite the population to make themselves capable
of managing their own affairs and of preparing the way for a
confederation of peoples? Let them see, through instruction,
science, moral health and patriotism, how to dispense with all
ministerial and constitutional hierarchy, while in the meantime
profiting from the little good it will do them.'

This letter is the first document in which Proudhon shows an
emphatic political attitude that, in its general outlines, anticipates
remarkably closely what he developed in later years. Eight years
before his first polemical essay, one recognises the Proudhonian
distrust of centralised authority and the desire to see the working
people learning to manage their affairs without the intervention
of governments. These, indeed, are the seeds of those theories of
anarchism, federalism and mutualism which were Proudhon's
contributions to the social thought of his time. It would be interesting to trace the filiation of such ideas, but there are few records
of his reading at this early period, and it is therefore impossible to
decide how far they were actually evolved out of his own observa-

tion of the ineptitude of officials and of the natural practical abilities of the peasantry to whom he belonged.

After further persuasion, Proudhon finally agreed to give a trial to the profession of editing; it lasted less than a day. Having written his first article, he handed it to the office boy, telling him to take it to the printer and return in a quarter of an hour. The boy replied that it would take more than an hour.

'How is that?'

'The Prefecture is not so very near, and the Prefect will need some time to read the article and give it his authorisation.'

This was enough for Proudhon. He threw his article in the fire and walked out of his office. ' Confess that in all the world I am the man most incapable of doing the work I had undertaken,' he wrote next day to Muiron. 'Besides, I believe our principles do not agree very well; and as I have told you, though I have no foregone conclusions about many things, I hold to my principles, I will never sacrifice them, whatever may happen to me; I am content with my position as an artisan.'

It was indeed to his trade that he returned. Immediately afterwards he was approached by Auguste Javel, a printer of Arbois, thirty miles from Besançon. Javel had been commissioned to print a great number of mediaeval documents in Latin and Comtois dialect. He could think of no compositor more capable of this task than his friend Proudhon, whom he immediately sought out. 'Arbois?' said Proudhon. 'The wine is good there, the wine growers are republican, the neighbourhood is picturesque. I accept.' Javel's account of this stay at Arbois is the best early portrait of Proudhon as a young printing worker with intellectual ambitions.

On departing from Besançon, Javel suggested that they should take the coach. 'Not at all,' Proudhon replied scornfully. 'I have good legs and ten leagues do not frighten me. Take the coach if you like.' He set off early in the morning on his walk through the Comtois hills, and arrived at Arbois by the evening, still fresh and inclined to talk. Javel offered him hospitality, but Proudhon refused, saying: 'You have a wife and children, you need your freedom, and I need mine. Help me to find a house where I can have a room of my own, where my meals can be served when I need them, without interrupting my reading. That is all I ask.'

Javel found him accommodation with an old crippled captain who had served through the Revolutionary wars and who now lived on his scanty pension, supplemented by the earnings of his daughters from embroidery, and by the produce of a tiny vineyard. They were a simple and friendly family, and Proudhon appreciated their hospitable consideration for his wishes.

He soon regulated his days in a manner which enabled him to make the most of his time. He would rise before dawn, start work early and then, at two or three in the afternoon, glance through the work he had done, set his case of type in order, and say: 'My day is ended.'

His afternoons were spent in walking, and it is characteristic of the way in which Proudhon loved to mingle opposites that his companion on these lengthy rambles was a notary who was reputed to be 'the gravest personality and the most obstinate conservative in all Arbois.' The notary was an amateur artist, and when they had found a pleasant place to rest he would sketch the scenery, while Proudhon would take out his notebook and jot down any ideas that occurred to him during the day. In his reminiscences Javel reproduces a page which he somehow acquired from this notebook and which gives an indication of Proudhon's thoughts at the time. It ran as follows:

'AUTHORITY. Right to respect? Yes, if elective, conventional, temporary. Senis si senis. CAPITAL. Its role in production (Malthus). Its dividend (study and repute the formulae of the sects). Negative. CLERICAL INF. Incompatible with human dignity, Civil Liberty, Economy.'

All the hints contained in these brief jottings of some summer afternoon in the Jura were to find their place, magnified into major arguments, in Proudhon's later and more mature writings.

In the evenings Proudhon would sometimes retire, after his meals, to read and study. On the other occasions he would encourage the captain to tell his reminiscences of the wars, and would sit smoking his pipe and listening silently, in his characteristic attitude, astride a chair, with his hands on the back, his bearded chin resting upon them. On Sunday evenings there would be parties to which the young friends of the family would come to play lotto, the loser paying for the chestnuts and the strong, straw-coloured Arbois wine that was consumed. Proudhon would join in amiably, but Javel noticed that whenever the other young people became flirtatious he would rise, politely wish everybody a good evening, and flee shyly to his room.

Yet his very quietness attracted the girls of the house, who nursed him when he developed a quinsy, and refused to take any gift in return for these friendly services. According to Javel, the younger daughter, Caroline, fell in love with him and remained so for years afterwards. When Proudhon departed, and embraced his friends with painful awkwardness, she said to him sadly: 'You will soon have forgotten us.'

'No,' he replied. 'One does not forget in that way the people whom one has become used to loving and who deserve it.' But Caroline seems to have remembered longer and more deeply than Proudhon. In his correspondence and notebooks we can find no sign that he recollected with any particular vividness these friends of a season. Caroline, on the other hand, followed his career with the closest attention, and for years afterwards would anxiously ask Javel for news of him. She remained single, and in 1849, when Proudhon was imprisoned, she travelled to Paris in order to see him. Having learnt that he had married, she returned and never spoke of him again. It was a devotion whose constancy Proudhon would have appreciated had he been aware of it, but, so far as we can tell, he never was.

6

Proudhon returned to Besançon early in 1833, and he was not long at home before the news arrived that his brother Jean-Etienne had died while undergoing his military training. 'That death,' said Proudhon years later, 'finally made me an irreconcilable enemy of the existing order,' and he told Alexander Herzen: 'Twenty years ago I lost a brother, a young soldier, through the tyranny of an embezzling captain, who wished to force him into becoming the accomplice of his peculations, and, by his vexations, drove him to suicide.'

Beyond this account we have no further details, and also no means of checking the accusation which Proudhon directed against the superior officer, though the corruption that existed in all branches of the state apparatus under the July Monarchy makes its correctness seem probable. Yet, in so far as the event affected Proudhon personally, these details are irrelevant; it is more important to imagine the feeling of powerless grief which this little family of Comtois peasants experienced, and to realise how the tragedy must have appeared to the already rebellious Pierre-Joseph a direct consequence of their position among the lowest class in a society whose activities militated against the poor and the honest. The state, with its compulsive machinery, had seized Jean-Etienne with no regard for his wishes or the feelings of his relatives, it had used and killed him, and now it would go on in the same way, seizing another young man to put in his place, and the process would continue indefinitely. On the other hand—and here was a second lesson—the state was by no means impartial in its operations. Influence could deflect it from its course and save the child of the wealthy. So the state, it became evident to Proudhon, was an instrument of the powerful, and henceforward the anarchistic tendencies which we have already seen appearing in his thought began to grow strong, and authority became the principal object of his attacks. The death of this beloved brother thus represents one of the most significant points of his development as a rebel.

The years that followed this tragedy are little documented and seem to have been almost completely uneventful. Of 1834 and 1835, indeed, Proudhon was content to remark in his autobiographical notes: 'Happy years because of my work.' When he returned from Arbois the economic situation in Besançon was greatly improved, and his old employers, the Gauthiers, were glad to take him back as a foreman. He received 120 francs a month, and was able to keep his family in more comfort than they had enjoyed since his early childhood.

The work of this period seems to have been the most satisfying of his career as a printer. The Gauthiers produced during these years not only a Vulgate Bible, which Proudhon regarded as his masterwork of craftsmanship, but also the *Dictionnaire Théologique* of the Abbé Bergier. Because of his knowledge of Latin and Hebrew, Proudhon supervised these books over the months of their composition and printing, and, though he did not regain the simple beliefs of his youth, he was tempted by his daily occupation to go back into the maze of theological speculation, and to acquire that mass of information on religions which later he used so effectively in his study of the nature of belief and in his criticisms of the Church.

On many points he disputed the ideas put forward by the Abbé Bergier, but he also developed a real respect for the man and his work, and would refer to him as 'my theologian in ordinary.' There were many points in common between the rebel and the churchman; both were of Comtois peasant race, and both had the brusque, outspoken manner of their country. Bergier had chosen, rather than revelling in the glory of fashionable pulpits, to spend his years among the farmers of the village of Franche-Rouge, tramping the roads in sabots and in his free hours studying the doctrines of the Church at their most ancient sources. An adversary of the worldly magnificence which attended the Gallican Church, he had been asked by d'Alembert to edit the theological items for the celebrated Encyclopaedia, and these articles formed the basis of the Dictionary reprinted by Gauthier. Proudhon's thinking on religious matters always bore the traces of his early encounter with this now almost forgotten theologian. Perhaps, indeed, it was Bergier's dedicated life, his love for the poor and his despising of magnificence, that really attracted Proudhon and made him credit the old scholar with a greater importance as a thinker than he really deserved.

During these years Proudhon seems to have made an effort to renounce his literary ambitions, and he even avoided contact with intellectual circles in Besançon. At times, however, the old dreams returned to torment him and never more than when he had news of Fallot. In the years since they had been together in Paris, Fallot had become librarian of the Institut de France, and at the beginning of 1836 Proudhon wrote and asked whether he could find him employment there. Perhaps he could become Fallot's secretary. Or perhaps he could work at the press that would produce his friend's philological treatise.

Fallot had not in fact become so influential a personage as he may have appeared from the shadows of a provincial printing shop, and he replied that not only was he unable to give Proudhon employment, but that he had not even found a publisher for his own book. Accordingly, Proudhon abandoned the idea of returning to Paris, and instead decided to advance himself by means of his trade into a position where he could earn the leisure that would enable him to carry on his studies. On the 17th February, 1836, Charles Weiss noted in his diary: 'Lambert and Proudhon, two foremen of the house of Gauthier, Proudhon a well-read workman,

Lambert highly instructed in ancient languages, have taken the Montarsolo Press on good conditions; they will begin by publishing a Notary's Dictionary.' Besides Lambert, a second friend, Maurice, went into the business as a sleeping partner. Lambert and Maurice appear to have put up almost all the capital, and the press was conducted in Lambert's name.

Of the early days of Lambert and Company no information exists, but it is certain that during the winter of 1836 to 1837 Proudhon suffered from an illness (its nature is not recorded) that forced him to abandon work for some months. It is possible that his business responsibilities may have combined with the shock of Fallot's death in the previous July to precipitate the disorder. He utilised his convalescence to make his first serious attempt at writing—'a few fairly happy essays in sacred criticism and philosophy'—which led him to devote his attention once again to 'grammatical researches.'

It is to the latter that we owe his first published work. In his admiration for Bergier, Proudhon persuaded his partners to reprint the theologian's outdated philological work, *Eléments primitifs des langues*, in which Bergier tried to find the common roots of the main world languages as a basis for determining the manner of their formation. To bring the book up to date, Proudhon himself wrote an *Essai de Grammaire Générale*, which was printed as a supplement to Bergier's text.

Later he disowned this essay as 'apocryphal,' 'perverse' and 'feeble.' But at the time he was delighted with it and with the fact that some Bisontin 'persons of merit' had, as he assured Just Muiron, found in it 'things which are entirely new and curious.' Its substance need not long delay us, since, as he himself later declared, it was based on 'a thesis definitely rejected by science', but there are several features which can profitably be brought out as having some bearing upon his later intellectual development.

The first is his attempt to confute the philologists who claim that the key word in all languages is *être*, by a rival claim that it is in reality *moi*. The psychological connotations of this argument seem to point back to the childhood of misery which toughened Proudhon's own ego, and forward, not only to the anarchism that is basic to his whole later teaching, but also to the highly personal and anti-systematic nature of his thinking in general.

More than once, as one reads through the antiquated philological reasoning of this essay, the potential rebel is recognisable, and, at times, the man who was later to declare himself at war with God seems amazingly near. 'Though we may never be present at a second dawning of flawless virtue,' cries Proudhon in almost existentialist tones, 'though chance and necessity may be the sole gods which our intelligence shall recognise, it will be good to bear witness that we are conscious of our night and, by the outcry of our thoughts, protest against our destiny.' As Sainte-Beuve remarked, 'an intellectual Prometheus growled already in the bosom of Bergier's disciple.'

Apart from the praises of local acquaintances, this essay passed unnoticed. Yet Proudhon was full of optimism, and already saw himself revolutionising the study of languages. He assured Muiron that he was on the verge of a grammatical revelation, and, like many other autodidactic thinkers, he became dominated by an almost mystical belief in the function of language as a key to the whole of philosophy. The man who discovered the secret of speech, he felt, would open up new vistas across the whole world of knowledge.

By the end of the year, lack of recognition had tempered his enthusiasm. To a new friend, the Alsatian poet Paul Ackermann, he boasted that he had 'enough ideas to feed two or three Château-briands,' but was inhibited by his stylistic shortcomings. 'I have a terrible itch to send literature to the devil; it bores me and it is beyond me . . . I would like to be able to speak in formulae, to put all I think on one page.' Yet he was obviously not discouraged enough to abandon his ambitions, and the mere fact of having published an essay which was appreciated by a few people whom he respected gave him the confidence to proceed with the larger plans taking shape in his mind.

7

The affairs of Lambert and Company had in the meantime shown little progress, and it became evident that even two working partners could not be maintained. Early in 1838 Proudhon therefore decided to return to Paris, partly in the hope of finding some work for his firm, partly to earn his living there as a compositor, and partly to see whether, with the added experience of six years, he could now begin a literary career.

This time he had no difficulty in finding work as a corrector, but, though he was not poor, his disgust with Parisian life appears to have been even greater than on his first visit. 'A thousand causes make me abhor living in the capital and inspire in me an inexpressible pity for its desperate population,' he complained to his old teacher, Pérennès. 'Everybody about me is singing and laughing and restless; it seems as though to enjoy themselves they must go into convulsions. The rich drain themselves to the point of exhaustion; the poor work and save for a month to be *happy* one night.'

He found a consolation in praising the French provinces and in concluding that 'the Franche-Comté can become an arch of the human race.' It was the exaggerated statement of a countryman lost in a metropolis, a defiant cry of mingled patriotism and homesickness, but it also anticipated that line of thought, springing out of a distrust for centralisation, which was eventually to make Proudhon one of the great prophets of regionalism.

This sojourn in Paris was ended abruptly when, a few weeks after his arrival there, the news reached Proudhon that his partner, Lambert, had disappeared from home. On the 9th April, he departed for the Franche-Comté, writing hurriedly to Pauthier: 'Lambert, my colleague, is at this moment either dead or in a state of complete lunacy. I am therefore going to replace him and to guide our unfortunate barque. Goodbye for a long time to linguistics and philosophy!' He reached Besançon by the 15th April. Shortly afterwards, Lambert's body was discovered in a wood two leagues from Besançon.

Proudhon immediately set to work putting in order the chaotic affairs of their partnership. But he had little zest for a business that had involved him already in so much disappointment, and he and Maurice decided to sell it at the earliest opportunity. This virtual failure of his efforts to become a successful master printer confirmed Proudhon in a decision, which he had already been considering in Paris, to abandon the workshop and embark on a life of scholarship. The Suard Pension, which Fallot had held, would become available again in 1838, and now, with one essay already published and a growing reputation among the Besançon intellectuals, he felt that he stood a much better chance of winning it than in 1832.

In this hope he was encouraged by Pérennès, who was now

Permanent Secretary of the Besançon Academy, and with whom he had already corresponded on the subject before Lambert's death. In February, he had outlined to Pérennès the studies he proposed to make in the event of his receiving the pension; it was philosophy he wished to pursue, using the study of languages as a point of departure. Soon after his return to Besançon he began to seek out the men who could best help him in competing for the pension, and very soon he prepared his letter of appeal.

Beginning with a declaration of his humble origin, he told the story of his life and education with such eloquence that Pérennès exclaimed in astonishment: 'Wherever did you learn to write like that?' He then detailed the course of studies which he had already described to his adviser, and ended with the celebrated dedication, the oath to his fellows in poverty:

'Born and brought up in the working class, still belonging to it, today and for ever, by heart, by nature, by habits and above all by the community of interests and wishes, the greatest joy of the candidate, if he gains your votes, will be to have attracted in his person your just solicitude for that interesting portion of society, to have been judged worthy of being its first representative before you, and to be able to work henceforward without relaxation, through philosophy and science, and with all the energy of his will and the powers of his mind, for the complete liberation of his brothers and companions.'

This open declaration of sympathies scared Pérennès as much as it delighted him, and, doubtless with a great deal of difficulty, he persuaded Proudhon to tone it down into a paragraph which expressed the same sentiment in a form less likely to arouse the fears of the committee in whose hands the decision would rest.

The Academy's decision was reached on the 23rd August, and, after two votes, Proudhon was chosen out of several candidates; in the report that was read the following day by Pérennès, it was stated that the Academy had been in favour of Proudhon, since he had over his competitors 'the incontestable and sad advantage of possessing less resources and of having been more rudely shaken by fortune,' and that his remarkable intellectual progress offered 'almost certain guarantees for success and for the future.'

Proudhon's natural delight at his success was mingled with annoyance, since the academicians insisted that he should go to Paris, while he wished to carry on his studies in Besançon. 'What they want of a pensioner,' he said angrily, ' is not only that he should become a savant, but that he should gain a *good position* in the world. It is far from such ideas to those of an *egalitarian*.' And when the bourgeois of Besançon took it upon themselves to congratulate him on having made the beginning of a great career, he was even more disgusted, and began after all to think Paris might be preferable to his native town. 'There is still, you tell me, intelligence and light in the capital,' he stormed three weeks later to Ackermann. 'As for me, I live among sheep.' More than two hundred people, he complained, had congratulated him on his chances of making a fortune and 'of participating in the hunt for places and great appointments, of attaining honours and brilliant positions.' Nobody had told him that he owed himself to the 'cause of the poor, to the liberation of the lowly, to the instruction of the people.' Nobody had told him to 'tell the truth and take up the cause of the orphan' without expecting any reward other than 'the blessings of his brothers.' Proudhon took very seriously the oath he had made in his application to the Academy, and nothing enraged him more than the insinuation of cynicism contained in these suggestions that he should follow the road to prosperity and power, regardless of the class from which he sprang. He was justified, for throughout his life he followed, according to his own highly individual lights, the path he had marked out for himself in 1838 when he wrote his application to the academicians.

8

In November, 1838, Proudhon made his third departure for Paris. But before we begin to narrate the further course of his life, there is a passage in his correspondence from Besançon that merits attention. It appears in the letter to Ackermann on the 20th August; the poet had been bewailing some reverse in his personal life, and Proudhon gave him stoical consolation, mingled with an elusively incomplete fragment of autobiography.

'It is not at the end of the way we follow that one meets happiness; sacrifices, rather—sufferings, insurmountable disappointments, desertions, despairs . . . I have written during these last days to my former mistress, at present in Lucerne; she is dying of boredom, and perhaps of love; she asked me for consolation. "Consider," I said to her, "what is passing around you; are you not gentle, chaste, hardworking, honest? How is it that you find it hard to live, while a crowd of prostitutes display their impudent luxury? I will explain this mystery to you. God has willed that when evil and vice have reached their height among mankind, the good shall be the first to suffer, so that they may awake and oppose the flood which is about to drown them. There are a hundred thousand young men in France who, like me, have sworn to fulfil that holy mission, and sooner or later they will know how to conquer or to die. It is for men of courage to fight with head and arm; but you, poor girl, must pray to God that he gives us intelligence and audacity, that he blesses our ardour and makes his cause triumph!" What do you think a young woman feels for a lover who talks to her in this manner?'

'What, indeed?' we may echo. But more interesting than the priggishness of the sermon is the hint it contains of an amorous relationship which had proceeded farther than the chaste infatuation of Proudhon's early twenties. Once again we are at a loss to identify the girl he addresses, but there are two passages in *De la Justice* which throw light on the incident as a whole. In the first he deals with the accusations which his critics had brought against the chastity of which he boasted, perhaps a little too extravagantly. He maintained obstinately that his life had indeed been chaste. But he brought a curious qualification into the argument.

'I am chaste; I am naturally so, by inclination . . . but above all through respect for women . . . However, this does not mean that I have always been of a perfect continence. There exists, you know, a great difference between these two things, chastity and continence, of which the one does not always presuppose the other . . . Very well, is that not a good text for declamation—that in a century of free loves, despite my natural chastity, I should have happened, doubtless on more than one occasion, to sin against the virtue of continence?'

Bearing in mind this definition of chastity as not necessarily implying continence, we come to a further passage, in which Proudhon criticises the idealistic conception of love and recalls the first infatuation of his own adolescence. 'As happens to many others, my youth began with a platonic love affair which made me very silly and very sad, but to which I owe, in compensation, the fact of remaining for ten years after my puberty in the state of *agnus castus*.'

A decade after Proudhon's puberty, the time in which he lapsed from lamblike chastity, coincides approximately with the period in which he was writing his singularly unencouraging letter to his 'mistress' in Lucerne. And of this time he gives the following description:

'That long crisis ended [the ten years], I believed myself free; but it was then that I was assailed by the devil who teased St. Paul, and, I may say, it was to my great displeasure. The devil, who had so long roasted me on the side of my heart, now roasted me on the side of my reins, so that neither work, nor reading, nor walking, nor refrigerants of any kind could give me peace. I was the victim of the senses against the spirit . . . The flesh said: I would; the conscience: I would not. Should I give way, or be consumed once again by that mystification to which I could see no end? To combat physical love by platonic love, that is not done by commandment; the latter exhausted, the other broke out with all its violence.'

The implication of these devious confessions seems to be that round about the end of the period in Besançon which lasted from 1833 to 1838 Proudhon became involved in a passionate sexual relationship. That the experience was pleasant does not follow; indeed, to a young man of Proudhon's extreme sensitivity it may have been humiliating, both in itself and as a surrender to physical demands, and the very form of his letter suggests a desire to escape from an unwilling obligation by pleading greater obligations elsewhere. Certainly, whatever may be the facts of this relationship, it provides the last recorded instance of women taking any intimate part in Proudhon's life until his marriage a decade later. And, since this period of sexual crisis was followed by a time of mental activity and productiveness, it is possible that Proudhon may have been able to sublimate a desire whose power he admitted only with the utmost unwillingness.

Here it is appropriate, in order to illustrate the rapidity with which Proudhon's ideas on women were crystallising, to mention a letter which he wrote in the summer of 1839 to a local priest who had written a manuscript 'on the Mystery of the Virgin.' It included a citation from George Sand, which Proudhon made the excuse for the first of many bitter criticisms of that authoress, and also for an early sketch of his theory of the position of women in society. As this passage gives a further hint of his own sexual experiences, I will quote it at length.

'George Sand has never appeared to me other than a kind of Mme de Staël who retains plenty of admirers among people enamoured of bombast and big words. The herd mistakes her exaggerated expression and violent epithets for energy of style, her generalisations and abstractions for depth, her balloons blown out with wind for sublimity, her bold denials of accepted maxims for novelty or fine observation. I could give you proofs of all that even in the fragment which you cite . . . "It is women who preserve for us across the centuries the sublime traditions of Christian philosophy." That means absolutely nothing, because it says infinitely too much. "It is they who today save the relics of spirituality." The contrary is rigorously true: women in general plunge themselves into the depths of sensualism and drag us with them. Look at the Saint-Simonian and Fourierist women. All that George Sand says on the equality of women is a trivial truth, if it means nothing more than what Rousseau developed in the last part of *Emile* with a marked superiority of reasoning and eloquence; if it does mean anything more, George Sand falls into falsehood. If one compares rights, men and women are equal; if one compares duties, they are still equal; if one compares sex with sex, women are inferior.'

From a literary viewpoint Proudhon's strictures on George Sand showed the emergence at this period of a rigorous sense of critical values. But biographically more interesting is the bitterness with which he talks of the constitutional sensuality of women, a bitterness like that of the Fathers of the Church, which one feels can only have arisen from personal experience, from temptation imperfectly resisted, and, ultimately, from a desire to lay elsewhere the responsibility for his own weakness.

From a conflict between sexual fear and republican principles arises the general opinion on women which Proudhon expresses at the end of the passage I have quoted. An egalitarian cannot deny equality of rights, even to people of whom he disapproves, and equality of rights implies equality of duties. But neither *necessarily* implies equality of intellectual or moral qualities.

Proudhon wrote so much on the comparative functions of the sexes that we shall often return to this abundant field of controversy. Here, however, it might be well to recall the fact that he had only just emerged from a working-class environment, and that many of his reactions were, and remained throughout his life, astonishingly true to the outlook of the Latin working man. At that time the idea of sexual equality was much less frequent in this social class than among the bourgeoisie, while 'free love' was more in vogue among middle-class utopians than among genuine proletarian radicals. This situation persisted throughout the nineteenth century; the early pronouncements of the French workers in the First International on the subject of women were strikingly similar to those expressed by Proudhon throughout his life. This point helps to explain rather than to justify the rigidity of Proudhon's outlook on the relationship of the sexes, which was shared by few socialists in his time, which was rejected by his anarchist disciples, and which would be accepted by few enlightened people today.

Part Two

THE CRITIC OF PROPERTY

I

PROUDHON reached Paris in the late autumn of 1838, and immediately established contact with Joseph Droz, who had been nominated by the Besançon Academy to advise him in his studies. Droz, a mild and honest savant who wrote innocuous essays on the Art of Oratory and the Art of Being Happy, was at first rather perturbed by the unpolished character of his pupil, but he saw clearly the excellent qualities that were concealed by this rough exterior. 'I believe I shall be able to announce to you before long,' he wrote to Pérennès shortly after meeting Proudhon, 'that, without shedding any of his excellent Franc-Comtois qualities, he will lose his wildness, and his timidity will become no more than the modesty that is proper in a man of merit.'

Through these remarks there runs a suggestion of the bewilderment Droz must have experienced on his first encounter with Proudhon, whose own comment on their relationship is even more illuminating. Droz, he told Pérennès, appeared to have come to the conclusion that 'I am a man of paradox, and he is not wrong.' This remark is worth noting; it shows the beginning of Proudhon's tendency to self-dramatisation, which in later years was to grow almost into a second nature. Yet one cannot deny the

36

justice of this self-definition, for it anticipated the most distinctive characteristic of his polemical technique—the powerful use of paradox, contradiction and antinomy to illuminate his reasoning and deepen his criticism.

It soon became evident, though Proudhon expressed a considerable personal regard for Droz, that the academician could give him little in the way of instruction, since they disagreed almost immediately on the aims of philosophy, history, linguistics and every other subject that Proudhon was studying; Droz seems to have argued that almost all had been said in these fields of knowledge, whereas Proudhon felt that they were capable of indefinite extension. Droz himself was sensitive enough to realise their incompatibility, and limited their contacts to twice-weekly conferences, which grew more irregular as Proudhon became engrossed in his individual pattern of work.

Nor were Droz's efforts to overcome his pupil's timidity by introducing him to the social life of intellectual Paris any more successful, for when he was invited to soirées Proudhon was too terrified to attend. 'Have you forgotten what it is to be a Franc-Comtois of pure blood and pure race, who has never lived except with his dreams, alone in contemplation between the sky and the pine trees?' he asked Droz in a letter of apology and explanation. 'I am still only that. For the twenty years since I reached the age of reason I have almost always lived alone, and you would transplant me suddenly into the most distinguished society! No, I could never endure such a trial!'

His excessive shyness impeded Proudhon's contact with scholars who worked in the fields that interested him; he became a solitary student, rarely indulging in the reciprocal process of discussion, and to this fact one can perhaps attribute the eccentricity of thought and the encyclopaedic indiscipline in presenting facts which so often mark his later works as those of an unprofessional philosopher. They are faults whose corresponding virtues are the equally individualist qualities of originality and flexibility.

In his own way he worked from the beginning of his stay in Paris with fervour and energy. He attended the public lectures at the Sorbonne, the Collège de France and the Conservatoire des Arts et Métiers, and sent back to his friends highly critical notes on the superficiality of the lectures and the backscratching cliquishness of the professors. But the greater part of his work consisted of reading in the Bibliothèque Royale and the Bibliothèque Mazarine. His activities during these early months of study had little appearance of integration. He thought of studying for his licenciate as the preliminary to an academic career. He contemplated a critical history of the Hebrews. He began to learn German and Sanscrit. But his principal work was still in the field of philology, and centred around the preparation of a thesis to compete for the Prix Volney, which was to be awarded by the Institut de France. For this purpose he elaborated and enlarged his earlier grammatical essay and presented it under the title of *Recherches sur les catégories grammaticales et sur quelques origines de la langue française.* The prize was not awarded, since the judges did not think any of the competing papers sufficiently elaborate, but Proudhon's manuscript was selected for honourable mention; the judges praised his ingenious analysis, particularly in the mechanism of the Hebrew language, but 'regretted that the author should have abandoned himself to hazardous conjectures and that he should sometimes have forgotten the experimental and comparative method which the commission especially recommended.'

Meanwhile, it was quickly becoming evident to Proudhon that his financial situation would not allow him to devote his whole attention to study. No doubt in ordinary circumstances during the 1830's a grant of 1,500 francs a year would have been enough for a scholar to keep himself frugally in Paris. Proudhon, however, was no ordinary, unburdened student. Not only did he send help to his parents, who were still in need, but in some way which it is now hard to determine he had assumed responsibility for a debt in connection with his printing press which involved the payment of at least 300 francs a year in interest. 'If I were foolish enough to forget my living by trusting to the Suard Pension,' he remarked, 'in six months I would not have a crust of bread.'

Not long after he reached Paris he was seeking evening work as a printer to double his income, and by March, 1839, he was writing articles on grammar, logic and philosophy for a Catholic Encyclopaedia, and reading proofs for a Legitimist paper, *L'Europe.* But these schemes for earning money were indifferently successful; the editor of the Catholic Encyclopaedia suspended publication without paying for all the articles he had commissioned, and by the end of the summer Proudhon was writing to ask Maurice for a loan of thirty francs; it was his last recourse.

Yet he did not allow poverty to interfere with his writing, and found time to prepare his first published article, on the letters of the alphabet, which was published in *L'Instruction Publique*. 'I have just crossed the Rubicon,' he announced when it appeared.

Later in 1839 a new opportunity to show the development of his ideas occurred when the Besançon Academy announced a competition for an essay on 'the utility of the celebration of Sunday in regard to hygiene, morality, and the relationship of the family and the city.' For a month he worked on his dissertation, until he was ill with exhaustion, but the completion of the essay gave him new confidence, and he saw it as the beginning of a literary career. 'If my first work gains some success,' he remarked, 'I shall soon be in the position of publishing something every six months. It is necessary to strike hard and quickly.'

De la Célébration du Dimanche, as his essay was called, presented an argument in which, as Sainte-Beuve justly observed, the subject was 'hardly more than a pretext for introducing his system of ideas, still obscure and half-concealed.' Proudhon approved of the institution of a day of rest, and much of his essay was devoted to an idyllic description of the peaceful rural life in which such a custom found its appropriate place. It was the nostalgic dream of a *paysan manqué*, of the man who had already the exile's eye for the beauties of the pastoral existence from which he was becoming irrevocably detached.

But in Moses, the institutor of such a beneficial custom, Proudhon saw not merely the religious leader, but also the father of social reform. He examined the patriarch's teachings, and from his own philological speculations drew the explosive contention that the meaning of the commandment, *Lo thignob*, is not 'Thou shalt not steal,' but 'Thou shalt not lay anything aside for thyself.' He added to this a declaration of the absolute character of moral law, and a categorical assertion that 'equality of conditions is . . . the aim of society.' Finally, he declared that 'Property is the last of the false gods.' He talked against 'cumulative proprietors,' he attacked the 'exploiters of the proletariat,' and he ended on the challenging note of an imaginary dialogue in which the poor cry out in defiance: 'Proprietors, defend yourselves!'

In this essay we find already formed much of the essential

outline of Proudhonian thought, his egalitarianism, his theory of property, his ideas of a natural, immanent justice. At the very beginning of his career, with only a comparatively slight preparation of experience and study, he had evolved the social attitude which he would maintain throughout his life; what he did in later years was to expand and illuminate it by insight, observation and study, and to extend it into new fields of thought.

Indeed, it is interesting to encounter here hints of even the minor arguments which Proudhon developed subsequently. For instance, his later condemnation of Rousseau's idea of the Social Contract is anticipated by a very perceptive passage on the faults of the eighteenth-century thinker: 'In founding right on human conventions, in making law the expression of wills, in other words, in submitting justice, and morality, to the decision of the greater number and the rule of the majority, he plunged deeper and deeper into the abyss from which he believed he was emerging, and absolved the society he accused.'

There is a provocative similarity between this criticism of Rousseau and that which William Godwin had made nearly fifty years before, and further parallels between the two writers appear in their ideas on equality and on the injustice of what Godwin called 'accumulated property.' Yet there is no evidence that Proudhon had read Godwin[1] and it seems likely that these closely similar thinkers reached their conclusions by mutually independent reasoning on the principles and events of the French Revolution.

Indeed, the search for shaping influences in connection with Proudhon's ideas is an involved and often thankless task. His thought seems to contain an unusually high proportion of genuine originality, and when he borrowed an idea he would work it over in his own mind to such an extent that it emerged in a state of renewal, adapted to suit that fluid dialectical battleground which represented the nearest approach to a Proudhonian system. He was, indeed, a voracious collector of ideas and information; his reading was vast, while he readily made use of his friends to inform him on questions where they had expert knowledge; Pauthier instructed him on Chinese philosophy, Tissot on Kant,

[1] In 1846, in *Les Contradictions Economiques*, he mentions Godwin while discussing Malthus, but since he classes him with Owen as a 'communist,' it seems probable that he had not read *Political Justice*.

Gruen and Bakunin on Hegel. At the same time, he often disagreed with his informants on the meaning of the facts they gave
him.

So far as general influences are concerned, he was a child of his
age to the extent of accepting the wider ideals of the French
Revolution, but even here he reacted against the Jacobin tradition, and rejected Robespierre as emphatically as he did Napoleon.
I have already shown how far Christian theology influenced him,
principally through Bergier, and his polemical style carries many
echoes of the minatory utterances of the prophets, but, while his
morality was often that of the Old Testament, he accepted and
used the Mosaic codes in a completely unorthodox manner.
The influence of classical antiquity was less prominent. He
rejected the authoritarianism implicit in Plato, and the Greek
philosophers with whom he had most in common were Heraclitus and the Stoics, yet even here the link seems adventitious—a
parallelism of attitude rather than a direct filiation.

Apart from the Bible, the only influences which Proudhon
admitted, when he talked on the subject to his disciple Amadée
Langlois in 1848, were Hegel and Adam Smith. Kant, Fourier
and Saint-Simon, however, were certainly evident, though un-
acknowledged, partners in his development. In later years he
grew steadily more independent of the theories of others;
Michelet and Herzen influenced him a little, but from the rest
of the leading figures of his day, whether liberal intellectuals like
Renan or professional revolutionaries like Blanqui, he reacted
with more or less violence.

Even in the cases where influence is evident, Proudhon never
stood in the relation of a disciple to a master; his attitude was
usually that of a critical and rather noisy student, and he ended
invariably by giving some individual twist to the doctrines of his
teachers. His dialectical method, for instance, seemed out-
rageously heretical even to such unorthodox Hegelians as Marx
and Engels, while Kantians like Tissot were equally distressed by
his cavalier use of the antinomies. Of Fourier and Saint-Simon
his treatment was yet more ruthless; acknowledging that they had
perceived certain things with an unusual clarity, he did not
hesitate to denounce their general systems as misapplications of
these insights, though he took from them what he found acceptable. In other words, Proudhon demonstrated a healthy eclectic

41

intelligence which accepted nothing without examination, but was not excessively scrupulous about appropriating suggestions it could use effectively.

2

The implications of the opinions on property and equality incorporated into Proudhon's discourse on Sunday did not escape the Besançon academicians, and the judge, the Abbé Doney, found danger in the 'digressions, the ill-sounding, audacious, temerarious, inadmissible propositions . . . the theories of politics and speculative philosophy, and systems of equality.' But he also praised the remarkable literary qualities which the essay displayed: 'A style always clear, natural, flowing, rapid, full of originality and distinguished by that warmth which is born of an ardent love of goodness and truth.'

Such a report was clearly meant as a warning to Proudhon that he had not been made a pensioner of the Academy in order to dabble in the perilous territory of radical thought, and its intention was endorsed by the rest of the academicians, who, instead of awarding him the crown of honour, merely gave him a bronze medal. The winner of the award was Tissot, professor of philosophy at Dijon, translator of Kant, and later a close friend of Proudhon.

Proudhon, who had returned to Besançon, in order to be present at the judgment, accepted the award with defiant equanimity. 'I much prefer the bronze medal which I have been awarded,' he told Ackermann. 'My memoir had been classed as apart and out of line; that is worth more, you will agree, than an *ex aequo*.'

He remained in Besançon long enough to print *De la Célébration du Dimanche* on his own press; in November he returned to Paris, took up lodgings in the Rue Jacob, and in a few weeks was announcing that he had suspended his philological studies so as to devote himself to Kant, 'whom I count, in the intoxication of my pride, on reforming once for all.'

But his thoughts were by no means entirely in the realm of philosophy. Away from the isolation of Besançon, which was very marked in the days before the railway had penetrated into the Jura, he began to observe the disturbed social conditions of the time, and to relate them to his own speculations. He was particularly concerned with the fermenting discontent among the unemployed Parisian workers. 'Their revolutionary exaltation seems to me bordering on despair,' he told Pérennès in December. 'They know that the plan of Paris is drawn by the government in such a way that it can suddenly occupy all the points of the town on the first rising; they know that they cannot rise today without being massacred in thousands. It is that powerlessness which makes them more terrible. . . It is indubitable that if they were the masters, their reign would not last a fortnight; they would disperse of their own accord, by the effect of their disorganisation, but they would have had the time to give a terrible lesson to the public men.' A few months later the rising known as the Conspiracy of the Seasons was to collapse for the very reasons which Proudhon had hinted—the lack of strategical power and the failure of cohesion among the insurrectionaries.

Meanwhile his own material condition was growing steadily worse. 'I write to you in the bitterness of my soul,' he told his new friend, Fréderic-Guillaume Bergmann, the Alsatian scholar, in February, 1840. 'You believed me poor last year; this year, if you come to Paris, you will see me penniless . . . I shall have 250 francs to live from the 20th March next to the 20th September. I have much to read, to write, to study, but I am oppressed, dismayed, and exhausted. Sometimes I stare at the Seine as I cross over the bridges; at other times I think of becoming a thief. The feeling of my poverty is so great that if I came into a fortune tomorrow, the nightmare that haunts me would not depart for two years.'

His anxiety was all the greater, since he did not know whether he would find a publisher for the new book he was preparing. He had been working on it assiduously for the past month, and his personal misery made it all the more challenging in tone and intention. 'This time I will not sing any *gloria patri*,' he told Bergmann. 'It will be a veritable tocsin . . . This is the title of my new book, which I would like you to keep secret: *What is Property? It is Theft*, or *A Theory of Political, Civil and Industrial Equality*. I will dedicate it to the Academy of Besançon. The title is frightening, but it will not be a reason to censure me; I am a demonstrator, I expose facts . . . Pray God that I find a publisher; it is perhaps the salvation of the nation.' Then, perhaps realising that his enthusiasm was rather far-flown, he added:

'I speak to you with my accustomed frankness; you know that I do not love false modesty; with you, who are my friend, any other language would seem to me hypocrisy and lies.'

His object, he told Bergmann, was ' to determine the idea of justice, its principle, its character and its formula,' particularly as exemplified in the institution of property. The style would be 'rough and sour,' and irony and anger might even be too evident, for 'when the lion is hungry, he roars.' Finally, Proudhon had no doubt at all of the originality and timeliness of his book. 'In the philosophic sphere,' he told Ackermann, ' there exists nothing like it.' He worked quickly at his task; the book was finished by the end of April and, a publisher having been found more quickly than Proudhon feared, it appeared at the end of June.

3

As the first book of a man, little more than thirty years old, who had educated himself under exceptionally difficult circumstances, *Qu'est-ce-que la Propriété* (*What is Property?*) was in every respect a remarkable work. The Proudhonian fire, the zestful writing, the love of paradox, the flair for the shattering phrase, the personal bitterness and the eloquent invective, all the qualities that inspired his best work were already there in full measure. For the quality of its prose alone, it could bear comparison with the work of many of Proudhon's better-known literary contemporaries; it had all the vigour of conception, the sense of structure, the verbal proportion, which made his most ruthless critic, Arthur Desjardins, admit in the end: 'This plebeian sculpts his phrases with a profound art, the art of the great classicists. He, no less than Molière, should have belonged to the Academie Française.'

As for the quality of the contents, and what perhaps concerned their author just as much, their originality, another enemy can testify—Proudhon's most bitter ideological rival, Karl Marx. Writing in the *Neue Rheinische Zeitung* in October, 1842, Marx was one of the first people outside France to recognise *What is Property?* He called it a 'penetrating work.' Three years later, in *The Holy Family*, he expanded this first comment by saying: 'Proudhon submits the basis of political economy, *property*, to a critical examination, and it is truly the first decisive, vigorous and scientific examination that has been made of it. Here is a great scientific progress, which revolutionises political economy and for the first time permits one to make a true science out of it.'

What is Property? opens with one of those bold passages which tended to become Proudhon's speciality in political writing. 'If I were asked to answer the following question: "What is slavery?" and I should answer in one word, "Murder!", my meaning would be understood at once. No further argument would be required to show that the power to take from a man his thought, his will, his personality, is a power of life and death, and that to enslave a man is to kill him. Why, then, to this other question: "What is property?" may I not likewise answer, "Theft"?'

Hardly noticed at first, 'Property is Theft' was to become one of the great phrases of the nineteenth century, bandied about between anarchists and conservatives, borrowed by socialists and communists, and suspended like a sensational placard above the popular image of its author. Ironically enough, Proudhon did not even mean literally what he said. His boldness of expression was intended for emphasis, and what he wished to be understood by *property* was what he later called 'the sum of its abuses.' He was denouncing the property of the man who uses it to exploit the labour of others without any effort on his own part, the property that is distinguished by interest, usury and rent, by the impositions of the non-producer upon the producer. Towards property regarded as 'possession,' the right of a man to control his dwelling and the land and tools he needed to work and live, Proudhon had no hostility; he regarded it as a necessary keystone of liberty, and his main criticism of the Communists was that they wished to destroy it.

However, this was by no means clear to those whose knowledge of his work was limited to a single phrase, and often, in his intense annoyance, he found himself classified with the Utopians he detested as an enemy of property in every form. Yet the more his celebrated maxim was misunderstood, the more closely he clung to it. One of his most bitter reasons for anger against the state socialist Louis Blanc was that the latter accused him of stealing the phrase from the Girondin Brissot, who had said, in his *Recherches philosophiques sur le Droit de Propriété et sur le Vol*: 'The measure of our needs should be that of our fortune . . . Exclusive property is a *theft* in nature.' Proudhon eventually solved this question to his own satisfaction by declaring that anyone who might previously have equated property and theft did not know the real meaning of what he said; by showing the true significance of the formula, he alone had discovered it, and it was his 'most precious possession.' For a man who was later to contest the conception of property in ideas as fervently as that of property in goods, this was certainly an odd exhibition of obstinacy.

Even when he was writing *What is Property?* Proudhon must have realised the effect his bold opening statement would have on many readers, for he hastened to reassure them by remarking, 'I am no agent of discord, no firebrand of sedition,' and to argue that in his work he was merely anticipating history and delineating the course of progress. He stood as an investigator, a seeker after truth, and denied any ambition to become a party leader, or the founder of a school. 'I build no system. I ask an end to privilege, the abolition of slavery, equality of rights, and the reign of law. Justice, nothing else. That is the alpha and omega of my argument: to others I leave the business of governing the world.'

Throughout Proudhon's career as a social thinker this conception of justice remained the most important of the few general principles between which, in his quasi-Heraclitian view, life moved as a kind of fluid equilibrium. And in this early work he described and praised it in words no less definite than he was to use in later years. 'Justice is the central star which governs society, the pole around which the political world revolves, the principle and regulator of all transactions. Nothing takes place between men save in the name of right, nothing without the invocation of justice.'

Justice is the social motive which man 'at war with himself' has perverted to his own detriment by making it subject to the fallible sovereignty of the human will, expressed in the principles of the French Revolution. It is upon a return to the idea of immanent justice that Proudhon bases his attack on property.

He begins by disposing of the three most familiar justifications for property. To the assertion that it is founded on occupation, he replies that 'the right to occupy is equal to all'; to the argument that it is based on civil law, he replies that the law is merely a convention which can be revised to suit social realities, and to the argument that it springs from work, he makes the obvious retort that all workers are not proprietors.

It is when he is discussing property in relation to work that Proudhon makes some of his most significant statements. He argues that labour alone is the basis of value, but that this nevertheless does not give the labourer a right to property, since his labour does not create the material out of which the product is made. 'The right to products is exclusive—*jus in re*; the right to means is common—*jus ad rem*.'

But *means*, as Proudhon points out, does not consist only of the raw materials provided by nature. It includes also the vast heritage of installations built by men in the past, the accumulated techniques and traditions of civilisation, and more important, the element of co-operation in labour which makes each man's work so much more effective than if he acted in solitude. This, according to Proudhon, is the real 'surplus value' of which the capitalist appropriates an unduly disproportionate share. 'Now this reproductive leaven—this eternal germ of life, this preparation of the land and manufacture of implements for production—constitutes the debt of the capitalist to the producer, which he never pays; and it is this fraudulent denial which causes the poverty of the labourer, the luxury of idleness, and the inequality of conditions. This it is, above all other things, which has been so fitly named the exploitation of man by man.'

In *What is Property?* we have thus not only a labour theory of value based on Ricardo and differing little from that of Marx— though antedating it by some years—but also a widely different theory of surplus value which seems a great deal more acceptable even in the undeveloped but provocative sketch Proudhon has given us. Marx's theory of surplus value is restricted to the particular relation of employer and employee. With its implicit connection with the nineteenth-century 'Iron Law of Wages,' according to which the workers are kept down to the mere necessities of living and procreation and all the rest of the product of their labour is taken by the capitalist, it has become outdated in modern society, for it is impossible to claim that the American worker is merely receiving enough to keep him alive—unless one stretches the point to include automobiles among the requisites of a subsistence existence. But in this culture where a relatively high standard of comfort is widely spread and where, far from the middle class becoming proletarianised, the proletariat has climbed towards the lower ranks of the middle class, Proudhon's theory still retains its validity. As he contended, all of us, workers and capitalists, producers and parasites, are everlastingly in debt to the past and to society. We live as we do by reason of centuries of common work; the labourer could not do the tasks which create 'surplus value' unless he had the tools and the co-operation provided by social effort, and it is thus in fact the social and not the personal element in work which the exploiter appropriates. He does not steal from a man the results of that man's personal labour; instead he takes for himself the extra productive power conferred on us by collective work.

Proudhon seems hardly to have realised the full import of this extremely illuminating hint. He made his point and passed on to a refutation of the anti-egalitarian arguments of the Saint-Simonians and the Fourierists, both of whom declared that, because men are unequal in capacity, they must receive an unequal return for their labour. Proudhon, advancing from the conception of the social basis of all labour, declares that, though men may indeed be unequal in capacity, in rights they must be equal, since it is not their own merits but the inherited traditions, techniques and means of production embodied in society which make it possible for them to develop their capacities. It follows that each man, in working according to his capacity, is only establishing the same right as his neighbour, however spectacular may be his contribution.

Following on these arguments, Proudhon declares that property is incompatible with justice, because in practice it represents the exclusion of the worker from his equal rights to enjoy the fruits of society.

But, since property is incompatible with equality and by implication with justice, and since our present social order is based on property, it remains to consider an alternative. Will it be communism? Certainly not, for, though man is a social being and seeks equality and justice in his relationships, he also loves independence, and society develops naturally in this direction. Communism, in Proudhon's eyes, is the primitive form of association, and property originates in man's desire to gain independence from its slavery. And here we come to a particularly interesting indication of his studies at the time, for he proceeds to reduce the proposition to what he calls 'a Hegelian formula,' with communism as the thesis and property as the antithesis. 'When we have discovered the third term, the synthesis, we shall have the required solution.'

The reference to Hegel is important, not only in illustrating the breadth of Proudhon's enquiries even in 1840, but also in solving the dispute which later arose as to who—Gruen, Marx or Bakunin —introduced him to Hegel. The answer is clearly that none of them did, for Proudhon met all these Left-Hegelians between 1844 and 1846, when he had already been well aware for some years of Hegel's basic ideas.

How he came to discover these ideas we do not know for certain. Evidently, he had not read Hegel's works in the original; he admits as much in a letter written in 1845 to Bergmann. It seems possible that he learnt a certain amount from friends and acquaintances familiar with German philosophy, such as Ackermann, Bergmann and Tissot, while in 1836 Willm had published an essay on Hegel in *La Revue Germanique*, which Proudhon certainly read, for he refers to it in *De la Création de l'Ordre*, completed in 1843. It would hardly have needed more to support the simplified version of the dialectic which we find in *What is Property?* It is certainly true that Proudhon later took advantage of his meetings with people who had studied Hegel in the original to expand his knowledge of that philosopher's work, but already he was adapting it to his purposes, and I think it might justly be said that Proudhon was never again so good a Hegelian as he was when, in 1840, he knew least about that philosopher's ideas.

Returning to the question of the ideal social pattern, Proudhon finally dismisses communism as a system which creates only a spurious equality and does not in fact abolish property. His criticisms have an uncommonly prophetic bearing on authoritarian communism as it has been practised in our own day.

'The members of a community, it is true, have no private property; but the community is proprietor, and proprietor not only of goods, but also of persons and wills. In consequence of this principle of absolute property, labour, which should only be a condition imposed upon man by nature, becomes in all communities a human commandment, and therefore odious. Passive obedience, irreconcilable with a reflecting will, is strictly enforced. Fidelity to regulations, which are always defective, however wise they may be thought, allows of no complaint. Life, talent and all the human faculties are the property of the State, which has the right to use them as it pleases for the common good. Private associations are sternly prohibited, in spite of the likes and dislikes of different natures, because to tolerate them would be to introduce small communities within the large ones . . . Communism is essentially opposed to the free exercise of our faculties, to our noblest desires, to our deepest feelings.'

But, if communism is to be condemned, even more so is property, which 'violates equality by the rights of exclusion and increase, and freedom by despotism.' In other words, it is a form of theft which, to preserve itself, is inevitably bound up with the power of the strong or the crafty. But in considering this point we are brought to the question of legitimate authority. And here Proudhon introduces a memorable dialogue and an historic definition.

'What is to be the form of government in the future? I hear some of my readers reply: "Why, how can you ask such a question? You are a republican." "A republican! Yes, but that word specifies nothing. *Res publica*; that is, the public thing. Now, whoever is interested in public affairs—no matter under what form of government, may call himself a republican. Even kings are republicans." "Well, you are a democrat." "No." . . . "Then what are you?" "I am an anarchist!" '

Proudhon imagines his interlocutor looking at him in astonishment and then taking for granted that he is jesting. Finally, he explains his statement, tracing the genesis of authority in the instinctive tendency of social animals and primitive man to seek a chief. As a man develops reasoning powers, he selects authority as one of the first objects of his thought, and out of this process spring protest, disobedience, finally revolt. This revolt is canalised by the appearance of political science and the realisation that the laws of social functioning are not matters for the opinion of some ruling individual or group, but exist in the nature of society. 'Just as the right of force and the right of artifice retreat before the steady advance of justice, and must finally be extinguished in equality, so the sovereignty of the will yields to the sovereignty of reason and must at last be lost in scientific socialism . . . As man seeks justice in equality, so society seeks order in anarchy. Anarchy —the absence of a master, of a sovereign—such is the form of government to which we are every day approximating.'

In this way Proudhon became the first man to call himself an anarchist. Others before him had attacked the idea of government, and Godwin in *Political Justice* had made a detailed criticism of society which entitles him to be regarded as the first libertarian theoretician. Some of the more extreme revolutionaries of 1793 were given the name of 'anarchists' by their enemies, but they never took to the epithet, and, for the most part, their ideas were far from anarchistic in the true sense, and much nearer to the concept of class dictatorship later put forward by Blanqui and the Marxists. But Proudhon was the first man voluntarily to adopt this name of 'anarchy' for the form of society he envisaged, and actually to mean by that word—philological stickler that he was— a society without government.

So we come to the final conclusion that neither communism nor property is suitable as a basis for a just society. Their aims are good, but their results are bad, because communism rejects independence and property rejects equality. But the synthesis of communism and property, which is 'liberty,' fulfils these deficiencies, providing a society where equality, justice, independence and the recognition of individual merits can all flourish in a world of small producers bound together by a system of free contracts.

In its rejection of government and of accumulated property, in its advocacy of economic equality and free contractual relationships between individual workers, *What is Property?* contains the basic elements of which all the later libertarian and decentralist theories—including even those of such maverick figures as Tolstoy and Wilde—have been built.

What, however, strikes one more immediately is the relatively undeveloped form of Proudhon's solution. As Theodore Royssen has remarked, there is a 'static' quality in the method of reasoning by axioms and corollaries which Proudhon borrowed from the seventeenth- and eighteenth-century philosophers; 'history in the real sense of the word occupies hardly any place in it.'[1] This fact cannot be dissociated from the sharply limited nature of Proudhon's approach to property. For it is clear that what he is discussing is above all property in land, and that his solution is almost wholly an agrarian one. It was perhaps an inevitable result of his background that he should look to a society in which every Claude-François would get his fair share of land and would never have to fear the threatening hand of the mortgage-holder. And, if almost no attention is given to industries which cannot be administered by one small artisan 'possessor,' we should bear in mind

[1] Introduction to the definitive edition of *Philosophie du Progrès*, 1946.

that up to 1840 Proudhon had probably very little chance of observing the new world of the industrial revolution. The railway, pioneer of industrialism, had not reached Besançon, which was still economically an island of workshops in a province of peasant farmers. Proudhon's acquaintance with such cities as Lyons, where industrialism was really beginning to grow, had so far been fleeting, and the part of Paris with which he was familiar has remained even to this day a stronghold of small workshops. Later, when he came to know the industrially developing areas more thoroughly, and to become involved in business ventures which brought a wider contact with the working life of his time, he made some very significant amendments to his theories which, as will become evident in considering *The General Idea of the Revolution*, destroy the arguments of those who, using *What is Property?* as their text, accuse Proudhon of having been retarded by a peasant outlook.

4

As he had threatened, Proudhon dedicated *What is Property?* to the Besançon Academy, and in a letter which he submitted to that institution at the end of June he tacitly acknowledged the academicians as the partners in and even the instigators of his inflammatory work. 'If, by an infallible method of investigation, I establish the dogma of equality of conditions,' he declared, 'if I annihilate property for ever—to you, gentlemen, will redound all the glory, for it is to your aid and your inspiration that I owe it.'

He decided not to wait in Paris for the Academy's reaction to this challenging gesture. He had again become tired of the capital, which he described to Ackermann as 'stupid, filthy, chattering, egotistical, proud and gullible,' and the troubles of his life as a provincial printer had grown dim in retrospect, so that recently he had been moved in his poverty to confess, 'I sigh for the day when I shall resume my paper cap.'

He set off on foot with an Alsatian painter named Elmerich, who was travelling to Strasbourg and agreed to go out of his way through the Franche-Comté in order to accompany Proudhon home. When they reached Besançon, about the middle of July, Proudhon found himself the subject of violent discussion among his fellow citizens. 'The effect of my book on the Academy has been terrible for me,' he wrote to Bergmann. 'They have cried scandal and ingratitude . . . I am an ogre, a wolf, a serpent; all my friends and benefactors shun me . . . Henceforward everything is ended; I have burnt my boats; I am without hope. They would almost like to force from me some kind of retraction; I am not read —I am condemned.'

One can readily imagine the timid priests and professional men of a small provincial city shuddering to see the way in which their protégé was growing up into an embarrassingly powerful critic of notions they did not dare or desire to question. Indeed, it is to the Academy's credit that many of its members were sufficiently unaffected by the general prejudice to remain friendly to Proudhon. Yet even these felt that he had written too violently. One of them was the urbane Weiss, who said to Proudhon: 'My dear friend, you do wrong to your cause by your manner of defending it. Have you forgotten the words of Henry IV—one catches more flies with a spoonful of honey than with a hundred barrels of vinegar?' 'It is not a question of catching flies, but of killing them,' replied Proudhon.

Nevertheless, he was influenced by the opinion of his friends, and perhaps a little sobered by the amount of hostility he had aroused, for he now proposed writing a second essay to dispel the misapprehensions that might have arisen in connection with *What is Property?* He mentioned this in a mollifying letter to the Academy, and promised to return afterwards to his studies of 'philology, metaphysics and morality.' 'Gentlemen,' he assured them, 'I belong to no party, no coterie; I have no followers, no colleagues, no associates. I create no sect, I would reject the rôle of tribune, even if it were offered to me, for the sole reason that I do not wish to enslave myself! I have only you, gentlemen, I trust only in you, I expect favour and solid reputation only through you. I know that you propose to condemn what you call my *opinions*, and to renounce all solidarity with my ideas. I persist nonetheless in believing that the time will come when you will give me as much praise as I have caused you irritation.'

The more hostile academicians were not won over by this approach, and on the 10th August Proudhon told Tissot: 'They think of withdrawing my pension; they no longer expect anything of me, at the very time when they should expect most; they will abandon me at the moment of my strength and productivity.'

However, towards the end of the summer his position began to improve markedly. *What is Property?* was at last arousing interest in Paris; it was mentioned in Louis Blanc's *Revue du Progrès* and other papers, and a Parisian publisher, Prévot, had offered to bring out a second edition of 3,550 copies.

At the same time, a group of academicians including, to Proudhon's surprise, the prefect of the department and the bankers and business men, had shown themselves inclined to support him against the hostility of 'the devotees, the lawyers and the pure men of letters'. The result of this division had been a number of angry sessions; 'finally, it was resolved to do nothing until I had been heard, and I am summoned to appear before our academic Senate during next December, to justify myself and to hear myself reproached for having written *an anti-social book, contrary to all the proprieties in form as well as substance.*'

He lingered in Besançon until the autumn, unable to make up his mind whether to stay and try to re-establish his printing shop. Then, having learnt that Bergmann was in Paris and would leave for Strasbourg on the 15th October, he decided to go back to the capital in the hope of intercepting his friend, with whom he was anxious to discuss the republication of *What is Property?* and the sequel he had in mind. 'Try to prolong your stay from the 15th to the 20th,' he begged, 'so that I can see you . . . It is for you that I am going to break my legs.' He left Besançon on the 11th October and tramped wearily into Paris on the 17th; Bergmann had been unable to wait for him, and the six days of effort his poverty forced upon him had been in vain.

In Paris he discovered that the prospect of losing the Suard Pension had not been the worst danger incurred in publishing *What is Property?* Its appearance had coincided with a spate of pamphlets directed against the July Monarchy, and the public prosecutor sent it to Vivien, the Minister of Justice, with a recommendation that a case should be launched against its author.

Proudhon was saved by a fortunate chance. He had sent a copy to the Academy of Political and Moral Sciences, and it had been assigned for review to the economist Jérome-Adolphe Blanqui, brother of the celebrated conspirator. Blanqui prepared a long report, in which he criticised what he regarded as the exaggerations of Proudhon's viewpoint. He claimed that to suggest the abolition of property because of its abuses was as foolish as to demand the suppression of marriage as a remedy for adultery, but at the same time, when approached by the Minister of Justice for his opinion of the seditious nature of the book, he declared that it was a philosophical treatise which appealed only to 'high intelligences and cultivated minds.' Vivien accepted his recommendation, and did not prosecute. Proudhon was fortunate; only two months later Lamennais was imprisoned for a year and fined 2,000 francs for his *Le Pays et le Gouvernement*, a work which involved no more formidable attack on the basis of monarchist society than the anarchist exhortations of *What is Property?* Yet from this time onwards the authorities remained suspicious of Proudhon, and when a few months later a worker named Darmés made an attempt on the life of Louis-Philippe, there was an ominous note in the remark of the investigator, Girod: 'How can one be astonished that there should be regicides, when there are writers who take for their thesis: Property is Theft.'

Proudhon was, and remained, grateful to Blanqui for his intervention. Nevertheless, he did not intend to let even this friendly critic's strictures pass unanswered, and he now decided that, instead of, as he had originally intended, addressing his second memoir to the Besançon Academicians, he would write it as a 'letter to Monsieur Blanqui.'

5

It was not entirely without misgivings that he began work on this essay. 'On the one hand,' he told Bergmann, 'the love of knowledge beguiles me and commands me to pass on to something else, making me believe that I have done enough on the question of property; on the other hand, the feeling of injustice and the ardour of my temperament draw me towards a new war.' The polemical urge was the stronger, and he gave only a brief thought to abandoning his further attacks upon the orthodox theories of property.

This time, he set to work with every intention of persuading his readers by sympathetic argument rather than by violent denunciation. 'Henceforward, instead of dipping my arrows in vinegar, I will dip them in oil,' he told Ackermann. 'The wound will smart less, but it will be as surely mortal.' Yet the personal discontent which had nurtured his rage in *What is Property?* had not abated, nor were its basic causes removed. He was as poor as ever, and desperately lonely. 'I am almost without society,' he told Ackermann, 'a hundred leagues from Bergmann, four hundred from you, deprived of Fallot, whose memory was never more painful; there are moments when I fall into an inexpressible forsakenness.' And in the bitterness induced by his personal difficulties he could not refrain from defending his past anger even while he promised to amend it. 'I have only one excuse,' he declared to Ackermann. 'When a man, nearly thirty-two years old, is in a state near to indigence without its being his fault . . . when, at the same time, he seems to notice among the advocates of privilege more impudence and bad faith than incapacity and stupidity, it is very difficult to prevent his bile flaring up and his style feeling the furies of his spirit.'

His contempt for the world, in fact, overflowed in every direction at this time, and he let loose not only at the perfidy of the reaction but also at the stupidity of his fellow republicans, whose Jacobinical methods made it impossible for sincere and sensible people to work at the reshaping of society. 'A year ago, one might have believed we were going towards reform; today we are marching to revolution,' he declared with prophetic insight.

Meanwhile, the dispute with the Besançon Academy had broken out anew. Proudhon, who had been requested to appear in Besançon during December to justify his right to continue as a pensioner, did not do so, and the academicians were enraged by what they regarded as a further affront to their corporate dignity. At the end of December Proudhon received a letter from Pérennès demanding an explanation of his conduct. He was once again thrown into a state of mingled fury and despair, and complained to Pérennès that he had been given orders, which he would disobey, and threats, which he would defy; in a separate official letter to the Academy he announced his intention, in the event of the pension being withdrawn, of bringing his case publicly before the people of Besançon.

On the 15th January, 1841, the Academy considered his letter. Those already opposed to him were more hostile than ever, but Pérennès and Weiss supported him, and Proudhon was saved by the rule demanding a two-thirds majority for withdrawing as well as granting a pension. He was surprised and relieved, and the successful outcome of this dispute made him look upon the future with a renewed confidence.

He even confided to Bergmann his hopes that the second essay on property would have the 'happiest effect,' not only on the people, but also on the authorities. 'I have such confidence in the certitude of my principles and the rightness of my intentions that I do not despair of obtaining one day some mission or other from those in power, *servatis servandus*, of course.' The thought of gaining official patronage certainly seems strange in a newly declared anarchist. But there was a curious vein of Machiavellianism in Proudhon's character which often made him think of using people of influence for furthering his own theories. Since his diplomacy was of a rather obvious kind, carried on with the bravado and whispered asides of a stage villain, and since he always regarded himself as having a monopoly of cunning, it was not surprising that in such manoeuvres he was almost invariably and often comically unsuccessful.

6

The *Lettre à M. Blanqui*, which appeared in April, 1841, did in fact moderate the bitterness that had characterised *What is Property?* yet there was little diminution in the actual vigour of Proudhon's style, and, though the men with whom he disputed have mostly dwindled into the obscurity of the past, his polemics still make excellent reading. For if he shows less rankling anger than before, he does not cease to ridicule his opponents—the phalansterians, whose system he stigmatises as 'stupid and infamous,' the orthodox economists ('insipid commentators' who are 'deprived of reason and common sense'), and above all, Lamennais, who comes in for the strongest attack of all, as an 'anti-philosophical' mediocrity, the 'tool of a quasi-radical party.' Finally, property itself is 'devouring and cannibalistic,' and in order to live, the proprietor 'must ravish the work of others, must kill the worker'; 'ruse, violence and usury' are the means employed for this despoilment.

Apart from these attacks, the *Lettre à M. Blanqui* is mostly an extended gloss on Proudhon's first essay, and there is little in it really new, except for an historical survey which the author himself has best summarised in a letter to Ackermann. 'I have developed new points of view: for example, that humanity, for the last four thousand years, has been going through a process of levelling; that French society, unknown to itself and by the fatality of Providential laws, is every day engaged in demolishing property (for example, by the laws of expropriation, the conversion of bonds, the protection of the labour of women and children).'

His self-defence is based on the contention that he has been generally misunderstood as a violent revolutionary, and that what he advocates is nothing more than a logical continuation of the historical process. He attacks 'competition, isolation of interests, monopoly, privilege, accumulation of capital, exclusive enjoyment, subordination of functions, individual production, the right of profit or increase, the exploitation of man by man,' and it is these evils he calls Property. On the other hand, he recognises a 'necessary, immutable and absolute' element in property which he is anxious to retain, and this he defines as 'individual and transmissible possession, susceptible of change but not of alienation, founded on labour and not on fictitious occupancy or idle caprice.' In other words, the means of production and living can be possessed by the peasant or the artisan, but nobody has a right to the property which enables him to exploit the labour of other men.

Proudhon denies any intention of arousing hatred against the proprietors as a class; it is property he attacks, and all are corrupted by it, according to their circumstances. He even calls upon the workers to forsake those who inspire them with revengeful desires. 'O! proletarians, proletarians! How long are you to be victimised by this spirit of revenge and implacable hatred which your false friends kindle, and which, perhaps, has done more harm to the development of reformatory ideas than the corruption, ignorance and malice of the government?'

And he ends his essay with an ironical passage in which, posing as a good patriot and a lover of order, he seeks to enrol no less a pillar of respectable society than Louis-Philippe, the Citizen King himself. 'Since we are a monarchy, I would cry, "Long live the King!" rather than suffer death, which does not prevent me from demanding that the irremovable, inviolable and hereditary representative of the nation shall act with the proletarians against the privileged classes; in other words, that the king shall become the leader of the radical party.'

The ambiguity of this appeal was to be echoed more than once when Proudhon hoped that the leaders of his own and other countries might be beguiled into supporting his plans of social reform. But the equivocal touch it gives to the final pages of the *Lettre à M. Blanqui* does not detract from the fact that, on the whole, this essay is a capable defence of the position outlined in *What is Property?* and a successful justification of its author as a serious scholar.

7

Proudhon had braced himself for a hostile reception of his *Lettre à M. Blanqui*, and a few days after its publication he was already describing with relish to his old school friend, Antoine Gauthier, the animosity that seemed to threaten him. 'On all sides I am told that I shall not be spared; the wind blows and the sky darkens; there will be heavy weather.' He shook himself with a defiant gesture against the 'clamours of the coteries . . . the conspiracy of scribbling journalists . . . the great beast that is called the public'; he declared that he had his compensation in the esteem of 'honest, independent men.'

But his apprehensive preparations for self-defence were pathetically inappropriate, for the *Lettre à M. Blanqui* was received with a scantiness of praise or blame that probably distressed its author more than any mass attack by hostile reviewers could have done. Apart from Blanqui himself, and some of the Utopian socialists (the Phalansterians in particular), few writers noticed the book, and it was neither sold nor read so widely as its predecessor.

Even the few influential people whom Proudhon had hoped to convert remained unmoved. Early in 1841 he had met Pierre Leroux, the former Saint-Simonian who had now become a leading Christian Socialist. Like Proudhon, Leroux had been a compositor, and the similarity of their plebeian backgrounds, as well as their common distaste for the extravagance of the Phalansterians and of Enfantin's Saint-Simonian hierarchy, formed a basis for mutual esteem. But the enthusiastic Proudhon mistook friendliness for partisanship. 'One of those for whom I can attest the full and perfect adhesion to my doctrines,' he told Tissot in April, 'is M. Pierre Leroux.' But a month later, when he mentioned Leroux to Ackermann and described him as 'amiable and witty,' he no longer talked of the identity of their views. Already had begun that realisation of divergent opinions which was later to make

Proudhon as distant from Leroux as he was from any other of the socialist writers of his time. Perhaps, indeed, it was not wholly a question of differing views, for there was more than disparagement in Victor Considérant's later description of Proudhon as 'that strange man who was determined that none should share his views.' Proudhon was never willing to enter into an alliance that might limit his individuality or compromise his liberty of action. He had no intention of becoming a follower, but equally he had no desire to be a leader, and when he did work with other people the resultant combination was much more a group of friends held together by affinity than a sect or an embryo party. For this reason he soon began to avoid any close association with those socialists who had already gained a position and a following, and even at this early stage it is possible that the failure of his first enthusiasm for Leroux may have been due as much to his instinctive shrinking from close alliances as to the gap which became evident between their views on socialism.

If he was unsuccessful in converting the socialist Leroux, he failed equally to influence his dedicatee, Blanqui. Blanqui read Proudhon's essay carefully, and wrote him a long letter of criticism. 'Although you have done me the honour of giving me a share in this perilous teaching,' he protested, 'I cannot accept a partnership which, so far as talent goes, would surely be a credit to me, but which would compromise me in every other respect . . . The terms in which you characterise the fanatics of our day are strong enough to reassure the most suspicious imaginations as to your intentions, but you conclude in favour of the abolition of property! You wish to abolish the most powerful motive of the human mind, you would arrest the formation of capital, and we should build henceforth on sand instead of rock. That I cannot agree to, and for this reason I have criticised your book, so full of fine pages and so brilliant with knowledge and fervour!'

Finally, Proudhon was the reverse of successful in winning the friendly attention he had hoped for among the 'men of power.' He had reckoned without the vindictive reaction that grew each year more oppressive during the final decade of the Orleanist regime; again he was almost prosecuted, and again he escaped through the intervention of Blanqui. This time the police conceived the crassly ludicrous idea that the dedication of the pamphlet constituted evidence of a plot between Blanqui and Proudhon, and wished to prosecute both. The folly of the suggestion was Proudhon's salvation, for when Blanqui made representations to the ministry on the absurdity of the conspiracy charge, the whole affair was dropped without any independent proceedings being initiated against the author of the book. Deprived even of the publicity of persecution, the *Lettre à M. Blanqui* remained in an obscurity from which it would hardly have emerged but for Proudhon's later celebrity.

8

'I am trying to reply to you on the most beautiful May morning one could hope to see,' Proudhon wrote to Ackermann in the spring of 1841. 'Above my window the sun is magnificent; only the nightingales and the roses are missing. Instead, I have curs and sparrows, which are hardly suitable to refresh the mind and divert the imagination.' Paris had once again grown stale, and Proudhon was suffering both from public indifference and from the drudging hack work by which he contrived to live at this time (he was ghost-writing a work on criminal law for a Parisian magistrate). Yet even out of his setbacks he drew an amazing confidence in his mission as a necessary critic of social evils. 'I cannot withdraw,' he declared at this time. 'I regard my task as too great and too glorious. It only remains to make myself worthy of it.'

He was preparing to retrieve his position by yet another attack on the question of property, and he first thought of making his new essay a blast against Lamennais, some of whose recent remarks he interpreted as an attack upon himself. But this intention was abandoned later in the summer when both of them were attacked in an anonymous phalansterian pamphlet, bearing the grandiloquent title: *Defence of Fourierism. Reply to Messieurs Proudhon, Lamennais, Reybaud, Louis Blanc, etc. First Memoir. Refutation of Absolute Equality. Solution of the Problems of Pauperism, of General Wealth and of Work by the Theory of Fourier.*

Proudhon was not merely first on the list of writers singled out for criticism; he was also the principal subject of attack, and we can assume that he welcomed this distinction. Certainly he made the most of the opportunity it presented by deciding to write his third essay, not against Lamennais, but against the disciples of Fourier. The person he chose to address was Victor Considérant, the leading heir of Fourier's ideas and editor of *La Phalange*. The real

61

author of the pamphlet to which he was replying appears to have been Claude-Marie-Henri Dameth, a socialist journalist who ended his career as a professor of political economy at Geneva, but Proudhon was not aware of this, and the fact that Considérant, even if he had not written the pamphlet, evidently agreed with its contents, seemed sufficient reason to regard him as symbolically responsible.

While Proudhon worked on this new essay on property through the summer of 1841, he also began for the first time to think of finding a new medium for his ideas in political journalism. It was perhaps natural that such an extreme individualist should think less of contributing to already established periodicals than of founding a magazine over which he would have control, and during July, 1841, he was tempted by proposals emanating from two widely different quarters. A certain Baron Corvaja approached him on behalf of a shadowy group of Milanese bankers who wished to start an unorthodox financial review, and a number of dissident Phalansterians started to make plans for a periodical in the editing of which, thanks to the lack of literary talent among its founders, Proudhon hoped he might take a leading part. The doubts of his editorial capacity which he had expressed to Muiron nine years before seem to have vanished, and he was anxious to avail himself of any opportunity to express his views, through active journalism, to a wider public than his books were likely to reach. Neither of the plans actually materialised, possibly because of differences of policy, but they implanted in Proudhon a growing desire to control some periodical in which he might relate his developing opinions on the nature of society to the daily pattern of events.

At the end of July the situation of his printing business forced him to leave Paris once again for the Franche-Comté. Heavy bills had fallen due, and he must either sell out in order to settle them or else find the cash in some other way. He sought in vain for either buyer or banker, and his friends pressed on him the drastic solution of marrying a girl with a dowry.

'But that would be the very devil!' he confided to Bergmann. 'I am not particularly amorous, I know nobody, and despite the small reputation I have acquired, I am, without exaggeration, a bad bargain for a girl. A poor girl would be no help to me, and I should be lost without any profit to her. A rich girl would demean herself by forming an alliance with me. A girl of medium fortune would sacrifice everything in paying my debts, after which she would find herself with nothing but an unresourceful husband.'

Instead, therefore, of seeking a wife, he worked hard at putting his business on a better footing, and did so with some success, for while on his arrival it was in a state of 'complete holiday,' by the New Year it was working fairly efficiently and once again he decided that he would probably be a printer for the rest of his life. By December, moreover, he had finished his essay, which he intended to call *Avertissement aux Propriétaires* (*Warning to Proprietors*), and his mood of increased well-being was shown when, at the beginning of 1842, he wrote a memorable letter to Bergmann, with whom, as with his other friends, his correspondence had lapsed during his provincial seclusion. His optimism was ascendant, and though he expected 'a rough year,' he believed it might be the last of its kind. For one thing, he felt that the Bisontins were not so unfriendly as he had imagined after his dispute with the Academy. 'Day by day I gain the sympathy of my neighbours,' he assured Bergmann. The municipal councillors, he said, were even considering finding him employment as a functionary, 'so as to keep me among them,' and his dreams became so vivid that he declared: 'In two years I shall be completely, bag and baggage, within the government.' What he meant by this is not easy to determine. He can hardly have expected that Louis-Philippe would suddenly invite M. Proudhon, the man of paradox and attacker of property, to sit as a minister in the royal cabinet, and we can probably take his remark to mean rather that he would be ideologically 'in the government,' that, as Sainte-Beuve has suggested, the authorities would recognise his true worth, would cease to molest him, and would even be influenced by him to deal with the economic problems which were the basic causes of popular discontent. Such illusions were very shortly to receive a salutary shaking.

9

The *Warning to Proprietors* appeared on the 10th January, 1842. It was shorter than the preceding essays, and more pyrotechnical, for Proudhon had abandoned all pretence of a memoir designed for the academicians, and had written his new essay frankly in the hope of enlisting the public in a militant crusade for changing the social order. Later he said of it: 'The dialectic intoxicated me: a certain fanaticism, peculiar to logicians, went to my brain.'

The actual points discussed in the *Warning to Proprietors* add nothing fundamental to the theory of property Proudhon had already outlined. The book begins with a short exposition of the evils of property and once again it is made clear that, despite the startling sallies to which he gives utterance, his battle is only against proprietors in the sense of non-workers. Possession cannot be divorced from work, for that would mean the return of usury and exploitation.

The latter part of the *Warning to Proprietors* consists mostly of a counter-attack on the Phalansterians and especially on their ideas of free love. 'Rather prisoner than courtesan!' Proudhon cries. 'Such is my opinion on all the theories of free love.' It was the first of a series of public skirmishes on this issue that was to continue throughout his life; all his peasant puritanism, all his sexual fears, drove him perpetually to war against this one liberty which to him was libertinage and nothing more.

But the most significant aspect of the *Warning to Proprietors* is that Proudhon no longer addresses the 'men of power,' no longer summons Louis-Philippe to lead the reform of French society. It is the populace to whom he now speaks. 'Rouse yourself, Briareus!' he calls, and ends with a passage of determined invocation in which he not only shows himself as the man of the people he always remained, but also gives the warning to the propertied classes that justifies his title and anticipates his more direct challenges to the bourgeois in the revolutionary days of 1848.

'Workers, labourers, men of the people, whoever you may be, the initiative of reform is yours. It is you who will accomplish that synthesis of social composition which will be the masterpiece of creation, and you alone can accomplish it . . . And you, men of power, angry magistrates, cowardly proprietors, have you at last understood me? . . . Do not expect either by concessions or by reasoning to make us turn back on what you call *fanaticism and dreams*, which are only the feeling of our just rights; the enthusiasm that possesses us, the enthusiasm of equality, is unknown to you . . . Above all, do not provoke the outbreak of our despair, for, even if your soldiers and policemen succeed in suppressing us, you will not be able to stand up before our last recourse. It is neither regicide, nor assassination, nor poisoning, nor arson, nor refusal to work, nor emigration, nor insurrection, nor suicide, it is something more terrible than all that, and more efficacious, something which is seen but cannot be spoken of.'

By this final mysterious threat, Proudhon assured Ackermann some months later, he meant a revival of something like the German Fehmgericht, the secret popular tribunals which dealt summarily with the petty tyrants of the Middle Ages. Just how he thought such institutions might operate in nineteenth-century France it is difficult to imagine, and the idea has that flavour of a boy's game which characterises so many of the more romantic schemes of early-nineteenth-century revolutionists. He does not appear to have spoken of this intention except in private, and for his readers the threat remained all the more sensational because of its vagueness. More than anything else he had written, it seemed to convey a direct defiance of existing law and order, an undefined but potent incitement to the disinherited, and what he had meant as a warning was immediately regarded by the authorities as a threat, to be dealt with rigorously and swiftly.

Proudhon had returned to Paris on the 10th January, the same day as the *Warning to Proprietors* appeared. On the 18th, the public prosecutor of Besançon seized the book and instituted proceedings with a precipitation that precluded any chance of intervention by highly-placed well-wishers. From this haste, Proudhon concluded that the order had not emanated from Paris, but had been given by the officials of the Doubs, inflamed against him, he suspected, by his enemies in the Academy. He claimed to Bergmann on the 23rd January, immediately after hearing of the seizure, that it was unexpected by him. But he seems to have anticipated trouble of some kind, for on the 20th January, two days before learning of the events in Besançon, he had sent a copy of the *Warning to Proprietors* to the Minister of the Interior in Paris. It was accompanied by a long explanatory letter that prejudiced rather than improved his situation by a series of criticisms describing the existing government as hypocritical, devouring, perverted and anti-national, and recommending it to overthrow its own legal system so as to prevent a more general *débâcle*. The ineffectuality of this appeal was demonstrated when, on the 25th January, the Paris police searched his rooms in the Rue Jacob and made domiciliary visits to a number of his friends.

The Besançon court, meeting on the 22nd January, remanded the case until the 3rd February, and Proudhon prepared to leave Paris in time to appear on that date. The prosecutors had originally brought nine charges of crimes against public security, under which he would have been liable to five years' imprisonment and a fine of 10,000 francs. 'I will do a month in prison and pay 100 francs fine,' he decided. 'But I prefer five years of exile in Lausanne, Neufchâtel or Geneva to a year of captivity.' The court, however, was more lenient, and when he eventually appeared only four charges were allowed to stand: 1, Attacking Property; 2, Troubling the public peace by exciting mistrust or hatred of the citizens against one or more persons; 3, Exciting hatred and mistrust against the King's Government; 4, Outrage to the Catholic religion. All these charges were based on laws which no longer operate in France. A condemnation might still involve five years' imprisonment and a fine of 6,000 francs, while the chance of leniency by the judges was lessened owing to a message from the Ministry of the Interior, which arrived as a kind of backhanded answer to Proudhon's letter and asked for the severest possible punishment in the event of the defendant being found guilty by the jury. Unexpectedly, however, he gained an acquittal because the jury found his ideas hard to follow and refused to risk a condemnation on what they did not understand.

He was singularly fortunate in this escape. The courts of that period, when the recurrent insurrections of the 1830's were still fresh in men's minds, acted with severity in political cases, and juries in towns under clerical influence, like Besançon, were always liable, when in doubt, to throw their support on the side of the government. Even Proudhon's defence, which, to judge from the account he printed immediately afterwards, certainly seems sufficiently technical to befog the average Comtois merchant, might have annoyed the jurors just as easily as it impressed them. He appears to have encountered one of those rare juries who had a sufficiently strong sense of justice to take literally their duty to indicate guilt only when it was proved, in the ancient phrase, beyond the peradventure of a doubt.

10

Acquittal was not the sole benefit Proudhon gained from his trial. As he observed at the time, it also conferred a celebrity greater than any of his works themselves had brought him. The government had considered him dangerous enough to prosecute, and, for once, had burnt its fingers, with the result that, despite his differences with the majority of his fellow socialists, he was suddenly a hero of the radicals, a man who had defied the dragon and escaped, a writer to be watched and taken seriously. His fame spread even into Germany, for it was in 1842 that Marx discovered and praised his essays on property.

Among the conservatives his name, and the disturbing doctrines he preached, began to gain notoriety. Like Lamennais, he became a bogy among the propertied classes and, realising that unpopular celebrity is better than a tolerated obscurity, he accepted his rôle and resolved to make the best of it.

But this increased fame did not bring an immediate change in his daily life. He still worked at his press, which limped along by producing catechisms at four sous apiece, and he began a philosophical treatise which would form a background to the theories he had sketched in his earlier writings. 'This time,' he explained to Bergmann, 'I am going to expose the economic and universal laws of all social organisations.' He had still a long task of study ahead before he could complete this work of 'transcendant human economy,' as he called it, and in his letters of 1842 we can trace the flow of influences in which it was being produced. He takes up and rejects philosophers, Kant and Hegel and Comte, and then, when he has cast aside all the material he has found inessential in their systems, he is as likely as not to reclaim the residue and integrate it into his own viewpoint. At the same time, he views his personal contribution to philosophy with a characteristic lack of undue modesty. 'If I do not deceive myself,' he tells Fleury, 'it should bring about a revolution in all the moral and philosophical sciences.'

But even when he was engaged in the vast amount of reading and preparation necessary for this ambitious work, Proudhon's mind was restlessly active in many other directions. The elections of 1842 prompted him to print a leaflet called *Avis motivé*; no copy of it seems to have survived, but he told Tissot that he took the opportunity to laugh at everybody, deputies, electors and government alike, and that it pleased few of his fellow citizens. He discussed literature extensively with Ackermann, and advanced some ideas on the universal presence of the germ of poetry which form an interesting anticipation of his later ideas on the rôle of the artist. 'We all have the innate feeling of poetry and a beginning of poetic talent,' he argued. 'Boileau thought so, do not doubt it, just like Goethe; but he did not admit that this germ in its ordinary proportion could become through work what one saw in Homer; that was all his thesis and I find he was right. We are all appreciators, because we all have the germ; we are not makers, because we do not all receive fertilisation.'

And, as always, he suffered from a sustained financial shortage, all the worse since his pension had ended without his shedding any of the burdens imposed by business debts or the needs of his family. This poverty and the cares of his press prevented him from travelling to Strasbourg in the autumn to attend a philological congress, and forced him to write to Antoine Gauthier asking him humbly for a loan of 150 francs.

Towards the end of the year his hopes of bettering his position were again centred around the possibility that he might obtain a position in the local government service. 'The most influential personages in the town' were using their efforts to help him; the Prefect seemed 'well disposed.' He had even heard that the Archbishop was supporting the idea of finding him a position; with such backing, he told Bergmann, he could not fail to succeed. 'To tell you the truth,' he admitted, 'my friends in Besançon think I am lulling myself with illusions. Perhaps they are not wrong. However it may be, there will be something new in my life before Easter.'

One cannot help feeling that Proudhon's friends were well justified in suspecting him of illusionism, for it is difficult to imagine that the powerful conservatives of Besançon did not see through the flimsy veil of respectability with which this ebullient iconoclast draped himself. It certainly seems unlikely that the Archbishop had in fact shown any inclination to favour him and, as for the Prefect, the inaccuracy of the rumour that he was 'well disposed' is shown clearly in the letter which Proudhon wrote to Bergmann in February, 1843, after he had learnt that he would not gain his appointment.

'The Prefect would not agree to grant me anything,' he related. 'I do not know his true motives. As my friends and sponsors all maintain a deep silence on the discomfiture of their hopes regarding me, I presume that the causes of my rejection come from my past and from the scanty hope they have of seeing me change my sentiments. What confirms me in that opinion is that when a member of our municipality suggested to the mayor that he should secure my services, the latter . . . replied that he feared I might make *fools* and *instruments* of them, as I had done of the Academicians.'

The mayor's attitude was less puzzling than Proudhon's own naïve optimism or the motives of those 'influential' friends who encouraged his expectations. The latter can hardly have been converted to his opinions, and perhaps the most reasonable explanation for their conduct is that they may have hoped his radicalism would be mitigated when he found himself in a secure position. This view is implied in the words of Dr. Delacroix, one of his sympathisers at that time, which are recorded by Sainte-Beuve: 'The day I saw Proudhon escape from us and throw himself once again into the fray, the day above all when I saw him led away by the daily struggle and obliged at the same time to face the world, I did not for one moment doubt his glorious and unhappy future. For me he was a man and a friend lost.'

Indeed, while Proudhon was far from being a 'lost man' in the larger sense, he soon became so to his provincial circle. He now realised that there was no hope of a career for him in Besançon, and his departure was facilitated in the spring of 1843 by the sale of his printing press to a workman named Bintot; the price was very low, and it left him 7,000 francs in debt, mostly to Maurice, who originally financed the business. It was an obligation that he never fully liquidated.

Very shortly afterwards, Antoine Gauthier offered him a secretarial position in Lyons; though never a disciple of Proudhon, Gauthier always appreciated his old school-friend's talents and sympathised with his misfortunes. Proudhon accepted, and towards the end of April he left the Franche-Comté. Except for brief visits, he never returned to the provincial life in which he had been bred. Yet, though his life henceforward was spent in large cities, Lyons, Paris and Brussels, the mark of his Franc-Comtois origin survived; fundamentally, his attitude on social issues was always that of the provincial regionalist in opposition to metropolitan centralism. Nevertheless, in that spring of 1843 he seems to have abandoned his native town with little regret, and with the knowledge that his real career lay in the centres of population where social and intellectual movements reach crystallisation.

Part Three

THE MAN OF AFFAIRS

I

DURING the 1840's, Lyons, more than any other city, was the centre of the French industrial revolution. Under the July monarchy, the financial and industrial magnates replaced the landed nobility of the Old Regime and the military lords of the Napoleonic interlude, and the manufacturing cities on which they depended began to expand and change in character. In none did this process go on more rapidly than in Lyons, and when Proudhon went there in 1843, it had all the pullulating life and emergent ugliness of the heedless, unplanned transition from a centre of hand-weaving to a complex of large-scale mechanical industry.

The firm of Gauthier Frères was one of the many new enterprises that flourished under these conditions. It carried goods and provided a tug-boat service on the inland waterways between Strasbourg, Bâle and Lyons, and traded in coal from the Ruhr and Lorraine. Its head office was on the Quai Sainte-Marie-des-Chaînes, in the old St. Paul's district of Lyons, and there Proudhon lived and worked at his secretarial and book-keeping tasks, except when he travelled on business to Châlon or Besançon, Mulhouse or Colmar. His employers soon learnt that their confidence in his capabilities had been justified, and they en-

71

trusted to him many responsible tasks of a quasi-legal nature, such as composing memoranda to government offices, writing brochures on administrative matters and preparing information for use in litigation.

He entered zealously into this work, for he was fascinated by the economic vistas that were opened to him by a direct contact with the life of an industrial centre. Yet he was by no means always content with his new life. His tasks were heavy, and consumed so much time that at first he had very little leisure and almost no facilities for the studies he had hoped to complete. He told his parents that he was forced 'to run around all day,' while to Maurice he made a bitter complaint of his intellectual frustration.

'In Lyons I am like a buried man. For a period I have renounced will, desire and passion; imagine what a hard sacrifice it is for a man as selfish, wilful and fiery as I. But in the face of necessity I swallow my courage and budge no more than a corpse. Without books, without solitude, without learned or literate society, I sink into eternal jesting and loafing. I begin already to get more familiar with debit and credit; I see closely the effects of competition, and am plunged in everything that is disgusting and ignoble in the commerce of Lyons.'

Lyons itself he detested from the start. A resolute provincial at heart, he had not yet learnt to tolerate large cities. His periodic outbursts against Paris illustrate this—and Lyons he found lacking even in the redeeming features of the capital, such as libraries and intelligent company. He denounced it as a 'dirty city,' grumbled about 'Lyons mud', and wryly remarked: 'God grant that the neglect of my wardrobe which has always been held against me does not degenerate into filthiness.'

Nor did he find the Lyonnais any more attractive than their environment. He had taken to wearing spectacles—the thin steel-rimmed lenses which appear in his portraits—and he complained that the results were regrettable. 'Before, all the women looked passable; now they seem atrocious to me. At first I accused my glasses, but one day when I was in the Museum I realised that beautiful things actually appeared very beautiful—more beautiful even than in nature, and that the ugly things were made more ugly.' As for the character of his neighbours, he decided they were a mixture of debauchees and bigots, over whom

the clergy seemed all powerful, and he remarked with icono-
clastic sarcasm: 'I have seen the finest processions in the world;
long lines of little boys and girls crowned with roses; one might
liken them to crowds of cherubim.'

Yet he soon found that even in Lyons reaction was not so
powerful as it had first appeared. The poverty of the factory
workers was already producing mass discontent, and Proudhon's
arrival in 1843 coincided with a considerable resurgence of
radical feeling. Flora Tristan, the half-Peruvian feminist-socialist
who claimed descent from Montezuma, was there; the Icarian
Communist, Etienne Cabet, visited the city and gained many
adherents; both the Phalansterians and the Saint-Simonians were
active. But the largest group, with which Proudhon soon made
contact, was the secret society of the Mutualists, led by working
men who had taken active parts in the risings of 1831 and 1834,
such as the weavers Joseph Benoît and Greppo. The members of
this society seem in some degree to have shared Proudhon's ideas
of the primacy of economic and social change, in contradiction
to the Jacobinical exaltation of the political revolution, and he
saw in them a vindication of his idea that out of the people could
arise the movement that would reform society.

Through these new friends Proudhon became aware of the
tendency towards revolt that was now arising among the French
people, a tendency accompanied by none of the violent manifestations frequent in the preceding decades, but perhaps for that
reason more widely spread. There is a very illuminating passage
in a letter written to Maurice in the summer of 1844, which not
merely describes with considerable accuracy the situation in the
French industrial cities, but also reveals the extent to which
Proudhon himself entered into the new working-class movement.

'While the head of society is going one way, the people go
another . . . They begin to doubt everything that is traditional,
which means that they are turning their backs on monarchical
and religious ideas. One might say that it is only now that the
spirit of '93 begins to infiltrate the people . . .

'When a thing has to happen, everything that is done to hinder
it merely helps it. Associations have been forbidden by law;
what is the result? Propaganda is carried out in broad daylight,
and the members of secret societies have become the travelling
salesmen of a reform which hopes to embrace the world . . .

It is a more enlightened and tenacious fanaticism than has ever been seen before. In 1838 there was not a single socialist in Lyons; I am assured that today there are more than 10,000 . . .

'All this, believe me, will end in something, and the movement is not falling off; on the contrary, there is progress, frightening progress. If you wish to know where you stand and how the wind blows, do not ask the men of power . . . Find out the state of the whispered propaganda that occurs spontaneously among the people, without leaders or catechisms or any yet established system, and try to understand its direction and meaning; that is the true political indicator.'

Proudhon's association with the Mutualists not only gave him insight into social undercurrents; it also provided his first appreciable audience among the working class. Before this time his works seem to have been read mostly by people of literary pretensions, or by professional revolutionaries; now, through personal contact, he was able to reach a broad and militantly inclined section of the new industrial proletariat. 'I begin to get a fair standing among the people, particularly in Lyons and the neighbouring towns and villages for fifty miles around,' he told his Besançon friend Tourneux.

Years later Proudhon partly repaid the debt to his old comrades of Lyons by naming his own proposals for social organisation 'Mutualism,' and there seems little doubt that the outlines of this theory of economic co-operation were sketched in those inspiring early days when he first saw the common action of working men on a large scale. It should be remembered that this was the only period when Proudhon became involved—to what extent we can only surmise—in an underground revolutionary organisation. He did so only because the Lyons Mutualists did not share the political romanticism which characterised the neo-Jacobin conspirators, and it is certain that he regarded their society not as an instrument for gaining political power, but as a means of giving the proletariat a consciousness of the economic realities underlying the social situation.

This attitude is reflected in his preoccupation at this period with the idea of an association of workers; if we can judge from his diary, this idea almost completely superseded his old hope of being able to effect the desirable social change by arousing the benevolent intelligence of the ruling class. Pierre Haubtmann has suggested that here we may detect the influence of Marx, whom Proudhon met during the winter of 1844. However, I think that in this, as in other points, Proudhon's debt to Marx is slight, if it exists at all, and that his concern with association grew mostly from his connections in Lyons.

There, an all-embracing association of working men was very widely discussed from 1843 onwards, before Marx and Proudhon first met, and Flora Tristan, during her association with the Lyons groups, actually wrote a book embodying the idea. Proudhon may have been influenced by her, though there is no proof of this, or they may both have developed an idea whose germ they found existing among the workers of the Midi.

A second reason for doubting Marx's influence lies in the marked difference between the methods advocated by the two men in connection with the idea of association. Proudhon was opposed to political action, and he hoped, unlike Marx, that the desirable changes in society could be brought about without violence. On the first point he remarks categorically in his diary for the spring of 1845: 'The social revolution is seriously compromised if it comes through a political revolution.' On the second point he notes: 'The workers, once they are organised and marching through work to the conquest of the world, should in no event make an uprising, but become all by invading all through the force of principle.' Again, he remarks: 'No hatred, no hatred. Eliminate by principle.' And he adds a hope of being able 'to dispossess the proprietors, at their solicitation and without indemnity.' The latter end he expects to achieve by the creation of economic associations for the exchange of products and for co-operative work, and the scene of the struggle he locates, not in the streets or the parliament house, but in the workshop. 'The new socialist movement will begin by . . . the war of the workshop.'

The associations, which he also calls 'progressive societies,' will resolve that antinomy of liberty and regulation which is one of the fundamental social contradictions, for their very nature makes them 'the true synthesis of freedom and order.' They will be formed on a 'collective and limited liability' basis, and Proudhon sees them organised as a network embracing all the industrial centres. Finally, he imagines their immediate and cumulative success. 'Appeal to the Phalansterians,' he notes, 'who will all come. Communists will come also. We are 100,000.' And he reaches the summit of confidence when he remarks: 'By 1860, the globe will be over-run in every direction by the association.'

It is needless to say that Proudhon did not even begin to fulfil his ambitions in this direction, but these notebook jottings have a particular significance because they reveal between 1843 and 1845 an attitude which anticipated not only his later efforts at associational organisation through the People's Bank, but also the foundation of the International Workingmen's Association a quarter of a century later under the leadership of men like Tolain and Varlin, who held views derived from those Proudhon evolved during his contact with the Lyons Mutualists in the early 1840's.

2

It was in September, 1843, while Proudhon was gaining his introduction to the world of working-class revolt in Lyons, that his philosophical treatise, *De la Création de l'Ordre dans l'Humanité* (*The Creation of Order in Humanity*) was published. The year of stability in Besançon, from the successful conclusion of his trial to the selling of his printing house, had enabled him to complete this ambitious treatise, wherein he sought to lay the foundations of a reconstructive philosophy, without which 'socialism would remain an object of pure curiosity, alarming to the bourgeoisie and useless to the people.'

As the time of publication drew near, he began to display that mingling of apprehension and extraordinary confidence which almost always heralded the appearance of one of his books. 'I have made it . . . so boring, so indigestible,' he told Maurice, 'that few people will have the courage to go on to the end.' But he promised the Swiss journalist, Delerageaz, that the new book would reveal 'the abyss of our ignorance' by 'uncovering a new world,' and by demonstrating 'the essential laws of creation, thought and social order.'

The Creation of Order did not achieve this high aim, and Proudhon himself admitted in 1847 to Alfred Darimon that it was 'a book that failed.' Its construction is sometimes chaotic, and the vigour and clarity that are generally Proudhon's most persuasive qualities are often obscured by turgid reasoning and submerged

under masses of ill-digested facts. 'I wanted to make an encyclopaedia,' he said ironically to Darimon; he almost succeeded, but
it was at the expense of his argument. Yet, despite the failure of
this attempt to embrace the salient facts of every field of knowledge within the covers of one book and within one philosophical
system, *The Creation of Order* remains by no means so unreadable
as its author claimed in his pessimistic moments.

Its systematic basis shows significant parallels with the theories
of both Comte and Fourier. Though Proudhon would have
denied the influence of Comte, it seems hardly accidental that he
should have chosen to place so much emphasis on the triad of
'Religion, Philosophy, Science: faith, sophism and method,'
which he declares to be the 'epochs of education of the human
race,' and which bear a striking resemblance to the three 'states' of
the positivists—the theological, metaphysical and positive. Both
religion and philosophy, in Proudhon's eyes, are necessary stages
in the progress of human understanding, and here their validity
rests, but they are destined to be superseded by science.

Fourier's influence is even clearer than Comte's, and is acknowledged with an emphasis which Proudhon later regretted. The
point of maximum contact lies in Proudhon's acceptance of the
'Serial Law,' the feature of Fourier's system which had struck him
most forcibly when he first encountered the Phalansterian in
Besançon, and the only major aspect of Fourier's work he did not
attack and reject.[1] He declared, it is true, that Fourier had not
in fact realised the full implications of the law he had discovered,
but gave him credit for having been the first to expound it.[2]

The Serial Law, Proudhon claimed, is the method by which
science can put into operation the attribute which distinguishes
it from philosophy—its lack of concern for questions of substance
and cause. Science seeks to discover, not why things exist, but

[1] A curious minor idea of Fourier which he also retained was the notion of
the 'Little Hordes,' by which the natural cruelty and love of dirt displayed
by most children could be put to social use by encouraging them to organise
into companies to undertake the community's scavenging and other functions which adults normally regard with distaste, but for which children are
often observed to display a somewhat incomprehensible liking.

[2] Pierre Leroux was later to show that the Serial Law, or its essential basis,
had existed long before Fourier; this is only one of the instances in which, in
this book, Proudhon claimed originality, on behalf of himself or others, for
ideas already in circulation but which the lag in his reading had not allowed
him to discover in writing.

how they exist, how they live, work and react on each other—in other words, their relationships. And the law of these relationships is the Serial Law, by which the objects of study can be grouped in 'series.' The series has no concern with cause or substance, but is a principle of order and hence the very basis of science. Each being, each thing, is in itself a series; in the human body the unit of the series is the organ, in a society it is the individual. To discover a series is to find a principle of order, an essential factor for understanding an object in its relationship to other members of the series, and for determining the direction of the unity that embraces them all. The Serial Law is the principle of unity in diversity, of synthesis in division.

A typical Proudhonian series is that of Liberty—the 'immortal series' as he calls it. Arranged historically, it runs as follows: liberty of persons; liberty of work; liberty of conscience; liberty of examination; liberty of voting. Failure to understand the unity implied in this series has in the past led the protagonists of various liberties into fratricidal strife, but the realisation that all kinds of freedom are mutually interdependent is the means by which this confusion can be ended.

The Serial Law, indeed, is itself a law of liberty, for it allows men to understand the co-existence of a principle of unity and a principle of differentiation, and thus makes it possible for them to live in society without losing their freedom. Here Proudhon takes up a position which distinguishes him from extreme individualists like Max Stirner. To Stirner the fundamental reality was the individual, and society was the enemy. To Proudhon the individual is the basic unit, but society provides the serial order within which each man's personality finds function and fulfilment. Individuals cannot live on their own—there is no such thing in nature as an isolated being or fact; all things, and all men, exist within serial groups, but the serial group does not constitute a totality in which individual differences are melted and merged into uniformity. Yet at the same time it is not merely a collection of individuals. Out of it emerges a collective force and a collective character which are distinct from those of its members. This idea of the collective force or consciousness was to become a constant and important element in Proudhon's thought.

The Serial Law is applied in human relationships by political economy. Proudhon here emerges, years before Marx and Engels wrote the *Communist Manifesto*, as the protagonist of an economic interpretation of history. Political economy, he declares, is 'the key to history, the theory of order, the Creator's last word,' and it will provide the means to organise the whole of society—government as well as work, family relationships as well as education. In this attitude there is much that resembles the Marxist doctrine of 'historical materialism,' but Proudhon was in no way a proto-Marxist, and both social determinism in the mechanistic sense and the nineteenth-century myth of the economic man were foreign to his viewpoint. In his opinion, the individual will exercises reciprocal action and reaction on the group's development; he never subscribes to the positivist idea of man as completely ruled by external social forces. It is the organisation of society that he regards as economic in basis and nature; the motives that move individuals, and the criteria of justice to which social changes should be subordinated, are not dominated by economics.

The key to the economic organisation of society lies in the integration of work, and the key to the integration of work is the principle of equality. To retain the advantages of the division and socialisation of labour while safeguarding the worker from their evils, to make a balanced apprenticeship the basis of education, to make woman not man's equal (which Proudhon regards as impossible because of their radically different natures) but 'the living and sympathetic complement which completes his personality,' to abolish the proletariat by ending inequality and industrial servitude—these are some of the social changes which Proudhon foresees from the application of economic science to the organisation of work.

How are such changes to be brought about? By the natural development of a collective consciousness of their necessity, through which society will move towards reform. But Proudhon has no fatalistic hope of this taking place without conscious effort on the part of individuals, for the collective will, if it is not the sum of individual wills, is an emergent from them. Revolution may become a necessity, a right and a duty, but it will be fruitless if it happens without the existence of the proper vision among the people, nor will it be consummated without an extension of these faculties. 'No revolution henceforward will be fruitful if a re-creation of public education is not its crowning feature . . .

The organisation of education is at once the condition of equality and the sanction of progress.'

The Creation of Order was received in France with silence or disapproval. Even Proudhon's friends were unenthusiastic. Tissot, from the Kantian standpoint, criticised it roundly; Ackermann declared that the execution was inferior to that of the essays on property; Leroux impugned its originality; Bergmann and Pauthier praised it with reservations.

Proudhon himself, as we have seen, soon became dissatisfied with it and admitted—even at times exaggerated—its faults. 'You are right when you say that my last work is less well written than the preceding ones,' he told Ackermann, in a fit of most uncharacteristic humility. Four years later, in the secrecy of his diary, he was even more severe. 'A recapitulation of the studies of a schoolboy, an ignoramus,' he remarked impatiently. 'The author thought he was inventing what was known before him.' Yet, for all his discontent with the form of *The Creation of Order*, he never abandoned its general arguments. The Serial Law, expressed henceforward with more reserve, remained prominent among the group of ideas which represents the nearest thing to a Proudhonian system, and *The Creation of Order*, far from making any break in the continuity of his development, in fact represents an important transition between the early works of destructive criticism and the 'constructive' books of his later decades.

Before leaving *The Creation of Order*, it should be noted that, though it aroused little attention in Paris, it made a considerable impression on writers in Russia and Germany; one of them, Alexander Herzen, wrote in his diary on the 8th February, 1845: 'This book is an extraordinarily remarkable phenomenon . . . Proudhon rises resolutely to the heights of speculative thought. He rids himself in a bold and cutting manner of the categories of the understanding. He shows admirably the weakness of casuality and substantiality . . . There is a prodigious quantity of luminous ideas in this book . . . His deduction is strong, energetic and audacious.'

Thus, several years before they actually met, *The Creation of Order* wove the first strands of an intellectual bond between these two important nineteenth-century social thinkers who were later to have a great influence upon each other's lives and ideas.

3

One of the conditions on which Proudhon had accepted his employment with the Gauthiers was that he should be free, for three or four months each year, to leave his desk at Lyons and go to Paris, where, while he attended to his firm's business there, he could also carry on his studies. He made his first trip in September, 1843, announcing his departure to Ackermann by declaring: 'Without a wife, without any attachment, with no passion but the love of truth, hatred of prejudice and an immense taste for walking, conversation and loafing, I hope gaily to lead my Bohemian life.'

Now he was no longer the student to whom Paris had seemed such a desolate and hostile city. He had an income which, though he still sent money to his parents and paid the interest on his debts as scrupulously as he could, allowed him to lead a fuller life than before, while his repute as a writer had won him many new friends. At the same time, he exaggerated to Ackermann the Bohemian and loafing aspects of his new life, for this period in Paris was actually characterised by an acceleration of his intellectual activity.

A new interest which his increased prosperity allowed him to follow at this period was the stage, and many of the more interesting entries in the diary he began this year are concerned with the theatre. He regularly attended the Opéra and the playhouses, and wrote perceptive and caustic comments on the performances. After hearing Rossini's *William Tell*, for instance, he noted with discrimination: 'Tragedy, comedy and music have independently reached a high point of perfection, but as they have not arrived there simultaneously, the performance cannot attain completeness.' And towards the great actress Rachel, whom he saw in *Phèdre*, he reacted in shocked hostility. She seemed to him a personification of the romantic excesses which he regarded as the great disintegrating factor in French art and literature. 'From the beginning to the end of the tragedy she acted like an old tart in love with a handsome boy, and in the grip of an attack of hysteria . . . When Rachel moves you, it is by grating on your nerves, not by touching your feelings.'

Yet, though he was critical of every piece he saw, his interest in the potentialities of the theatre remained strong, and for a time he even saw himself as the writer who might start the necessary revolution in dramatic forms. He went so far as to sketch several scenarios—among others, for a tragedy on Judith and Holofernes and for a play on the trial of Galileo, subjects close to his own rebellious turn of mind. It seems to have been the pressure of other affairs rather than doubts of his own ability that prevented him from completing these works.

In the winter of 1843 this ambition to write for the theatre was by no means the only preoccupation that distracted Proudhon from his studies. The news that Ackermann had married a young poetess brought him back to the problem around which he prowled in these years like a beast around the fire that scares and attracts.

'At last you are married!' he wrote. 'I received this great news without surprise and without pleasure; without surprise because it was in your nature to end up in that way; without pleasure because with my thirty-four years soon completed I am more disposed to pity lovers than to feel a real sympathy for their pretended happiness. This does not hinder our friend Pauthier from writing that he is holding at my disposition a pretty peasant girl of Neuilly-sur-Marne; he pretends that in the way of a wife a peasant girl is all a philosopher needs. Indeed, I do not accept that ambitious title, but we shall see the little girl, and, by God, if it is written that I shall marry, I will accept my fate with a completely philosophical resignation.'

Nothing more was heard of the girl from Neuilly, but the question of marriage and its effect on husbands still troubled him, and a year afterwards he remarked to Ackermann that, of all their old group in Besançon, he himself was the only one who had remained unmarried, and also the only one who had remained consistent in 'the philadelphic bond' of friendship. 'I notice that marriage operates in a strange way on you other gentlemen, who have taken wives. At first you begin by wishing your friends as much happiness as has come to you; then, withdrawing gradually into the household, you end by forgetting that you were companions. I used to believe that love and paternity augmented friendship among men; I see today that this was only a paradox, an illusion. Love is thus as limited in man as his intelligence.'

But, though he seems here to reject it as an enemy of the higher relationship of friendship, it is evident that love, or at least its physical manifestation, had not rejected him, and early in 1845 there appears in his diary a laconic note, 'work induces chastity,' which reveals a world of inner struggle where the devil who tempted St. Paul was still lurking.

These disturbances of his personal equanimity seem to have stimulated Proudhon's mental activity, and immediately after completing *The Creation of Order* he was already planning a new work. His commercial activities had made him more conscious than ever of the contradictions which existed beneath the apparent unity of the capitalist economic structure, and he proposed to make these the basis of a new book. As usual, Bergmann was one of the first to whom he confided his plans, in a letter written on the 24th October, 1843. 'I am going to show that all the hypotheses of political economy, of legislation, of morality and of government, are essentially contradictory . . . I shall also present the theory and example of the synthetic resolution of all the contradictions.'

At the same time, his growing repute as a rising social critic had brought him to the attention of the editors of the left-wing press, who began to make tentative suggestions of collaboration. The Republicans of the Mountain were contemplating a new journal, *La Réforme*, and Proudhon told Ackermann: 'I am called to it by the entire managing council.' And then there was Cabet's *Le Populaire*, whose editors also were anxious to gain his help in turning their paper into a daily.

Martin Nadaud, the mason who became a member of the revolutionary Assembly in 1848, was one of the two friends of Cabet who went to negotiate with Proudhon on the last project. They found him living at No. 36, rue Mazarin, in a tiny, dark room, on the ground floor, lit only by a small window that gave on to a narrow court. Nadaud remarked that 'Proudhon, by reason of his bearing and his large, rather chubby face, had the air of one of those childlike peasants who come home happy from market when they have driven a good bargain.'

Proudhon carried on a peculiar kind of intellectual coquetry with his visitors. He began by praising Cabet, whom he claimed to regard as an honest man, and then suddenly, when the Icarians expected a willing collaboration, he turned to a bench loaded with thick files of papers and remarked: 'Gentlemen, these papers are meant to combat you.' Despite this indecisive meeting, the flirtation with the Icarians continued for some time, and appears to have been taken seriously on both sides, for in Proudhon's diary we find, in a long list of 'works to be done,' a note of 'one piece a week' for *Le Populaire*. When he returned to Paris in the spring of 1844 he again visited Cabet, and in July, when the latter went to speak in Lyons, he made a great deal of Proudhon. 'The good man designates me his successor in the apostolate,' said Proudhon to Maurice. 'I will hand over the succession to anybody who buys me a cup of coffee.' By now he had realised the impossibility of two such incompatible attitudes as the communist and the anarchist being able to work together.

Yet the idea of a collaboration between all the socialist sects and tendencies, in which he would play a leading part as unifier, continued to tempt him. As early as October, 1844, he gave Ackermann the most glowing picture of the prospects for unity: 'What today is called in France *the socialist party* is becoming organised. Already several writers have come together; Pierre Leroux, Louis Blanc, several others of whom you have not heard, and your unworthy friend. The people call upon us only to give them an example of unity and to educate them. George Sand has completely entered into our ideas.'

Socialism, he declared, numbered more than a hundred thousand adherents—perhaps even more than two hundred thousand, and in this mass of confused opinions he saw himself (strangely enough for a man who could rarely collaborate) as the great go-between. 'I work with all my strength to bring an end to the dissensions between us, at the same time as I carry discord into the enemy camp.'

Though he was mistaken in his own rôle, Proudhon was not wholly wrong in detecting a unifying influence at work among the jarring sects who represented the French left of the 1840's. But it was less an internal urge than a tendency imposed from outside, by a growing realisation of the scanty hope of seeing social reform granted freely by the entrenched bourgeoisie. This realisation swept Phalansterians, Icarians, neo-Jacobins, Saint-Simonians, feminists, Republicans and unattached anarchists like Proudhon on the same wave of popular awakening and indignation. As always, the revolutionary thinkers and talkers had produced no situation; they were responding to a situation that grew out of the people's discontent, and, while Proudhon was right when he remarked to Ackermann, 'the half-century will not pass, I am sure, without European society feeling our powerful influence,' the influence of the radicals was to be felt in 1848 only as a reflection of a general movement within European society.

It was characteristic of Proudhon's paradoxical nature that in the same letter as he declared himself a unifying agent, he also complained against those with whom he hoped to ally himself. The republicans had little use for him because he was not 'a blind partisan of war.' The Communists regarded him almost as a man of the centre. 'I am in the most unfortunate position; I must be right against everybody at once; otherwise I am lost.'

In such circumstances it was inevitable that the truce between Proudhon and his fellow socialists should have been temporary. Already in March, 1845, he remarked indignantly in his diary that the republicans and Cabet had done 'an immense wrong to progress' by pressing for the re-arming of the Paris forts, which he justly regarded as a dangerous piece of sentimental Jacobin bellicosity, and round about the same time he noted his specific distrust of Cabet. 'He is religious, dictatorial, intolerant, haughty, intriguing . . . Beware!' In the suspicion of this remark were embodied all those individualist factors which prevented Proudhon from ever collaborating satisfactorily with his fellow revolutionaries, but which also preserved the independence and originality of his own thought.

4

At the end of February, 1844, Proudhon was again in Paris. He met Pauthier, Tissot and other old friends, continued his fruitless negotiations with Cabet and, perhaps most important, made the acquaintance of a number of orthodox political economists.

This he achieved through Joseph Garnier, a celebrated economist with whom he began to exchange letters during 1843. Early in this correspondence he defended his non-academic status with almost aggressive fervour. 'For my part, I dare to say that, with my turn of imagination, I see more things from my office than a professor from his chair.' Evidently this approach did not alienate Garnier, who wrote for the *Revue des Economistes* a sympathetic review of *The Creation of Order*. 'I do not meet such justice among the radicals and independents, who call me *brother* and *citizen* Proudhon,' said the author in gratitude. But he added a complaint that 'no idea is accepted, no book will sell, unless the author belongs to something: to the university, the press, the administration, the clergy, to some coterie or corporation.'

It was perhaps in the hope of dispelling this sense of grievance that in March, 1844, Garnier invited Proudhon to attend a gathering of the Société des Economistes at the Café des Panoramas. Proudhon was delighted by the gesture, and out of their academic chairs he found the economists 'good fellows, educated men, of sound sense, and good taste, whom it is a pleasure to meet.' But the main practical advantage of the encounter was the contact he made with the publisher Guillaumin, who produced most of the important treatises on political economy that appeared in France. Garnier had predisposed Guillaumin in Proudhon's favour, representing him as a man whose ideas, despite the aggressiveness of their expression, deserved consideration. Guillaumin 'made advances,' and in a very short time had agreed to publish the work on economic contradictions which Proudhon had described to Bergmann in October, 1843.

This success in placing his book before it was completed stimulated Proudhon to work, but, though his situation in the summer of 1844 seems to have been more auspicious than for a long time before, he still found plenty of cause to bewail his fortune. He was not wholly unjustified, for his debts and family obligations formed a burden other men might have found crippling. Yet at times one has the impression—an impression that recurs in studying his later life—of a discontent which, though rooted in sound causes, had tended to become self-perpetuating. For instance, shortly after successfully completing his negotiations with Guillaumin, he wrote to Tourneux in the tones of a man whose future had been blasted by the prejudices of his enemies. 'I am simply an excommunicant. The appearance of my booklets has put me everywhere on the index; anger and the feeling of injustice have embittered me, and, like Raspail, with all my capacity and zeal I achieve not a quarter of what I wish.' To an extent this attitude can be traced to that feeling of inferiority which a man with little formal education often experiences in the presence of those whom chance has given the advantages he has missed.

But if at times Proudhon's discontent became tiresomely

manifest, it did not corrode his ideals. He found individual men faulty and erring, he saw the flaws in corporate institutions, but he never lost his faith in humanity, or in the ideals of justice, equality and freedom which in his mind assumed such concrete forms, nor did he abandon that pure patriotism which, for all his internationalism and his Franc-Comtois provincialism, still made him acutely conscious of the glories of France. When Ackermann, who was now collaborating with Alexander Humboldt in Berlin, ventured to blame his country for the neglect he himself had experienced, Proudhon took him to task. 'You are always accusing France, as if France, as if a whole nation, the most intelligent and generous of nations, could be the same, in the eyes of its children, as the governments who dishonour it, the coteries who abuse it, the charlatans and rascals who exploit it.'

Proudhon never lost this pride in his country and his people, but it was a patriotism that did not decline into uncritical chauvinism, and when the rulers of France, or the French people, did anything that was unworthy, Proudhon was the first to call them to order in the name of that revolutionary tradition which he regarded as the true tradition of France.

5

In September, 1844, Proudhon made another visit to Paris, and this sojourn of several months is of particular interest, since it was now that he made the acquaintance of the German Left-Hegelians and of the Russian revolutionary, Michael Bakunin. To Micaud he wrote in December, 'I know more than twenty Germans, all of them Doctors of Philosophy.' These included some of the most important German revolutionary figures of the century—Marx, then twenty-five, Heine, Arnold Ruge, editor of the *Annales Franco-Allemandes*, the younger Fichte, Karl Gruen and his friend Ewerbeck. Two of these men, Ruge and Gruen, together with Bakunin, were later to assist in spreading Proudhon's ideas, while Marx became his most celebrated enemy. As it is from the three-cornered encounter of Proudhon, Bakunin and the German Left-Hegelians that one can date the beginning of the great nineteenth-century split between the libertarian and authoritarian socialists, I shall discuss in some detail the events of this time.

Karl Gruen was the German who first sought out Proudhon, and in *Die Soziale Bewegung in Frankreich* he describes their earliest meeting. Proudhon was living in 'a student's room,' with a bed, a few books standing on a cupboard, and a table spread with newspapers and reviews of economics. Gruen saw him as 'a tall, sturdy man ... dressed in a knitted woollen jerkin, with clattering sabots on his feet.' He had 'an open face with well-sculptured brow and fine eyebrows,' a domed cranium and a massive lower face. But the feature that fascinated Gruen was the slight cast in the 'fine, clear eyes.' Proudhon's way of speaking was energetic, with a peasant vigour and clear pronunciation, and his language was 'crowded and concise, with an exquisitely appropriate choice of expression.' He gave the impression of calm and self-assurance.

Proudhon showed a particular eagerness to discuss German philosophy, and Gruen told him of the ideas of Feuerbach, declaring, 'And thus anthropology is metaphysics in action,' to which Proudhon replied, 'As for me, I am going to show that political economy is metaphysics in action.' The conversation then turned to Hegel, whose ideas Proudhon had already encountered through Willm's expositions. He was now anxious to find out from his new German friend whatever he might have missed in Hegel's thought. 'He was greatly relieved,' says Gruen, 'when I told him how criticism dissolved the Hegelian bombast.'

Proudhon, indeed, discussed questions of this kind with all his new friends, and the dialectic seems to have become the principal subject of the interminable conversations in their dingy little hotel rooms of the Left Bank. Marx and Bakunin, as well as Gruen, took part in these discussions, and the former claimed, when he delivered a final attack on Proudhon after the latter was safely dead, that he personally 'injected him with Hegelianism, to his great prejudice, since not knowing German, he could not study the question in the original.' In disposing of this claim we may note not merely Proudhon's interest in Hegel as early as 1840 and his conversations with Gruen before he actually met Marx, but also the fact that the all-night conversations on Hegel also went on with Bakunin.

According to Herzen, Proudhon was very intimate with Bakunin, and the references to the latter that appear in Proudhon's correspondence certainly lead one to believe that a great deal of affection existed between the two great anarchists. In 1851 Proud-

hon wrote to Herzen that he had been weeping over Bakunin's
'slow assassination' in the fortress of Schluesselberg; 'Herzen,
Bakunin, Edmond, I love you!' he cried, 'you are there, enshrined
in a heart which for so many others seems to be of marble!'

When Herzen arrived in Paris during 1847, some years after
Proudhon's original meeting with Bakunin, the latter was living
with the musician Reihel in the Rue de Bourgogne. 'Proudhon
often went there to listen to Reihel's Beethoven and Bakunin's
Hegel—the philosophical discussions lasted longer than the
symphonies . . . In 1847, Karl Vogt, who also lived in the Rue de
Bourgogne, and often visited Reihel and Bakunin, was bored one
evening with listening to the endless discussions on Phenomen-
ology, and went to bed. Next morning he went round for Reihel,
as they were to go to the Jardin des Plantes together; he was surprised to hear conversation in Bakunin's study at that early hour.
He opened the door—Proudhon and Bakunin were sitting in the
same places before the burnt-out embers in the fireplace, finishing
their brief summing-up of the argument started overnight.'

It seems evident, then, that at this time many people talked to
Proudhon about the Hegelian philosophy, and increased his
knowledge of its implications, but none of them, despite the
Marxist claims, introduced him to Hegel. As a final point in this
controversy, it should also be remembered that Proudhon never
admitted to being a Hegelian in the full sense. Some of Hegel's
forms of argument appealed to him, but he adapted them deliberately to his own philosophical attitude rather than, as Marx
suggested, distorting them through ignorance. This is evident
from the following passage of *De la Justice*: 'The Hegelian formula
is a triad only by the sweet will or an error of the master, who
counts three terms where only two exist, and who had not seen
that an antinomy cannot be resolved, but that it indicates an
oscillation or an antagonism susceptible only of equilibrium.'

Thus the criticism of Proudhon which Marx later made in *The
Poverty of Philosophy*, for not having 'been able to rise higher
than the first two rungs of the simple thesis and antithesis,' and
for 'being stricken with sterility when it is a question of giving
birth to a new category through the labour of dialectical confinement' is devoid of point, since Proudhon never set out to become
a Hegelian acrobat; the fact that the perpetual antinomy can
always be detected in his thoughts is not a product of mis-

understanding, as can be seen from another passage in *De la Justice*, where he says: '*The antinomy cannot be resolved.* There lies all the imperfection of the Hegelian Philosophy.' Thus the debate on who taught Proudhon Hegelianism dwindles into pointlessness.

In general, Proudhon seems to have found his philosophical discussions with the German expatriates more stimulating than convincing. 'You can say almost the same about their philosophy of history as you can about their dialectic,' he remarked. 'It makes one think; it brings out the truth; it has nothing absolute about it, and, too frequently, nothing certain either.' Yet these encounters broadened his philosophic viewpoint and helped to systematise his thought, so that he never again produced a book as chaotic as *The Creation of Order*.

A lesser, but perhaps more gratifying, result of Proudhon's meeting with the Left-Hegelians was the realisation that he had already a considerable reputation in Germany, where he was regarded by many younger thinkers as the best of the French socialists. This interest merits some explanation. The whole of the German Left-Hegelian school—Ruge and Gruen as well as Marx and Engels—was dominated by the idea of building a world brotherhood of socialists. With this aim in view, they founded the *Annales Franco-Allemandes* as an organ of international co-operation. Their initial effort was disappointingly unsuccessful. They secured the collaboration of only one important non-German, Michael Bakunin, who delivered in the pages of their review his famous dictum, 'The urge to destroy is also a creative urge,' and the *Annales Franco-Allemandes* appeared, ironically, without a single French contributor. Even settlement in Paris did not bring the German socialists into much closer contact with their French counterparts, with the sole exception of Proudhon, and the reasons for this failure are fairly clear.

First, as Pierre Haubtmann has pointed out, while the Germans regarded anti-religious propaganda as a necessary part of their revolutionary programme, almost all the leading French socialists claimed at least a quasi-religious inspiration. The disapproval felt by the Germans for this flirting with religion was shown in a letter written by Engels in 1843: 'It is . . . entirely remarkable that . . . the French Communists, who belong to a nation famous for its unbelief, are themselves Christians.' Only Proudhon stood aloof from this tendency. Even he did not agree with German 'atheist humanism,' but he regarded religion critically as a passing phase in social evolution, and his mind was therefore open to the arguments of the German anti-religious socialists.

Secondly, the French socialists still moved mostly in the Jacobin tradition, which nurtured the assumption that France was the world centre of revolution, and when the solemn German doctors of philosophy came to Paris with their baggage of wordy dialectics and tried to teach the French how the revolution should be carried out, the latter merely ignored them.

Only Proudhon, anti-clerical, anti-Jacobinical, and not at all patriotic in the narrow way of his fellows, was ready to welcome them. And even he had a peasant's eye to the intellectual main chance, for he w; s much more concerned with what he might learn from the Germans about philosophy than with how he might help their schemes for international co-operation. For, though the idea of an association of the working classes was very much in his mird during the years when he knew Marx, it was not an organisation for political propaganda, as conceived by the German socialists, that he envisaged, but an association for economic action, based on the workshop.

In the long conversations in that winter of 1844–5, Marx doubtless realised these Proudhonian reservations. But he seems also to have decided that Proudhon was more likely than any of the other French socialists to, fall in with his own ideas of an international network. How far this aim was discussed during their direct acquaintanceship in Paris is unrecorded. It does not, however, seem likely that anything definite was proposed, for though Marx was expelled from France in February, 1845, it was not until the 5th May, 1846, that he actually wrote to Proudhon suggesting co-operation. This letter and the reply are of great importance in socialist history.

Marx proposed to establish a 'sustained correspondence' among socialists, concerned with the discussion of scientific questions and with the problems of socialist propaganda. 'But the principal aim of our correspondence will be that of putting the German socialists into touch with the French and English socialists, so as to keep foreigners informed of the socialist movements which are operating in Germany, and to inform the Germans within Germany of the progress of socialism in France and England. In that manner, differences of opinion can be brought to light; one can achieve an exchange of ideas and an impartial criticism. It will be a step forward for the socialist movement in its "literary" expression, a step towards shaking off the limitations of "nationality." And at the moment of action it is certainly of great importance for each of us to be informed on the state of affairs abroad as well as at home . . . Our relations with England are already established; as for France, we all believe that we can find there no better correspondent than yourself—you know that up to the present the English and German socialists have appreciated you more than your own fellow countrymen.'

Proudhon accepted this approach without enthusiasm, and his reply revealed a number of aspects of his character which Marx had evidently left out of consideration. Proudhon's native shrewdness made him detect the latent authoritarian traits which were to become so prominent in Marx's subsequent activity, and his innate independence made him cautious about entering into commitments that might compromise his freedom of judgment. His letter laid down clearly and frankly the differences that divided him from the authoritarian socialists. He began by expressing his willingness to participate, but at the same time made a series of significant reservations.

'First, although my ideas in the matter of organisation and realisation are at this moment more or less settled, at least as regards principles, I believe it is my duty, as it is the duty of all socialists, to maintain for some time yet the critical or dubitive form; in short, I make profession in public of an almost absolute economic anti-dogmatism.

'Let us seek together, if you wish, the laws of society, the manner in which these laws are realised, the process by which we shall succeed in discovering them; but, for God's sake, after having demolished all the *a priori* dogmatisms, do not let us in our turn dream of indoctrinating the people . . . I applaud with all my heart your thought of bringing to light all opinions; let us carry on a good and loyal polemic; let us give the world the example of a learned and far-sighted tolerance, but let us not, because we are at the head of a movement, make ourselves the leaders of a new intolerance, let us not pose as the apostles of a new religion, even if it be the religion of logic, the religion of reason. Let us gather together and encourage all protests, let us brand all exclusiveness, all mysticism; let us never regard a question as exhausted, and when we have used our last argument, let us begin again, if necessary, with eloquence and irony. On that condition, I will gladly enter into your association. Otherwise—no!

'I have also some observations to make on this phrase of your letter: *at the moment of action*. Perhaps you still retain the opinion that no reform is at present possible without a *coup de main*, without what was formerly called a revolution and is really nothing but a shock. That opinion, which I understand, which I excuse and would willingly discuss, having myself shared it for a long time, my most recent studies have made me completely abandon. I believe we have no need of it in order to succeed; and that consequently we should not put forward *revolutionary action* as a means of social reform, because that pretended means would simply be an appeal to force, to arbitrariness, in brief, a contradiction. I myself put the problem in this way: *to bring about the return to society, by an economic combination, of the wealth which was withdrawn from society by another economic combination*. In other words, through Political Economy to turn the theory of Property against Property in such a way as to engender what you German socialists call *community* and what I will limit myself for the moment to calling *liberty* or *equality*. But I believe that I know the means of solving this problem with only a short delay; I would therefore prefer to burn Property by a slow fire, rather than give it new strength by making a St. Bartholomew's night of the proprietors.'

This letter ended all direct communication between Marx and Proudhon. Marx never replied, and we are told that he was disappointed by Proudhon's attitude. It is more likely that he was enraged, and it seems certain that he realised he had been trying to deal with a man whose character was as strong as his own and whose ideas of social morality made their co-operation impossible. Since Marx believed fervently that all who were not with him were against him, it was not long before the failure of communication that ensued broke into open hostility. Marx only waited for an incident that he could use as a pretext for war.

6

During these years when Proudhon was gaining his introduction to the literary-political world, he did not cease to be concerned for the welfare of his family—his parents, who were growing steadily more afflicted by age, and also his brother Charles, whose ability to earn a living was reduced by recurrent sickness. Throughout 1844 his letters to them contained, interspersed with domestic requests for such things as cravats and flannel undergarments, many anxious protestations of his desire to provide more fully for their welfare. 'Believe always, my dear father and mother,' he wrote from Mulhouse in February, 'that my efforts will ever turn towards making your life more agreeable.'

Later, he decided that his parents would be better off if they returned to the country, and at the end of 1845, after a year of persuasion, they finally left Battant for Cordiron, where Charles was working as a blacksmith, and where Pierre-Joseph, once they were established, wrote to them in solicitous enquiry: 'Let me know if your habitation is warm and not damp, if you have your supply of wood, how you are provisioned, finally, how you are living . . . I am afraid you may be bored. If that happens, you must return to Besançon. I did not wish to tell you in advance that in going to Cordiron you would only be making an experiment; the idea of an experiment would have stopped you from trying anything. But believe me, I do not intend to make you die in a solitude, and if in the spring the air of the fields does not suit you, I repeat, you will be able to take up your lodging in town. Keep warm in the meantime, and cover yourselves well. I hope that if you can pass happily through the first quarter of 1846, your life will then have more purpose.'

But the retirement to country tranquillity came too late to help Claude-François Proudhon; he did not even live through that first quarter of 1846, and died at Cordiron on the 30th March, 1846. His calm death seemed to Pierre-Joseph the model of a stoic's end. 'Friendship, a clear conscience, the hope of a better future for those he left behind, united to give a perfect calm to his last moments. The next day my brother wrote to me: "Our father died bravely." The priests will not canonise him, but I who knew him proclaim him in my turn *a brave man*, and hope for myself no better funeral oration.'

This was written a decade afterwards; at the time Proudhon felt that curious mingling of sorrow, self-reproach and relief which young people often experience on the death of their parents. Particularly he regretted his own failure to make his father's happiness more complete. 'I had promised myself,' he told Bergmann, 'that my situation would change before my father's death, in such a way that the poor old man would carry with him in dying the satisfaction of his son reaching a respectable position. Heaven disposed otherwise, and I felt greatly mortified.' But to Ackermann (himself marked to die of consumption before the year was out) he confessed the sense of liberation which this event also brought him. He had abandoned now any idea of returning to live in the Franche-Comté, and 'for the consideration of a small living allowance I make to that dear woman (his mother), I am as free as if I were absolutely alone in the world and without family connections, like grandfather Melchisedek.'

7

From the latter part of 1843 until the autumn of 1846, Proudhon was working continuously on *Contradictions Economiques*, and directly or indirectly almost all his activities seemed to have a bearing on his literary work. His experiences as a transport clerk, his meetings with the orthodox economists, his philosophical discussions with the German socialists, his collaboration with the Mutualist workers of Lyons, and his critical observation of the French socialist theoreticians, all went to influence the contents and mould the form of this book, which he imagined would become his definitive masterpiece.

By March, 1846, his work was far enough advanced for a draft to be handed to Guillaumin. The latter seems to have been disconcerted by Proudhon's attacks on the orthodox political economists, for on the 4th April the author penitently promised to change any passages that might offend. 'I will profit by your warning,' he added, 'for, as I have said many times, nobody is more convinced than I of the probity, honour and virtues of the economists I have had the occasion to meet.' But when Guillaumin's objections continued, Proudhon reacted in stubborn protest. 'You insist on seeing in my book nothing but a kind of satire on political economy; you will be completely surprised when, in the end, except for a few explanations which our century must be given, you will see there, fundamentally, only its apotheosis.'

Despite his doubts, Guillaumin found the manuscript sufficiently interesting to keep his promise of publication, and he offered a thousand francs for the first edition. 'A thousand francs!' Proudhon complained disgustedly in his diary. 'Now I understand how the Government counts on the fatigue of socialism, on the exhaustion of courage!' He considered the offer for three weeks. Then he gave in and remarked bitterly: 'I accept. If a second edition materialises, it cannot be worth anything more to me, after which all will be said. Two thousand francs for ten years of study!'

During the remaining months while Proudhon finished his book, his mood swung continually between confidence and pessimism, and at times attained an unusually humorous detachment in which he jested at his manifestations of both the more extreme moods, for in July he told Ackermann: '. . . a year from now I shall either have fallen completely into absurdity and ridicule through my theories, or I shall have inaugurated the greatest, the most radical, the most decisive revolutionary movement that has been seen in the world. Perhaps, however, I am neither bordering on a downfall nor near an apotheosis, and it may be with my plans as with so many things that appeared mountains to their authors when really they were only molehills.'

The System of Economic Contradictions, or, The Philosophy of Poverty, appeared in October, 1846, and Proudhon, sending a copy to Bergmann, announced it as marking a decisive moment in his life; from its success or failure he would discover whether he should continue as a business man or whether he would fulfil 'a nobler rôle.'

Within the two volumes of this ambitious work Proudhon set out to investigate the whole economic basis of contemporary society. Into the social vision of every philosopher, no matter how much honest reasoning and painstaking observation may have gone to make it, there enters always an important element derived from the particular bent of his personality. Authoritarians, like Plato, direct their ideas towards a static social order. The doctrines of Hegel, and their Marxian derivatives, are also of this nature, striving to arrest the movement they see in society into a final synthesis where, since the contradictions are resolved, movement will presumably end. Other philosophers, like Heraclitus, see in struggle and movement basic elements in the natural order. Proudhon was one of these, and, while in his *Economic Contradictions* there indeed appears the hint of a synthesis, it is kept very

Portrait of Pierre-Joseph Proudhon
by Gustave Courbet
Drawing, Musée de Montpellier

far in the background. It is the actual play of Contradictions in which Proudhon is really interested; the thread of Hegelianism that runs through his book is both tenuous and alien. Indeed, he draws more from Kant than from Hegel, and one can foresee the later stage of his development in which he would abandon the idea of synthesis for that of a dynamic equilibrium between eternally opposing forces.

Proudhon's world view was in fact essentially Zoroasterian, dominated by the vision of a new struggle between Ormuzd and Ahriham in the guise of clashing economic and moral trends. Though suggestions of reconciliation appear in his book, its main purpose was to show the great panorama of the world of contradictions, and he had too much love for the vision he created to mitigate its portentous quality. Just as Milton and Dante allowed no heavenly beatitude to break the impressive horror of their hells, so Proudhon did not spoil his spectacle of the earthly inferno of economic chaos by the celestial light of a Utopian solution. He promised to resolve the contradictions at a later date.

It would be hard to compress into a few pages an adequate summary of this sprawling, vigorous and combative work. But in his final chapter, Proudhon fortunately provided a brief recapitulation of his theme, and I begin by quoting from this.

'The essential contradiction of our ideas, being realised by work and expressed in society with a gigantic power, makes all things happen in the reverse way to that in which they should, and gives society the aspect of a tapestry seen the wrong way round or a hide turned inside out . . . The non-producer should obey, and by a bitter irony it is the non-producer who commands. Credit, according to the etymology of its name and its theoretical definition, should be the provider of work; in practice it oppresses and kills it. Property, in the spirit of its finest prerogatives, is the making available of the earth, and in the exercise of the same prerogative it becomes the denial of the earth.'

Economic Contradictions discusses all these phenomena, both as regards their potential value to humanity and their actual malignancy, and, in the process, shows the fundamental division within the communist solution which, taking fraternity for its principle, destroys it and leads to monopoly. But the section written with the greatest vigour, destined (and doubtless intended) to shock readers more than any other part of the book, is that 'On Providence,' in which Proudhon dissects the conception of God as shown in theology, and argues that the religious attitude perpetuates the contradictions within human society and serves as a prototype for injustice. If God, or Providence, is actually responsible for the world as it is, Proudhon contends that he is an influence irrevocably fatal to humanity. 'We reach knowledge in spite of him, we reach well-being in spite of him, we reach society in spite of him. Every step forward is a victory in which we overcome the Divine.'

And here Proudhon issues a passionate call to liberation from the reactionary idea of deity. 'God is stupidity and cowardice; God is hypocrisy and falsehood; God is tyranny and poverty; God is evil,' he declaims. 'Where humanity bows before an altar, humanity, the slave of kings and priests, will be condemned; where any man, in the name of God, shall receive the oath of another man, society will be founded on perjury; peace and love will be banished from among mortals. Retreat, God, for today, cured of your fear and become wise, I swear, with my hand stretched out towards the heavens, that you are nothing more than the executioner of my reason, the spectre of my conscience . . .

'I affirm that God, if there is a God, bears no resemblance to the effigies which the philosophers and the priests have made of him; that he neither thinks nor acts according to the law of analysis, foresight and progress, which is the distinctive characteristic of man; that, on the contrary, he seems to follow an inverse and retrograde path; that intelligence, liberty, personality are constituted otherwise in God than in us; and that this originality of nature . . . makes of God a being who is essentially anti-civilised, anti-liberal, anti-human.'

These are not the statements of an atheist, any more than Baudelaire's Satanism, which on occasion seems to resemble Proudhon's, is atheistical. Rather, we are in the presence of the final contradiction—God and Man. And whether we regard God as an objective reality or as a projection of human beliefs and traditions does not matter a great deal. The important thing is that a principle of evil and a principle of good appear as active and rival entities in Proudhon's world. This interpretation is supported by the two extracts from his diary during the year 1846: (1) 'God and man neither is more than the other; they are two incomplete realities, which have no fulness of existence.' (2) 'God is necessary to reason but rejected by reason.'

As the positive element in his world view Proudhon sets up man. But, since man's actions are thwarted and turned to evil, the other side of the contradiction, responsible for these miscarriages, must itself be evil. And since God, the complement to man, is the other side, God must therefore be evil. In Proudhonian logic the conclusion is inescapable, and, if it needed any reinforcement, the idea had that element of high paradox which Proudhon could never resist. Like *Property is Theft, God is Evil* was a phrase to startle and provoke the world.

The title page of *Economic Contradictions* bore the motto *Destruam et Aedificabo*. Proudhon destroyed to great effect, but the building is less evident, and it is not easy to decide in concrete terms what Proudhon had in mind for the solution of social problems. Such familiar Proudhoniana as the equalisation of property, the dissolution of government, and free credit, push their way rather feebly through the rank tangle of false theories which Proudhon fells with such prodigal zeal. An even more significant idea is little more than sketched in when he talks of the organisation of work, and declares that here is no place for capital or government to interfere; the organisation of work is the business of the workers themselves.

In general, his conclusion is variously expressed in the terms 'synthesis' and 'equation.' For instance, he declares: 'It is not towards destroying monopoly, any more than work, that we should tend; it is, by a synthesis which the contradictions of monopoly renders inevitable, towards making it produce in the interest of all the riches which it now produces for a few.' But, as we have seen, the synthesis, at least in the Hegelian sense, is not a concept which Proudhon adopts in any full sense. The idea of balance is much more to his taste, and rather than imagining a reconciliation of opposites, I think we can reach a much better idea of what he had in mind if we conceive the contradictions brought into a dynamic equation which has the effect of raising their struggle to a higher plane where it will become a regenerative and constructive rather than a stultifying and destructive force.

Proudhon reverts to his days among the Lyons workers when he gives us the hint that this dynamic equation will be found in 'a theory of MUTUALITY.' This Mutuality he defines as 'a society not merely conventional, but real, which changes the division of labour into an instrument of science, which abolishes slavery to machines and halts crises before they appear, which makes competition a benefit and monopoly a pledge of security for all, which, by the power of its principle, instead of demanding credit from capital and protection from the State, submits both capital and State to labour . . .'

We are given little more in the way of constructive hints; the rest is promised for a later book. And, in fact, Proudhon worked a great deal of the destructionism out of his system by writing *Economic Contradictions*. It is more completely devoted to criticism than any of his later works, and in other volumes we shall find constructive suggestions which have greater substance than these vague sketches. But it would be unwise to forget that Proudhon was essentially an anti-systematic thinker who hated static solutions. The dynamic society was always his ideal, the society kept alive and in movement by perpetual criticism, and such a society can never be built according to a foreordained plan.

Economic Contradictions gained a success that was largely of scandal, but, while it increased Proudhon's notoriety, it also placed him firmly among the leading intellectuals of the French socialist movement. As events in 1848 were to show, it greatly augmented his following among the literate workers, and in Germany it increased the Proudhon vogue, for by the middle of 1847 no less than three translations had been announced.

On the other hand, it aroused many people against its author. The pious were infuriated by his attacks on God. The economists were annoyed by his polemics against themselves. Most of his fellow socialists disagreed with him either for his denunciation of Communism or for his anti-religion. Guillaumin, who was overwhelmed with protests, became querulous, and an exasperated exchange of letters took place between publisher and author. 'I insult no person, no class of society, no religion,' Proudhon protested. 'I have the right to discuss all principles, to combat them, to renovate them, etc. . . . and if I have chosen a completely dramatic form, that is only a question of literature and taste.'

It was not surprising, after so many attacks, that Proudhon should have felt a return of his recurrent sense of isolation. 'I have earned the antipathy of everybody,' he told Maurice early in 1847. 'The repulsion I inspire is general, from the communists, republicans and radicals to the conservatives and Jesuits, including the Jesuits of the University.' Yet there was a perceptible change in his attitude towards his critics. The tendency to conciliate had gone; now he almost gloried in the feeling of being opposed, and when the Comtesse d'Agoult deplored his talent for making enemies, he answered: 'The number of adversaries frightens you; I, on the other hand, am animated by it.'

But it was still with little equanimity that, nearly a year afterwards, he read what was not only the most scathing criticism of his book, but also the most ruthless attack he experienced during the whole of his career. It will be remembered that Karl Marx never replied directly to the letter in which Proudhon had so clearly underlined their differences of outlook. In June, 1847, the reply was made indirectly, when Marx, in a volume of 220 pages, applied his critical rod with stinging violence to his former friend's new book.

In parody of Proudon's sub-title, Marx called his book *The Poverty of Philosophy*, and the very name suggests its tone, the carping, vicious superiority of a man who prides himself on his academic learning, laying down the law with blistering sarcasm to the self-taught writer who presumes to tread on the sacred ground, not merely of philosophy, but of German philosophy. This can be illustrated fairly by a brief passage from the preface: 'M. Proudhon has the misfortune to be singularly unrecognised in Europe. In France he has the right to be a bad economist, because he passes for a good German philosopher. In Germany he has the right to be a bad philosopher, because he passes for one of the strongest French economists. We, in our quality of German and economist at one and the same time, wish to make our protest against this double error.' Such heavy debating-society wit, interspersed with occasional bursts of personal vituperation, persists to the end of the book.

Much of Marx's attack is based on what we have already shown to be the irrelevant accusation that Proudhon had founded his dialectic approach on a misunderstanding of the Hegelian theory. But *The Poverty of Philosophy* broadens soon into a more general attack on Proudhon's real and apparent inconsistencies, and here it must be admitted that any book by Proudhon contains enough chaos in its argument, and enough overdone violence of expression, to make it a prize for the stickler for systematic thinking and hairsplitting arguments. In criticising these inconsistencies, Marx scores a number of minor points against Proudhon, but all the time, eluding such a mind as his, there is the fact that the very disorderliness of Proudhon's thinking is a necessary accompaniment of its remarkable fertility, originality and plasticity—qualities in which Marx's own thought was markedly lacking.

Marx also objected to the fact that Proudhon was not only unable but also unwilling to abandon his essential moralism, and he was clearly exasperated by what he called the 'economico-metaphysical' methods used in *Economic Contradictions*. Indeed, as Pierre Haubtmann has indicated, the core of Marx's attack is really to be found in his detection of an idealist under-current in Proudhon's thought, verging at times on the mystical and expressed in a language that betrays the Bible student of long standing for whom religion was an inescapable and perpetually important factor in human life. Marx's objections on these grounds are, of course, not without their ironical elements, when one considers the strong 'economico-metaphysical' element that eventually emerged in his own theory of historical materialism.

The Poverty of Philosophy aroused little interest when it appeared and subsequently can have done little harm to Proudhon's cause, since the only people who read it with enthusiasm were already fanatical Marxists. However, there is no doubt that Proudhon was intensely vexed by the character of Marx's attack. 'I have received a libel by a Doctor Marx,' he told Guillaumin in September, 1847. 'It is a tissue of abuse, calumny, falsification and plagiarism.'

He read carefully and annotated profusely his own copy of *The Poverty of Philosophy*, which has been preserved by his descendants, and this fact leads one to suppose that he intended, at least at the time of reading, to make some reply, while his diary yields enough references to Marx to make it seem certain that he was by no means so untouched by the attack as his absolute silence in print and relative silence in letters might suggest. On the 20th September, for instance, he remarks: 'All those who have spoken of it (*Economic Contradictions*) up to now have done so with extreme bad faith, envy or stupidity'; Marx's name stands at the head of the list of critics which follows this remark. Three days later appears a hastily pencilled note: 'Marx is the tapeworm of socialism!' Why Proudhon did not make a more public refutation of *The*

Poverty of Philosophy is a question we may validly ask. Benoît Malon has suggested that, since Marx was an unknown in France and Proudhon a celebrity, the latter calculated that it was better to leave his 'terrible contradictor's' book in obscurity rather than draw attention to it. In fact, however, Proudhon never flinched from replying to his critics, no matter how formidable or how obscure, while a glance at his annotations of Marx's text shows that, unlike Malon, he does not appear to have regarded Marx's work as a 'terrible contradiction,' but rather as a tissue of irrelevancies, calumnies and insults.

The lack of a published answer seems, indeed, more explicable by reference to external events. Proudhon, if we can judge from his letter to Guillaumin, does not appear to have studied *The Poverty of Philosophy* until September, 1847. Within the next two months he experienced an acute family crisis, which I shall describe shortly, and no sooner had he passed through this than the February revolution swept him into a period of intense activity that lasted several years, until the memory of Marx's attack had ceased to trouble him. We can legitimately regret that Proudhon did not undertake an answer, for it might have provided a valuable critique of the Marxist position at an early stage of the conflict between authoritarian and libertarian socialism. But we must also grant that circumstances in all probability rendered it difficult or impossible for him to make such a reply at a time when it would have seemed relevant.

8

For more than a year after the publication of *Economic Contradictions* Proudhon was so occupied with the extra-literary side of his life that he was unable to pay any close attention to the plans he had already made for a book that would serve as a constructive supplement to his destructive criticisms of society. The last six months of 1846 were spent almost wholly in the Midi, where the court cases of the Gauthiers required his continual presence, and he began to grow impatient even of the relaxed tyranny which his part-time transport work imposed upon him. 'I can no longer endure Lyons,' he complained to his mother in the autumn. 'I would much rather be a country policeman at Cordiron than live as I do. I am submerged in commerce and all its villainies, and I breathe only for the day when I shall say goodbye to the office.'

Even when he returned to Paris in January, 1847, it was to become involved in 'a new, monstrous affair' for his employers. The Gauthiers were appealing to the government for two thousand draft horses to operate a plan for the carriage of wheat on the Rhône. The scheme had some urgency, for during the winter of 1846-7 Eastern France underwent a severe famine owing to the bad harvest of the previous autumn, and the price of bread more than doubled. The government imported wheat to ease the situation, and it was in the distribution of this that the Gauthiers proposed to make such an economy that the price of a loaf would be reduced by half. For more than a month Proudhon was in daily contact with the Chamber, but nothing came of the scheme he fostered. 'We were welcomed by the deputies,' he recollected, 'but politely shown out by the ministers; that was to be expected.' It is impossible now to say whether the government of Louis Philippe had rejected an idea that might have helped it to solve the dangerous situation which existed in the country at this time —for the famine of 1846-7, badly managed by the Ministry, certainly intensified the long economic crisis that led up to the Revolution of the next year.

But neither economic crisis nor the attempts of benevolent capitalists to alleviate it, played the most dramatic part in Proudhon's return to the capital in 1847. Rather, it was his conversion from a cautious bachelor into an enterprising and original suitor. Several years earlier, while he deplored the restricting effect of marriage on many of his friends, he had already begun to hint that he had by no means ruled out this condition as a possibility for himself. In the autumn of 1844, for instance, he remarked to Tourneux: 'I shall occupy myself with gathering all the elements of success that crop up. God will do the rest. Afterwards, if I meet some poor and tender creature who wishes to entrust her cares to me, I shall try to enable her to live as little badly as I can. That is all I can say.' Finally, after years of indecision, he suddenly decided that the time to marry had arrived.

At this time he had acquired a certain eccentricity of manner and appearance which doubtless went well with the unorthodoxy of his opinions but which made him an odd-looking figure even in the Latin Quarter. A few months before, a young admirer, Alfred Darimon, had encountered him at an eating-house called the Restaurant Beaurain in the Rue Notre-Dame-des-Victoires.

Here, among a mixed clientele which included commercial tra-
vellers, artists, and the editors of *La Réforme*, Proudhon frequently
ate the excellent dinner provided for 1 fr. 60 c. and afterwards
took coffee and chatted with his friends in the little garden behind
the establishment. Darimon, having already formed an admiration
for 'the hardy reformer,' was delighted to meet his intellectual
hero, but also somewhat surprised to find him such an 'original'
in appearance. His head was submerged in a great hat with
a broad brim, his bony body was enveloped in an enormous
olive-green frock-coat that reached almost to his heels, he wore
heavy, laced shoes, and his trousers, which were too short, revealed coarse grey stockings. In a Paris where even the journalists
of the Left aspired to a certain sartorial elegance, Proudhon remained the uncompromising provincial, careless of appearance
and, in the privacy of his room, lapsing into the blouse and sabots
of his peasant childhood. In addition to the roughness of his dress,
Darimon found that Proudhon had carried into the days of his
Parisian celebrity the brusque manner, curt speech and contempt
for compliments that were typical of the Jura mountaineers.

It was this arresting figure who, on the 6th February, 1847,
decided to put his resolution regarding marriage into effect in a
manner as strange as his appearance. On that morning, in the
environs of the Rue Mazarin, he accosted a young woman whom
he had previously observed, but to whom he had never spoken
before and whose very name was unknown to him. All he did
know was that her bearing marked her as a self-reliant member of
that class of working women to which his mother had belonged
and from which he had decided that he must seek a wife who
would be an adequate partner. In addition, she was pleasant-
looking; the critical Darimon, who first saw her two years later,
went so far as to call her 'a beautiful person with blonde tresses,
resplendent with strength and health.'

Proudhon, having quickly satisfied himself that his impressions
were not demonstrably incorrect, led the conversation into an
abrupt proposal of marriage. There is, unfortunately, no record of
the emotions which the young woman felt on being approached
in this unorthodox manner, but she appears to have preserved
an equanimity in keeping with Proudhon's own forthrightness,
for she answered his questions with the greatest frankness. Her
name was Euphrasie Piégard, she was fourteen years younger than

Proudhon, and her parents kept a lace-trimming establishment. She was the youngest member of a family of six, and, as she told her relentless questioner, she could earn from ten to twelve francs a day by her trade, provided she found the work. Finally, she gave Proudhon her father's card, and this strange first meeting was ended.

The prospective suitor was not a man to delay, and on the following day he wrote to Euphrasie a long letter, setting down with the greatest sangfroid his reasons for wishing to marry her. It is a letter of proposal which, for sheer oddity, bears comparison with those curious epistles that had been written by the English romantics a generation before to the ladies of their reasoned choice, such as Peacock's letter to Jane Gryffydd or the pleas of Godwin to Harriet Lee. 'Mademoiselle,' Proudhon began, 'I must appear to you a singular eccentric, and you must have found my conduct yesterday most strange. To accost in the street a young person of whose position, family and name I am ignorant, and immediately to make propositions of marriage! Indeed, if that is not crazy, it is perhaps at least suspect. It is therefore as much an explanation that I have to give you, Mademoiselle, as a declaration of my feelings.

'But first of all, if you can in all conscience swear that your character, your heart and your reason are equal to your face, is it not true that you will begin to believe that my action is not, after all, as thoughtless as it seems? . . .

'I had, in principle, resolved to settle down. Reasoning on this question, I told myself that if I took a wife I would wish her to be young and even pretty. These qualities, believe me, neither exclude nor take the place of others in my mind, but I felt that I needed a spouse for my eyes as well as for my heart and mind . . .

'As for fortune, through philosophy or, if you like it better, through necessity I set little store by it. I know that most dowries are worth, and what obligations they impose on the husband, but I am determined to change nothing in my modest habits. From that, Mademoiselle, you will conclude that the woman who marries me must, like myself, resign herself to modesty; with that quality she will seem to me rich enough.

'After the considerations of age, fortune, face, morals, come those of education. On this point you will permit me to say, Mademoiselle, that I have always felt an antipathy for the high-toned lady, the female artist or writer; the best educated, without excepting the most illustrious, have always seemed to me poor in genius . . . But the working woman, simple, gracious, naïve, devoted to work and to her duties, such, in short, as I believe I have seen exemplified in you, gains my homage and my inclination . . .

'I would like a wife with your figure, your face, your hair, your expression, your voice, your modest and intelligent air; with these advantages, the only ones I have had the chance to appreciate in you, it seems to me that such a wife would infallibly be industrious, gentle, devoted to her husband as you are to your parents, severe with herself, and indulgent with everybody else. Above all, I would like her to have a calling at which, in case of need, she would be ready to work without regret and without murmuring.

'What I would have to offer such a wife would be the love of a man: for me, Mademoiselle, that word alone says all.'

This letter, in a sudden fit of caution, he signed with the name of 'E. Gauthier,' posing as one of his employers because he feared his own notoriety might scare Mlle Piégard before he had been able to establish a satisfactory initial relationship. The bad impression that might have been created had Euphrasie or her family discovered the deception before he chose to reveal himself evidently did not occur to him.

His approach seems to have been received with understandable reserve. For days he was kept waiting; then Euphrasie sent him a message that one of her brothers would reply on her behalf. The reply did not come, and at last Proudhon could no longer bear his suspense. On the 26th February he wrote, inviting the brother to dine with him. 'This,' he remarked, 'would bind nobody more than is agreeable, and might illuminate the question much better than six months of reciprocal enquiry, while I would know whether or not I should cease to concern myself with you.'

This brusque ultimatum evidently convinced the Piégards of the seriousness of Proudhon's intentions, and by the following month he was accepted as Euphrasie's suitor; the fact was celebrated by the revelation that the eccentric E. Gauthier was none other than the man of paradox, Pierre-Joseph Proudhon. The Piégards do not appear to have been greatly shocked by the discovery. Euphrasie's father was a staunch royalist who had suffered in the cause of the Comte de Chambord, the Legitimist king over the border, but he was tolerant of Proudhon's radical reputation; perhaps the common desire to undermine the existing regime drew them together with a bond that withstood merely partisan differences. It seems certain at least that, while Proudhon felt the traditional detestation of his future mother-in-law because of the bullying way in which he thought she behaved towards Euphrasie, he always maintained a cordial, if impatient, attitude towards M. Piégard, who had more than a little of his own impetuous Quixoticism.

Proudhon kept his betrothal a close secret. Only his mother was told; and none of those intimate friends with whom he had been in the habit of discussing his most private affairs was given the least hint of this departure from the old rhythm of his life. Why he should have acted thus can only be a matter for speculation, but one might justifiably conjecture that he may have felt his relationship was only tentative and might end in humiliating failure.

As a lover, Proudhon was formal and rather patronising. From the start he seems to have been anxious to establish the patriarchal position which his theories on marriage demanded. In his letters to Euphrasie there are none of those literary expressions of tenderness or passion, which he regarded as degenerate and which he associated with the detested Romantics. 'Profound respect,' 'sincere and entire devotion,' were as far as he would allow himself to go, and for two years he addressed Euphrasie merely as 'Mademoiselle.' At the same time, he showed a close interest in her wellbeing. He enquired perpetually of her health, and prescribed a treatment for migraine based on the methods of the socialist Raspail. He sided with her against her mother, and accepted without recrimination her intellectual shortcomings. Some years later he told Bergmann that he was governed in his attitude towards her, not by passion ('you understand without difficulty of what nature my passions are') but by 'sympathy for her position, by esteem for her person.' Yet if he was never led into transports of love, there are enough indications to suggest that he was a more hopeful and a happier man for having met Euphrasie. A passage in his diary for July, 1847, indicates this in an oblique way. 'A man marries a woman ten or twelve years younger than himself, in order that his youth may be prolonged all life long . . . Up to 15 or 16 years, he has his father, mother and teacher, from 16 to 30 he is young, from 30 to 40 he is young again through his wife, after 40 he is so through his children. Thus youth exists always for man; it is a miracle of love and sympathy.' Euphrasie was fourteen years younger than Proudhon, and he was clearly hopeful of a renewal of mental vigour from his relationship with her.

The success of his courtship resulted in a marked strengthening of Proudhon's preference for working women and of his hostility towards blue stockings. It was at this time that he made the acquaintance of one of the most formidable of this class, the Comtesse d'Agoult, mistress of Liszt and later historian of the revolution of 1848 under the pen-name of Daniel Stern. The Countess became interested in Proudhon's books and wrote, expressing her agreement with many of his ideas, but, like other of his well-wishers, deprecating the violence of expression he sometimes used. Finally, she invited him to visit her, so that they might discuss their differences. Proudhon replied in a tone that put the extension of their relationship out of all question.

'I should be happy, I should be proud, Madam, to obtain the support of a reason as balanced as yours, and for that I should like to profit by your amiable invitation to go and talk with you,' he declared. 'But I feel, on the other hand, that once we began to dispute I would concede nothing to you; that the intolerance of my judgments would break out with you as with M. Blanqui and Père Cabet; that instead of an agreeable visitor you would have only a tiresome disputer. Your education, your habits, everything separates you from a man who has nothing in his favour but an immense anger and for whom study, philosophy, political economy, the arts, are instruments of conspiracy. To meet for an instant and then not to see each other again would be as little worthy of one as of the other: curiosity on your part, vanity on mine, and in the end reciprocal disgust and misunderstanding. For myself, I am tired of these visits, and do not want any more encounters, except with my collaborators and my adversaries.'

It is difficult to accept this protestation at face value, for Proudhon by no means always avoided the company of those with whom he disagreed, nor did he find difficulty in associating with people whom education and habit separated from him. With his male acquaintances such considerations seemed to have relatively little significance. Noblemen by birth, naturalised into the freemasonry of the revolutionary movement, like Bakunin and Herzen, were his close associates, he did not discourage the attentions of Tolstoy, and in later years he did not refuse to visit Prince Jerome Bonaparte. As for the Bohemia to which Madame d'Agoult belonged by habit, it would be difficult to find a more startling citizen of that world than Courbet.

It seems likely then that his emphatic desire to avoid personal contact with the Countess was due to her largely unjustified moral reputation. Proudhon was generally over-eager to see support even where it was not offered, and one cannot help regarding it as significant that, on the single occasion when a distinguished woman showed a marked inclination to accept his beliefs, he should so pointedly have stopped any further contact. The panic of an exaggerated sexual puritanism seems, indeed, the sole likely explanation of the strange abruptness with which he repulsed this fine and talented woman.

9

In publishing his *Economic Contradictions*, Proudhon had promised his readers a sequel that would give his positive ideas on social reconstruction but, while he worked out the plans of this work during the ensuing year, his desire to give a more popular expression to his ideas led him once again to consider the possibility of a journalistic enterprise.

After his failure to reach agreement with Cabet and the editors of *La Réforme*, it became evident that the only way of obtaining the platform he desired would be through a newspaper over which he had virtual control, and he began to shape his plans in that direction. At first he thought of producing a weekly, which, by certain adjustments of time, he might be able to fit in with his business obligations, and by June 1847 his project had become more detailed. The journal would be called *Le Peuple* (*The People*) and it would appear in November, or at the latest in December.

Earlier papers called *Le Peuple* had appeared, each for a few issues, in 1836 and 1846. The editor of the latter, and probably of the former as well, was a journalist called Ribeyrolles who, like Proudhon, frequented socialist circles without being linked exclusively with any sect, and it is possible that there may have been a connection between the two men. This conjecture is given a certain plausibility by a remark to Bergmann later in the year, when Proudhon was replying to his friend's criticism of the proposed title: 'This title was imposed on me; it is by way of a tradition, or, if you like it better, a resurrection. It was hoped to recommend it to all the readers and subscribers to the former paper called *Le Peuple*.' At the same time he remarked that the actual business control was not in his hands, but added: 'I am the only one who can give life and success to the enterprise.'

Since *Le Peuple*, and variants thereon, became the title with which Proudhon's entire journalistic career was to be associated, it is worth recording that, while he did not defend to Bergmann the actual reasons for which the title was chosen, he declared, in words reminding one of Michelet, that he had already taken his stand upon it. 'The People will become the subject of my first numbers; the People, a collective being; the People, an infallible and divine being—here is what is dominant in my work, but developed, of course, from a completely different viewpoint and in a different manner from *The Social Contract*. Just as the old theories on the sovereignty of the people are empty and vague and completely false, so I hope you will find my ideas clear, positive, immediate and easy to realise.'

As the year ended and the publication date for *Le Peuple* was pushed constantly forward, Proudhon's ideas on its potential importance grew steadily more elevated. In October he noted in his diary: 'Yes, the publication of *Le Peuple* will be the inauguration of the social revolution. The doctrine of equal exchange . . . a doctrine intelligible to the masses, will cause panic among the bourgeois classes and consternation among the barons of finance and agriculture.' And shortly afterwards he indulged in one of those lapses into vanity which he reserved for the private pages of his journal: 'The representative of the people, it is I. For I alone am right.'

This curious spurt of arrogance seems to have been provoked by the appearance during October, 1847, of an independent socialist paper called *Le Représentant du Peuple* (*The People's Representative*), under the motto: 'Every man has the duty to work, so that all shall have the right to the products of work.' Its editors, Charles Fauvety and Jules Viard, if not then actual Mutualists, were certainly in close sympathy with Proudhon's ideas. This paper, which lapsed after two specimen numbers, clearly seems to have aroused Proudhon's interest and to have piqued his pride that other editors should have anticipated him with a publication so similar in title and approach to the journal he himself envisaged. He immediately made contact with Fauvety and Viard, and on the 29th December the lapsed *Représentant du Peuple* and the unborn *Le Peuple* were fused. 'We shall start off with 3,000 subscribers,' Proudhon noted in his diary. 'It is a fair nucleus for foundation. We count on 6,000 in the first six months, and if the subscription grows, the paper, without ceasing to be a weekly, will become a daily.' The first issue of the reconstituted *Représentant du Peuple* was published on the 27th February, 1848, and thus the further history of Proudhon's journalist ambitions belongs to the period that followed the outbreak of the Revolution. In the meantime, however, there remain certain incidents in his personal life which precede that event and demand more than a passing mention.

Closely connected with his decision to found and edit a newspaper was the final termination of his connection with the house of Gauthier. Already in May he had discussed with Maurice the difficulties he experienced in ordering his life, and in June, having spent a whole month in Dijon looking after his employers' affairs, he complained to Bergmann that his duties kept him from following the studies he had planned. By October, after a frustratingly busy summer and some differences of opinion with his employers, he finally decided to abandon caution and leave Gauthiers without waiting to find an alternative means of existence. 'I have been long enough in the service of others,' he told Bergmann. 'I want to be master in my turn, even if it is only of a savage's hut and a fishing line. And if I must ever again endure employment, I shall be careful to take for my employer a stranger, unknown to me, who is neither my companion, my fellow-believer, nor my friend, who never sets foot in my house, who is not interested in me, and whose house I do not enter.'

The decision was doubtless inevitable, yet it involved a certain moral courage, for at present Proudhon had no source of income other than that provided by Gauthiers. He could expect nothing from his projected newspaper until it had become established, while, owing to his inability to do any writing since the appearance of *Economic Contradictions*, he had no manuscript on hand that might be immediately remunerative. He confided to Bergmann that he was leaving his position with only 200 francs in his pocket. The sole means of earning any money in the near future was through his publisher, for Guillaumin offered to pay a small advance on his next book and to take articles for the *Journal des Economistes*.

Proudhon did not escape from Lyons as quickly as he had anticipated, and the slowness of winding up his connection with the Gauthiers was doubtless due to a conscientious desire not to embarrass them by leaving any of his tasks uncompleted. On the 15th November, he was still writing to Euphrasie from Lyons, and he did not leave that city until at least a week afterwards. In the end he appears to have parted cordially from his employers, for his friendship with Antoine Gauthier continued to the end of his life.

From Lyons Proudhon went first to the Franche-Comté, where he was anxious to finish the sequel to *Economic Contradictions*. But on arriving he found his mother seriously ill—'in a reverie or lethargy that removed her from the things of this world—an apprenticeship to death.' When the need to organise *Le Représentant du Peuple* made it imperative for him to return to Paris, a deceptive appearance of recovery on his mother's part led him to suppose he could leave her until the spring. Two days after his arrival in Paris, she was dead. 'Sorrows and misfortunes killed that woman,' he remarked in a note where his inner sorrow percolates through all his imposed restraint. Her death renewed his guilty feeling that the life he chose had prevented him from giving his parents either the material comforts or the pride in his success which they might justly have expected. 'I have been cheated of my dearest hope, that of proving to the authors of my days that I was not deceived in my economic studies, and of letting them enjoy the fruits of my work.' His sense of solitude became more poignant than ever. 'I die by degrees and today I have hardly any further ties with the world,' he noted. 'I can call myself free. But what freedom!' And to Maurice he wrote: 'I tell myself in vain . . . that I no longer have either family, or home, or status, or position; I cannot believe in this complete denuding.'

There was indeed a peculiar fatality about Proudhon's situation at the end of 1847. Deliberately he had cut himself off from his business life in Lyons and had embarked on a career in Paris in which his economic interests, as well as his daily occupation of writing, would inevitably be bound up with the trend of political reform that was mounting towards the crisis of the ensuing year. For the rest, with the dissolution of his family, he stood almost nakedly independent, since his feelings for Euphrasie Piégard were certainly not strong enough to deflect him from the path of a reformer which he had chosen to follow. Indeed, despite his tacitly established position as her suitor, he seems even now to have been undecided whether to marry her, for when he recorded his mother's death he added the significant note: 'I hope, *if I ever marry*, to love my wife as much as I have loved my mother.'

Thus, though Proudhon had no direct part in fomenting the great events which shook France and Europe in the following year, and even foresaw them with apprehension, he had at this time become so detached from the associations of his past that he was able to accept without any hindering obligations the peculiar opportunities and responsibilities which history was shortly to place upon him.

Part Four

THE VOICE OF THE PEOPLE

I

THE Revolution of February, 1848, though it appears to have taken the French government by surprise (Louis-Philippe told a Prussian diplomat in January that revolution could not happen again in France) was not unexpected by more astute observers. Men of insight who had watched the steadily deepening economic crises from 1845 onwards, who had observed the diminution of wages and increase in living costs under the Citizen King, were aware of the emotions that were being kindled in the hearts of the poor and the aims that were taking shape in their minds.

The suicidal insurrections of the 1830's were not repeated, but the secret societies were still at work, and the producing classes were beginning to ask, not only for political rights, but also for social security. The demand for the right to work, which dominated the actions of the Paris workers from February to June, may seem almost retrogressive at a time when the English workers were already making the more revolutionary demand for the right to shorter hours and less work, but it was symptomatic of the economic conditions of France in the 1840's and of the desperation of the poorest class, who asked rarely for more wages or more leisure, but always for the chance to work for a subsistence, for the right not to starve in idleness.

It was not merely the revolutionaries who foresaw that this situation could not continue without some violent outcome. Even the conservative Thiers prophesied civil war, and on the 27th January, 1848, Alexis de Tocqueville made his speech of warning in the Chamber of Deputies. 'You say that there is no peril because there are no riots; you argue that as society is calm on the surface, revolution is an age away. But you are utterly mistaken. It is true that there is no visible sign of disorder, but that is because the disorder is deep in people's hearts. Try to see what is going on in the hearts of the workers—who I admit seem peaceable enough at the moment. It is true that they are not torn by political passions as they used to be. But do you not see that their aims are now social, not political?'

Proudhon, the man who more than any other in France expressed in his writings the social as distinct from the political principle of revolution, was as much aware as de Tocqueville of the storm that was brewing in the first weeks of 1848. He looked towards it with mixed and apprehensive feelings, for despite his destructive way of speaking, he feared social conflict, and always hoped to find a means by which the changes he thought necessary could be achieved without violent disruption. So, on the last day of 1847, he noted in his diary: 'One dreads the year that is coming.' 'Be on your guard, workers,' he added, and a flash of insight led him to see through the partisan struggles of the time into the ominous future, for there is a remarkable anticipation of the Bonapartist ending to the drama of 1848 in this entry from early January: 'If we follow the inspiration of the parties, France, brought low by them alone, will seek through twenty-five years of war and poverty what should not cost her a centime.' '*What should not cost her a centime*' means the social solution Proudhon believed could be brought about by goodwill and reason. But he despaired of these qualities having any part in the forthcoming struggle. 'In the scuffle,' he told himself on the 18th January, 'there is no longer any room for reason. I am more and more convinced that I have no place in this situation.'

More than a year later Proudhon wrote, in *Le Peuple* for the 19th February, 1849, an account of his reactions during the days leading up to the revolution; its frankness makes it a revealing document of the changes in his attitude during these weeks, and I am therefore quoting the more important passages.

'Placed at the bottom of the social edifice, in the heart of the working masses, myself one of the leading miners who was sapping its foundations, I saw better than the statesmen who disputed on the rooftops the approach of danger and all its consequences. A few more days, and at the least parliamentary storm the monarchy would collapse, and the old society with it.

'The tempest began to blow at the banquets for reform. The events in Rome, in Sicily, in Lombardy, added to the ardour of the parties; the Swiss civil war excited public opinion by carrying to its height the irritation against the ministry. Frightful scandals, monstrous trials, added ceaselessly to the public anger. The Chambers had not yet met for the session of 1847-48 when I judged that all was lost; I went immediately to Paris.

'The two months that passed before the explosion, between the opening of the Chambers and the fall of the throne, were the saddest and most desolate I have endured in my life . . . A Republican of yesterday, and of the day before yesterday, a Republican of college, workshop and study, I shuddered with terror when I saw the Republic approaching! I shuddered that none around me believed in the advent of the Republic, at least in an advent as close as it was. Events were on the march, destinies were being accomplished, and the social revolution was rising up, without anybody, high or low, appearing to be aware of it . . .

'I wept for the poor worker, whom I considered given up in advance to unemployment, to years of poverty . . . I wept for the bourgeois, whom I saw ruined, pushed to bankruptcy, excited against the proletariat, and against whom the antagonism of ideas and the necessity of circumstances would force me to fight when I more than anybody was disposed to pity him . . . Before the birth of the Republic, I went into mourning and did expiation for the Republic. And who, once again, with the same foreknowledge, would not have given himself up to the same fears? . . .

'In that devouring anxiety, I revolted against the march of events, I dared to condemn destiny . . . I longed to have an organ in which to wage mortal combat on *Le National*, *La Réforme*, all the republican and reformist organs of opinion . . . My spirit was in agony: I carried in advance the weight of the sorrows of the Republic and the burden of the calumnies that were going to strike socialism.

'On the evening of the 21st February I again exhorted my friends not to fight. On the 22nd I breathed with relief on learning of the retreat of the opposition. I thought myself at the end of my martyrdom. The 23rd dissipated my illusions. But this time the die was cast, *jacta erat alea*, as M. de Lamartine said. The volley in the Capucines changed my attitude in an instant.'

Looking back over a chaotic year, Proudhon had smoothed and simplified the course of his actual thoughts during those formidable days, when the Revolution was breaking out in the streets, and the opposition, having decided to withdraw strategically, discovered, like the sorcerer's apprentice, that something had been released which it could not control. As event piled upon event, as the government of Guizot fell, as the workers built their barricades with skill and experience in the little mediaeval streets of pre-Haussmann Paris, as the bourgeois National Guard threw in its support for the Revolution, his feelings were not quite so sharply defined, nor did they change with such abruptness, as he has suggested. For, while it is true that when the soldiers fired on the people in the Rue des Capucines he instinctively turned to the support of the class from which he sprang, and while he welcomed the fall of Louis-Philippe he did not accept everything that happened without criticism; he made a distinction between the Revolution and the latter-day Jacobins who became its leaders. On the very day the Republic was established, the 24th February, he noted angrily in his diary: 'The mess is going to be inextricable . . . I have no place in it . . . They have made a revolution without ideas.' And the following day he added contemptuously: 'There is nothing in their heads.'

Nevertheless, during the days of insurrection he could not keep away from the scenes of action. On the 22nd he went to the Chamber of Deputies and found all Paris afoot and expectant. On the 23rd he saw the barricades rising in the Marais. On the 24th he was present at the storming of the Tuileries and described it as 'a devastation' rather than 'a capture,' the people having entered without firing a shot. He walked in the streets and squares which, with their innumerable barricades, he likened to 'a labyrinth of five hundred Thermopylaes.' By midday, like many other socialists who had no other prearranged rendezvous in this revolution which had taken them by surprise, he gravitated to the offices of *La Réforme*, which had become the temporary unofficial centre of government so far as the left-wing republicans were concerned. He was appalled and also a little amused by the confusion with which the revolutionary leaders tried to decide how they would dispose of this almost unwelcome gift of fate.

It was in this muddled situation that Proudhon was called to perform his most important act of the day of Revolution. 'After the President, Flocon, had fortified us with a quotation from Robespierre, like a captain making a distribution of rum to his soldiers, I was charged to compose at a printing house these great words: *Citizens, Louis-Philippe will murder you like Charles X; send him to join Charles X!* This, I believe, was the first republican manifesto. "Citizen," said Pére Flocon to me in the printing shop where I was at work, "you occupy a revolutionary post; we count on your patriotism." "You can be sure," I told him, laughing, "that I shall not quit my task until it is finished."'

Afterwards, as he wandered again through the streets, Proudhon was moved to action by the spirit of the day. He helped to uproot trees and force railings, he carried paving-stones for the assiduous architects of the barricades. Out in the enthusiastic streets it was impossible for a revolutionary of such conviction not to respond to the sense of liberation that was abroad.

But when he returned to his room and began to write to his friends, his enthusiasm tended to wane, and what he thought on the day after the Revolution was what other less perceptive men were not to realise until months afterwards. 'They have made a revolution without ideas'—that was the truth which dawned on him on the very evening of victory, and his life for the next year was devoted to supplying the lack.

The first person to whom he communicated his thoughts was Maurice; on the 25th February he told him that 'a revolution is a thing which fatigues one's spirit prodigiously by its confusion and emptiness when one witnesses it.' He found intrigue everywhere, chattering triumphant. 'It is necessary to give a direction to the movement and already I see it lost beneath the waves of discussion.' The workers, indeed, were worth more than their leaders, he thought; they were 'gay, brave, jesting and honest,' but, for all their audacity, they had triumphed only because the monarchy in its weakness had opposed no serious resistance to the Revolution.

2

On the morrow of the Revolution, Proudhon decided that he would remain in his solitude until he found a positive direction for his activity. 'Perhaps I shall be employed by the new order of things; who knows? Perhaps I shall go into opposition; again, who knows?' He did not wait long in doubt. On the 25th February he was sitting in the room he now occupied at the Hôtel de la Côte d'Or. It was, Darimon tells us, 'the mean hotel of the penniless student and the petty clerk.' The stairs were steep and ill-lit, and Proudhon's room, on the fourth floor, was 'not in the proper sense a room at all, but rather a closet.'

As he worked at his table, one of his admirers, George Duchêne, ushered in a deputation of four workers, who entered carrying the muskets with which they had guarded the barricades. They were all compositors—Vasbenter, Debock, and the brothers Nicholas and Joseph Mairet—and they came to raise the question of immediately publishing *Le Représentant du Peuple*, so that there might be an adequate forum for the social ideas to which the Revolution had so far given little expression. Duchêne offered to bear managerial responsibility, while the compositors undertook to assemble the necessary workers, and it only remained for Proudhon to accept editorship. Characteristically, now that the newspaper he had longed for was at last realisable, he asked for time to think. 'The title of the paper did not suit him,' Joseph Mairet recollected. 'The people, he said, should not have a representative; they should affirm themselves; the title should be replaced by a shorter and more expressive phrase—*The People*.'

However, by the time his visitors departed, Proudhon had tacitly agreed to meet their requests, and a month later, when the paper began to appear as a regular daily, his name was at the head of the editorial board. Vasbenter was manager, and the editors included not only Viard and Fauvety, founders of the original *Représentant du Peuple*, but also Darimon, Amadée Langlois, a former ship's officer who became one of Proudhon's most faithful disciples, and Jules le Chevalier, a dissident Phalansterian.

But although during the first month of the Revolution Proudhon did not begin the career of independent journalist that made him such a celebrated figure in the Paris of 1848-9, his position as a leader of radical thought was recognised from the beginning. He frequented several of the hundred political clubs which had taken the place of the old secret societies, and although he often came home appalled by the follies he had heard spoken in the Club of Clubs or the Club of the Revolution ('It is laughable, it is mortifying, it is terrifying,' he noted one evening in his diary), he was popular among their members. When the clubs held a great demonstration on the 17th March to demand the withdrawal of the army from Paris, his name appeared, without his consent or knowledge, on the lists of a proposed new government which were passed from hand to hand by the leaders of the manifestation. And in the dispute between the two revolutionary paladins, Blanqui and Barbès, over the obscure Taschereau affair[1], it was he who was chosen to act as a kind of revolutionary arbitrator and try to bring about a conciliation. Finally, when the elections for the Constituent Assembly took place in April, he was nominated in five districts, including Lyons, Besançon, the Pas de Calais and two Parisian constituencies, and it was to the electors of the Franche-Comté that, on the 3rd of April, he issued a manifesto that for the first time set forth publicly his attitude towards the Revolution. 'The Fatherland is in danger,' he warned. 'It can only be saved by the integral reform of our economic institutions.' Like most of the socialist candidates, he was defeated by the swing against extremist policies which set in after the first heady enthusiasms of the Revolution.

While he was engaged in these varied activities he found time to write three pamphlets dealing with the issues of the Revolution, which appeared in quick succession on the 22nd, 26th and 31st March, as the first titles in a weekly series that was abandoned when he started regular journalistic writing. The first two, entitled respectively *Solution of the Social Problem* and *Democracy*, dealt with the immediate problems of the time, and the main conclusions Proudhon reached were that the provisional govern-

[1] Early in 1848 Taschereau, editor of *La Revue Retrospective*, printed a document which he claimed had been taken from Guizot's office during the insurrection; entitled 'Declaration made by XXX before the Minister of the Interior,' it contained information about the Conspiracy of the Seasons which Barbès claimed was known only to Blanqui and him. The suggestion that Blanqui was an informer did him great harm in 1848, but it is difficult to believe—and Proudhon seems to have shared this view—that such a dedicated revolutionist would have betrayed his associates in this way.

ment, with its policy of herding the unemployed into national workshops, was erring by seeking to palliate the social situation without touching the basic contradictions underlying the prevalent economic distress, and, secondly, that the deification of universal suffrage betrayed a failure to realise the important truth that 'social reform will never come out of political reform; political reform must, on the contrary, emerge from social reform.' Within a few months the June rising was to prove Proudhon right on the first point, and the election of Louis Bonaparte through the institution of universal suffrage was to justify him on the second.

These two pamphlets attacked the immediate topical issues of the day; the third gave the first sketch of his long-promised constructive suggestions for the reform of society. With perhaps an excess of descriptive volubility, it was entitled: *The Organisation of Credit and Circulation and the Solution of the Social Problem without Taxation, Loans, Specie, Paper Money, Price Control, Levies, Bankruptcy, Agrarian Law, Poor Law, National Workshops, Association, Sharing or State Intervention, without Impediment to Commerce and Industry, and without Attacking Property.* It was a vast programme, but Proudhon summarised it in the following sentence: 'What we need, what I call for in the name of all workers, is reciprocity, equity in exchange, *the organisation of credit.*'

To achieve this organisation of credit, Proudhon proposed that there should be an immediate reduction of interest rates, dividends, rents and wages, accompanied by a simultaneous reduction of prices which, he held, would solve the difficulties the country was undergoing owing to the scarcity of circulating media. But the main basis of his proposals lay in the Bank of Exchange or, as he was later to call it, the People's Bank. The scheme of the People's Bank remained a favourite social panacea to which Proudhon continually returned, but it was not one of his most influential ideas, and for the moment we can confine ourselves to its basic outline.

In substance, it was Mutualism put into more concrete form. Proudhon envisaged an organisation in which the workers, as members, mutually guaranteed each other. Credit would no longer be a matter arranged by financiers or the State; it would rest on the mutual support which the workers were willing to organise. In order that there might be neither shortage nor surplus, credit must be unrestricted and its scope must be equal to the productivity of society; instead of being subjected to usury, it must be gratuitous. To realise this end, the actual products of the workers should become, in a sense, current money. This could be achieved by the use of coupons, handed to each worker on the basis of his production, as an issue of gratuitous credit, by means of which he would be able to buy the products of other workers.

The further ramifications of the Bank of Exchange's activities included the buying and selling of consignments as a means of relieving over-stocked warehouses, loans on mortgage, and the encouragement of workmen's productive co-operatives. There is no need to go into these matters in any great detail, and for the present it is enough to point out that in the idea of credit based, not on specie, but on productivity, Proudhon was anticipating not only many recent theories of extended credit, but also actual measures of credit reform to which contemporary governments have resorted in order to avert financial catastrophe or to ease industrial crises complicated by an insufficient flow of money.

Proudhon put forward his scheme as one which should be carried out by the Provisional Government, with the Bank of France becoming the nucleus for the Bank of Exchange. It was with this in mind that, on the 8th April, he wrote to Louis Blanc, the socialist member of the Provisional Government—whom he had already lambasted in print on more than one occasion for his utopian authoritarianism—pointing out the virtues of his plan and suggesting that Blanc should sponsor it before the government. Blanc did not even reply, and Proudhon therefore decided to create the Bank of Exchange by a direct appeal to the public. But before this further effort of Proudhon the constructor was launched, Proudhon the critic had once more taken the scene, and it is to his début as the most eloquent opposition journalist of 1848 that we must now turn our attention.

3

The regular issues of *Le Représentant du Peuple* commenced on the 1st April, bearing the banner motto: 'What is the Producer? Nothing. What should he be? Everything!' and in the latter part of the month began the signed articles in which, sustained by a great indignation against those in power, and also by a feeling that he represented the innermost inclinations of the working people, Proudhon stood forth to voice the conscience of the Revolution. He spoke with a clarity and a lack of fear that soon took him and his paper to the forefront of public attention, for there was no other journalist able or willing to wield so assiduously and so unerringly the flail of criticism. Among the 171 papers that appeared in the first months of the Revolution, *Le Représentant du Peuple* rapidly became distinguished for its liveliness, and the Comtesse d'Agoult, who had no reason to remember Proudhon with pleasure, could not restrain her admiration when she discussed it in her history of 1848. 'Of all the newspapers,' she said, 'the only one that was produced with a quite extraordinary originality and talent was *Le Représentant du Peuple* . . . From the depth of his retreat he [Proudhon] agitated public opinion more strongly, more deeply than was done by the men who mingled most with the multitudes.[1] *Le Représentant du Peuple* took paths to which the Press was unaccustomed. It ranged itself under no banner. Attacking with a haughty spiritedness the majority as well as the minority in the government, chiding the clubs, the newspapers, the civil service, judging disdainfully and rallying pitilessly the Republicans of *Le National*, the Jacobins, the Communists, each morning M. Proudhon surprised his readers, who had difficulty in reconciling the tone and manner of his polemics against the revolutionaries with what was known of his ultra-radical theories . . . [His] unexpected and striking manner of speaking . . . excited the curiosity of the public to the highest degree.' Gustave Lefrançais, the Communard, declared that in 1848 *Le Représentant du Peuple* was soon more in demand than any other radical paper, and was eagerly torn from the hands of the vendors as soon as it appeared on the streets.

Indeed, there is no doubt that, while Proudhon's journalistic activities had little result in the sense of establishing a Proudhonian party or collecting a great many disciples (the first he did not

[1] While it is true that Proudhon mingled little with the factions of the time, his influence among the militant workers was considerable even before he became a journalist, for Engels complained to Marx in January, 1848, on the eve of the February Revolution, of the 'Weitlingery and Proudhonistery' which were rampant among the members of the Communist League in Paris.

desire and to the second he was relatively indifferent), they certainly had an enormous effect in stimulating public opinion, and in making the more acute among his fellow socialists realise, if events had not already taught it to them, that it was not enough to expect the mere founding of a republic and the expression of a few radical sentiments to bring about a genuine social revolution or even an appreciable amelioration in conditions.

Right from the beginning, his articles took on the tone of a direct challenge to the government and the Old Guard of the Mountain, and from the first he raised the anarchist cry of direct action—'the proletariat must emancipate itself without the help of the government.' After the elections of April had confirmed the temporary decline of the left republicans, he published a long essay, entitled *The Reaction*, in which he analysed the deterioration of the revolutionary situation and demonstrated that it sprang more than anything else from an unrealistic reliance on political means and, in particular, on what seemed to him the most egregious of political illusions, universal suffrage. This article displays Proudhon's incisive form of criticism at its best, and it shows him making at the time and on the spot the kind of perceptive analysis of the situation which other people were to make after the events had long been past.

'The social question is adjourned,' he declared. 'The 16th April has nullified the socialist candidates. The cause of the proletariat, proclaimed with spirit on the barricades of February, has just been lost in the elections of April. The enthusiasm of the people has been succeeded by consternation. It is the bourgeoisie which, as in the past, will regulate the condition of the workers . . .

'One of the first acts of the provisional government, that on which it has been most applauded, was the application of universal suffrage. The very day on which the decree was promulgated, we wrote these words, which then might have passed for a paradox: "Universal suffrage is the counter-revolution." One can judge, after the event, whether we were wrong. The elections of 1848 have been made, in the great majority of cases, by the priests, by the Legitimists, by the dynastics, by all that France contains of the most backward and conservative. It could not have been otherwise!

'Is it so hard, then, to understand that in man there exist two instincts, one for conservation, the other for progress; that neither of these two instincts acts in the interests of the other; that thus each individual, judging things from the viewpoint of his private interest, understands by progress the development of that interest; that, such interest being contrary in direction to the collective interest, the sum of votes, instead of expressing general progress, indicates general retrogression?

'We have said it and we repeat it: the Republic is the form of government in which, all wills remaining free, the nation thinks, speaks and acts like one man. But in order to realise that ideal it is necessary that all private interests, instead of acting in a contrary direction to society, should act in the direction of society, which is impossible with universal suffrage. Universal suffrage is the materialism of the Republic. The longer this system is employed, the longer the economic revolution remains an unaccomplished fact, the more we shall go backwards towards royalty, despotism and barbarism, and that all the more certainly in so far as the votes are more numerous, more reasoned and more free.

'You blame the incapacity, the indifference of the proletarian! But that is just what condemns your theory. What would you say of a father who left to his young children the free disposition of his means and then, ruined by them, blamed the inexperience of their youth? And what an argument against you is the indifference of the proletariat!'

It may be contended that this article was in part motivated by Proudhon's personal disappointment at not having been elected to the Constituent Assembly in April, and that it was somewhat inconsistent for a man who denounced universal suffrage so emphatically to make use of it in the hope of getting elected. The first suggestion may be partially true; as for the second, though at first sight Proudhon does seem inconsistent, he would probably have defended himself with the contention that, if universal suffrage exists, it had better be used by a man who is aware of its dangers and will try to mitigate them. But even if the criticisms are admitted, they do not invalidate Proudhon's actual contentions. It was one of the prime illusions of the men of 1848, as of the Chartists in England, that universal suffrage was a sovereign remedy for social ills. It took the staggering majority that confirmed Louis Bonaparte's *coup d'état* three years later to convince most of them that such political devices, unless accompanied by profound changes in social life, are often worse than useless. It is to Proudhon's credit that, almost alone among the men of his time, he saw immediately the dangers of such a fallacy.

Proudhon's articles in *Le Représentant du Peuple* continued in this uncompromising style, commenting on events, advancing his cherished theories, and occasionally making turbulent sorties into places outside the field of political commentators. Writing of this kind appealed to Proudhon's readers. The circulation of *Le Représentant du Peuple* rose steadily, and Proudhon, even though he still had no standing as a partisan leader, nevertheless became recognised as one of the leading men in the socialist movement, and that despite the fact that he did not make the least effort to placate his readers, and was just as liable to rail at the workers as to praise them.

One sign of his growing reputation appeared on the 15th May, when a demonstration led by Blanqui and Barbès, Sobrier, Raspail and Huber, invaded the Constituent Assembly and demanded a series of extravagant steps, including the abolition of poverty, the organisation of labour and the declaration of war to rescue the Poles; finally Huber declared the Assembly dissolved, and then, at the Hôtel de Ville, the demonstrators proclaimed a new government of nine members, including Proudhon's name on the list with acclamation. The insurrection, if so noisily ineffective an incident deserves such a title, was quickly crushed by the National Guard. The leaders were arrested and the radical clubs were closed down. Proudhon himself was fortunate in having denounced the demonstration in advance and in having kept away from the Hôtel de Ville; otherwise, he would almost certainly have shared the imprisonment of Blanqui and the other leading demonstrators.

4

On the 5th June a new election was held to fill a number of vacancies in the Constituent Assembly, and Proudhon was once again a candidate. He took his nomination very seriously, and prepared an elaborate address to the electors of the Seine which was published in three issues of *Le Représentant du Peuple*. It must have been an indigestible election manifesto for the average man in the street, for it ran into almost twenty thousand words and contained a detailed description of Proudhon's ideas on finance, government, the family, etc. He insisted once again on the need to turn the Bank of France into a Bank of Exchange, and talked of the State, in a well organised society, being reduced to 'nothing.' But there were also some notions that sorted oddly with his avowed anarchism. Thus, while he asked for a simplification of the legal system, he opposed abolishing the death penalty, and, in calling for an end to the old forms of conscription, he retained enough Jacobinical militarism to demand that each citizen should do one or two years' militia service.

Baudelaire, who edited *La Tribune Nationale*, was among those who supported Proudhon's candidature, and the electors were sufficiently impressed by his personality and his journalism to elect him with more than 77,000 votes. The ten companions who accompanied him into the Assembly were an oddly mixed group of, for the most part, distinguished names—Victor Hugo and Thiers, Pierre Leroux and the sinister and corsetted General Changarnier, who represented the most unrelieved reaction. Finally, most significant of the confusion into which the Revolution had entered in its fourth month, there was Louis-Napoleon Bonaparte, posing as a reformed adherent of the Republic. Proudhon was suspicious from the start of the intentions of this last colleague. 'The people have just got rid of one princely fantasy,' he remarked. 'God grant it be the last!'

Recollecting his election a year afterwards, Proudhon remarked with some justification: 'When I think of all I have written and published for ten years on the rôle of the state in society, on the subordination of power and the revolutionary incapacity of government, I am tempted to believe that my election was the effect of a misunderstanding on the part of the people.' One might add that it seems to have been the effect of a misunderstanding on his own part as well. But, at the time, he accepted it, and the responsibilities it conferred, with the utmost conscientiousness, though not without misgiving.

Just after the election, Darimon called at the Hôtel du Côte d'Or. He found Proudhon moved to a fine room on the first floor. 'It is my landlady who has made me come down here,' Proudhon jested. 'She pretends that it is not proper for a representative of the people to keep on living in a garret.' But when Darimon started to congratulate him on his election, Proudhon interrupted sharply. 'My dear fellow, I cannot accept compliments. A crushing task has just been imposed on me, and I am very much afraid of sinking under the burden.'

On the whole, he found no reason to change his attitude; in 1854 he recollected his period in the Assembly as 'a life of hell,' and in *Confessions of a Revolutionary* he described in detail the mental effect of parliamentary life.

'I entered the National Assembly with the timidity of a child, with the ardour of a neophyte. Assiduous, from nine o'clock in the morning, at the meetings of bureaux and committees, I did not quit the Assembly until the evening, and then I was exhausted with fatigue and disgust. As soon as I set foot in the parliamentary Sinai, I ceased to be in touch with the masses; because I was absorbed by my legislative work, I entirely lost sight of the current of events. I knew nothing, either of the situation of the national workshops, or the policy of the government, or of the intrigues that were growing up in the heart of the Assembly. One must have lived in that isolator which is called a National Assembly to realise how the men who are most completely ignorant of the state of a country are almost always those who represent it . . . Most of my colleagues of the left and the extreme left were in the same perplexity of mind, the same ignorance of daily facts. One spoke of the national workshops only with a kind of terror, for fear of the people is the sickness of all those who belong to authority; the people, for those in power, are the enemy.'

Proudhon, in fact, put himself in a totally false position by joining the Assembly, and when, a very few days after his entry into that body, the differences between the workers and the government burst out in the civil war of the June days, this fact was brought home to him with terrible emphasis.

5

On the 15th June the banker Goudchaux, who had been elected to the Assembly on the same day as Proudhon, demanded that the national workshops, which had been established after the Revolution to provide work, should be abolished. There was much to be said in criticism of these establishments, which for the most part applied the classically futile remedy of employing men to disturb dirt in order to keep them occupied. They represented a trend towards governmental regimentation without any of the positive advantages that in other circumstances have sometimes arisen from national public work projects. Unwillingly, the men employed in them were forced into the position where they actually earned the title of 'loafers' which de Falloux contemptuously fixed upon them, while their situation was so demoralising that there was reason in Victor Hugo's warning that this army of paupers might become the nucleus of 'a new dictator's praetorian guard.'

But, for all their faults, the national workshops still fulfilled a temporary palliative function by keeping thousands of men from complete despair, and if they were to be abolished it should have been in favour of some scheme by which the energy of the unemployed would be put to more constructive use. Instead, on the 21st June, the Assembly abolished the workshops, proposed to conscript the workers between eighteen and twenty-five, and declared that the rest would be sent out of Paris to work as navvies. It was a decision bred of fear, and it produced the very result which the more honest among its supporters had wished to avoid, a wholesale uprising of the Paris slums. On the 23rd June the barricades rose again, around the Bastille, in the militant St. Antoine quarter, and on the Left Bank between the Rue St. Jacques and the Jardin des Plantes.

Proudhon, like many other left-wing representatives, was completely bewildered by the rising. 'I thought it was a conspiracy of pretenders leaning on the workers of the national workshops,' he wrote later. 'Like others, I was wrong.' As the days progressed, his attitude changed rapidly. Showing a coolness remarkable in a man who had never taken part in fighting, he took advantage of his representative's insignia to walk in the areas where the combat was in progress. General Negrier was killed only a few paces from him, and Proudhon, weeping at what he saw (he was normally a man of few tears), helped to carry the body to the Hôtel de Ville.

On the second day of the rising he ceased to believe that it had been provoked by political intriguers. 'I became convinced that the insurrection was socialist . . . Its first and determining cause was the social question, the social crisis, work, ideas,' he told the commission that later investigated it. He was thus ahead of most of his contemporaries in recognising that a new element had entered into revolutionary history; and as the bloody days continued towards their catastrophic climax, as Cavaignac's forces implacably encircled and crushed the insurgents, as the bourgeois National Guards fought against the men who had been their comrades in February and the members of the working-class Garde Mobile killed their neighbours and kin, Proudhon became steadily more enlightened on the issues which the June rising placed before the men of his time.

On the 23rd June he entered in his diary: 'The Terror reigns in the capital, not a Terror like that of '93, but the Terror of the civil and social war . . . What is happening here is what has always been seen: each new idea has its baptism; the first to propagate it—misunderstood and impatient, get themselves killed for too much philosophic independence.'

When the last burst of fighting took place on the 26th June around the Bastille, Proudhon was again there, in the hope, as he told the investigating commission, of 'leading the strayed sheep back,' and as soon as the last barricade on the Rue St. Antoine was breached he went through it, to question the shopkeepers and to take help to a socialist friend who lived in the area. Evidently there were no longer any rebels in a fighting mood, for he suffered no ill consequence, and was able to confirm his impression that what inspired them was indeed 'the social idea—vague and general.'

It was only afterwards that his temerity on this occasion put him in danger, for when the commission held its investigations a strong attempt was made to implicate him in the responsibility for the rising, on the alleged grounds that he had been within the barricades before the soldiers entered. He combated this accusation successfully, but another sensational charge remained; a hostile representative declared that Proudhon, on being questioned about his purpose at the Bastille, replied grandly: 'I am listening to the sublime horror of the cannonade.' It was a phrase so Proudhonian that its authenticity cannot be doubted, but it shocked his fellow deputies and added to the ogreish image of him that was growing up in the minds of the Parisian bourgeoisie.

Even if they could not lay upon him any blame for organising the insurrection, his enemies in the Assembly were intent on according him at least a share of moral blame, and it was with this aim in mind that Senart, the President of the Assembly, brought into the Address to the Nation, which was read to celebrate the victory of 'order,' a remark stigmatising 'savage doctrines in which the family is only a name and property a theft.' The Abbé Lacordaire recorded that at this unfair thrust (for it would be hard to find a more fanatical supporter of the family than Proudhon) 'the whole hall turned its looks towards the bench where M. Proudhon sat.' He did not flinch, but showed his dissent by remaining seated while the rest of the representatives rose to approve the Address.

Thus, while he was not so emphatic as Lamennais, who cried out to his colleagues: 'God will call you to account for all this bloodshed,' in his own way he expressed the change that had taken place in his attitude during these four terrible days. Now he recognised the Assembly as a body whose purpose was opposed to his own, and saw that his rôle within it must be an isolated and rebellious one. In his diary for the 28th June he noted: 'The ill will of the Assembly was the cause of the insurrection.'

On the 6th July he finally took his stand in public beside the calumniated and defeated victims of June. During the fighting *Le Représentant du Peuple* had taken no clear position, and even afterwards the editors confined themselves to expressing pity for the victims of a savage repression. For this slight departure from the prevalent attitude of total condemnation they were violently attacked in the conservative *Journal des Débats*, which again tried to associate Proudhon with the insurrection. This was too much for him, and in a furious article in the form of a letter to the editors he cried out in anger against the policy of the government.

'Four months of unemployment were suddenly converted into a *casus belli*, into an insurrection against the government of the Republic; there is the whole truth of these funereal days . . . The English proletarian lives nobly on the poor rate; the German journeyman, loaded with money and clothes, does not blush to beg, from workshop to workshop, the cost of his travel; the Spanish beggar does more—he asks *caridad* at the point of a blunderbuss; the French worker asks for work, you offer him alms, and he rebels, he shoots at you. I prefer the French worker, and I glory in belonging to that proud race, inaccessible to dishonour . . . '

6

Proudhon spoke late, but he spoke with effect at a time when his was almost the only voice raised to defend the persecuted. And, having spoken, he did not cease, for he chose this moment to make an appeal for drastic action to avert the worsening economic conditions which had already bred the bitterness and violence of the June days. Quarter day, the day for settling bills and paying rents, would fall due on the 15th July, and Proudhon dreaded the hardship it might cause at such a time. On the 8th July he published a manifesto in which he called the people of France to demand that the government should decree a third reduction in all payments falling due. It was bold at such a time to suggest anything so radical, for the state of siege was still in full force, but Proudhon did more, for his article was worded as a direct call to the National Guard to intervene in the situation.

'Go then, misled National Guards, ask for work, credit and bread from your pretended protectors! . . . It is no longer a question of saving the proletariat; the proletariat no longer exists, it has been thrown on the garbage heap. We must save the bourgeoisie, the lower bourgeoisie from hunger, the middle bourgeoisie from ruin, the upper bourgeoisie from its infernal egotism. Today the question is for the bourgeoisie what it was on the 23rd June for the proletariat.'

Cavaignac, whom the Assembly had given dictatorial powers to administer the state of siege, immediately suppressed this issue of *Le Représentant du Peuple*. Thereupon the editors, feeling that the situation did not allow them sufficient freedom of speech, decided to suspend the paper voluntarily. two days later, and it did not appear again for almost a month. Proudhon himself was shielded from prosecution, for the time being at least, by his parliamentary immunity.

But he had no intention of abandoning his proposal, and elaborated it into a memorandum to the Assembly. He suggested that creditors should be asked to surrender a third of what was owed them over the past three years, half to be returned to tenants, debtors, etc., to re-establish their positions, and the rest to go to the State as a fund to restore the standard of living which had existed before the revolution.

Judged by modern practice, it seems a plan which, if perhaps unworkable in the form Proudhon suggested, at least contained a germ that was worthy of consideration. It was in fact a tax on unearned income of which half was to be used to subsidise farming and industry, and its close relatives in taxation and subsidy have become familiar in the modern world. But the members of the Finance Committee, to whom the plan was referred, were hostile from the start, and however reasonable and conciliating Proudhon tried to be, they refused to see any good in his proposal and accused him of trying to associate the legislators with his attacks on property. The discussions soon shaped themselves into a duel between Proudhon and Thiers, who suggested that the proposal was really an attempt 'to agitate and raise the masses,' and who later reported to the Assembly in general in a manner which sought to discredit Proudhon's plan by a minute criticism of its figures and a contemptuous dismissal of its basic principles. Proudhon heard the speech in silence and, according to one satirical commentator, shook himself like a wet dog; he was becoming used to public denunciation. He asked for time to prepare his reply, and on the 31st July appeared at the Assembly to defend his proposition.

It was a crowded session, for public expectation had been raised to a considerable height by rumours of Proudhon's demands. The orator mounted the tribune clad in a black frock coat. His thin hair, Victor Hugo remembered, was 'ruffled and ill-combed, with a curl on his high and intelligent brow.' Hugo saw 'something of the mastiff in his flattish nose and of the monkey in his whiskers,' and noted that his thick lower lip gave his mouth a look of perpetual ill-humour. His gaze, the novelist decided, was 'humble, penetrating and steady,' and his expression was one of 'mingled embarrassment and assurance.'

All the eye-witnesses agree that Proudhon spoke badly, and, with the friendliest intentions, one has to agree with Lord Normanby, the British Ambassador, that the text of his speech, which lasted three and a half hours, was 'irremediably dull.' Yet the scene in the Assembly did not reproduce this dullness. Proudhon's colleagues had gone there to laugh, but soon they were provoked to anger by the speaker's statements.

Having defined his aim as the reduction of property to possession by the abolition of revenues, he went on to say that the 'liquidation of the old society,' which had begun on the

24th February, would be 'stormy or amicable, according to the passions and the good or bad faith of the parties.' He asked the Assembly to aid the peaceful completion of the transition by agreeing, as a first step, to his proposition of a levy on income. The proprietors should be summoned 'to contribute, for their part, to the revolutionary work, proprietors being responsible for the consequences of their refusals.'

Proudhon's colleagues shouted for an explanation, and he replied: 'It means that in the case of refusal we ourselves shall proceed to the liquidation without you.'

'Whom do you mean by *you*?' came the shouts.

'When I used these two pronouns, *you* and *we*,' said Proudhon, 'it is evident that I was identifying *myself* with the proletariat, and *you* with the bourgeois class.'

There was an uproar. 'It is the social war!' the enraged conservatives shouted. 'It is the 23rd June at the tribune!' Proudhon's proposition was rejected almost unanimously, but the upholders of order wanted more than that, and the session broke into a bedlam as the representatives competed to find a suitably insulting way of expressing their hostility. Finally, it was resolved that Proudhon's proposition 'is an odious attack on the principles of public morality, that it violates property, that it encourages scandal, that it makes appeal to the most odious passions,' and, finally, 'that the orator has calumniated the revolution of February, 1848, by pretending to make it an accomplice of the theories which he has developed.'

The majority was overwhelming: 691 voted to condemn Proudhon and only 2 dissented. They were Proudhon himself and his old friend from Lyons, the weaver Greppo. Of the remaining socialists, none was prepared to support him, even though the issue was not one of accepting his proposition, but merely of defending him against insult. Sixty of them abstained, but Louis Blanc carried personal enmity so far as to join in the vote of censure. From afar another enemy, the exiled Marx, admitted grudgingly that, in the circumstances, Proudhon's motion had been an act of high courage.

This debate crowned Proudhon's notoriety in respectable society. 'From the 31st July,' he declared, 'I became, according to the expression of one journalist, the *terror-man* . . . I was preached upon, acted, sung, placarded, biographised, caricatured, censured, insulted, cursed.' He was a regular subject for the newspaper artists; pious ladies sent him holy medals; anonymous letter-writers dedicated him to the wrath of God or threatened more immediate and earthly punishments; no less than four petitions to the National Assembly asked for his exclusion from that body, and the Spanish Ambassador, Donoso-Cortes, declared that never had any being sinned so gravely against humanity and the Holy Spirit, and suggested that, even if Proudhon were not a demon, he must certainly be possessed by one!

'I am like a Salamander, I live in the fire,' Proudhon wrote almost enthusiastically to his Comtois friend, Dr. Maguet. 'Abandoned, betrayed, proscribed, execrated by everybody, I stand against the whole world and hold at bay the reaction and all the enemies of the Republic. The people, who regard me henceforward as their sole representative, are flocking to me *en masse*. They swear only by or against me.'

7

As usual, Proudhon exaggerated when he described his popular following, but it is true that, in August, the circulation of *Le Représentant du Peuple* rose to a peak of 40,000, a very high figure for the Paris of a century ago, particularly when one considers the high proportion of illiteracy at that time. When the paper reappeared on the 9th August, after its month of silence, Proudhon was in a more truculent mood than ever, and the motto on the head of the first page was significantly enlarged by the words: 'What is the capitalist? Everything! What should he be? Nothing!'

He was not allowed to continue long in this vein, and *Le Représentant du Peuple* had reappeared for little more than a week when it was seized on three consecutive days. The excuses for suppression were in each case flimsy. On the 16th August it was an alleged attack on property contained in a letter from the politically radical but artistically conservative sculptor, Antoine Etex. The next day it was a letter from a prisoner in the Conciergerie which was construed as a provocation of hatred between classes, and on the 18th it was an 'enquiry into the events of June' which the editors had begun.

Proudhon did not take these attacks passively. On the 21st

August he published an article defending his paper in general and the suppressed items in particular; in answer, the government finally suppressed *Le Représentant du Peuple* altogether. Proudhon called personally on Cavaignac; the general accused him of being 'at odds with the country,' and said that to maintain order was impossible while papers like his existed. 'I know you well,' he added. 'From the point of view of principles, you are inflexible. If I lifted the suspension, you would be worse than ever.' According to his own lights, Cavaignac was correct.

Total suppression was an eventuality which Proudhon and his friends had anticipated, and they immediately made plans to start a new paper, *Le Peuple*. On the 2nd September Proudhon told the Besançon lawyer, Abram (an old school-friend), that 'the best future is assured us,' and suggested that a little outlay on propaganda would result in a circulation of 50,000. But, although three isolated issues of *Le Peuple* appeared, undated so as to avoid the laws relating to periodicals, there was a long delay in collecting the bond now needed for regular publication. Eventually, after Proudhon had put into the fund 3,000 francs from the sale of his books, and a young Breton nobleman, Baron Charles de Janzé, had provided 6,000 francs out of admiration for Proudhon, the paper was able to appear in the middle of November. By the time the bond was paid the coffers were empty, for the 100,000 francs in capital which the editors had hoped to attract was not forthcoming, and they started operations with 35 francs towards production costs. But the public interest in Proudhon and in his journalism was worth more than cash, and the editors were reassured when the 40,000 copies printed of the first issue sold out immediately. Meeting a friend, Proudhon remarked in mock sadness: 'My paper is now going to make money . . . Remember that any paper worth a thousand francs is lost to its party.'

8

One of the more curious incidents in the latter part of 1848, and one of the most productive in calumny, was Proudhon's meeting with Louis Bonaparte. The story is told in a letter written in July, 1849, to refute an accusation Emile de Girardin had made in *La Presse* that Proudhon himself had sought to see the future emperor.

'It was on the 26th September, 1848, that, to my great surprise, I was asked to visit M. Louis Bonaparte . . . The conversation turned on the organisation of work, finance, foreign policy, the Constitution. M. Bonaparte spoke little, listened to me amiably and appeared to agree with me in almost everything. He was not at all misled by the calumnies spread against the socialists; he blamed unreservedly the policy of General Cavaignac, the suspension of the newspapers, the state of siege, and that army of the Alps which seemed to say to an Italy risen for independence: *My heart would and would not* . . . In all, we were given reason to believe that the man who posed before us had no longer anything in common with the conspirator of Strasbourg and Boulogne, and that it was possible that, as the Republic had once perished by the hand of a Bonaparte, it might be made secure in our own day by the hand of another Bonaparte . . .

'I find in my notebook, under the date of the 26th September, these few lines, which I reproduce exactly: "Visit to Louis' Bonaparte. This man appears well-intentioned, chivalrous head and heart; more filled with the glory of his uncle than with a strong ambition. At the same time, a mediocre intellect . . . For the rest, be on your guard. It is the custom of every pretender to seek out first of all the heads of the parties".'

Meanwhile, the legislative machine creaked on towards the elections on which Louis Bonaparte was basing his plans. After months of committees, in which the right wing had progressively weeded out every mildly revolutionary clause, the Constitution that the Assembly had been elected to formulate was finally approved on the 4th November, by 739 votes to 30. The minority consisted of 14 Royalists and 16 Democratic Socialists; Proudhon was among the latter, but whether he acted from the same motives as his companions seems doubtful when one reads his statement to *Le Moniteur* on that day:

'I voted against the Constitution because it was a Constitution. What makes the essence of a Constitution—I mean a political Constitution since there can be no question of any other—is the division of sovereignty, in other words, the separation of powers into legislative and executive . . . I am convinced that a Constitution whose first act is to create a Presidency, with its prerogatives, its ambitions, its culpable hopes, will be a danger rather than a guarantee to liberty.'

From this time onwards he had little use for the Assembly; a few days later he told his old employer, Javel, that the spirit of the Revolution must not be sought there, but in the 'subterranean movement of ideas.' However, he continued to attend its sessions with comparative regularity, and before the year was ended his parliamentary activities had involved him in a further series of disputes, this time with his neighbours on the left.

After the debate of the 31st July, he had patched up his differences with the Mountain, and particularly with the Democratic Socialists. When elections were held on the 17th September to choose a further thirty members of the Assembly, he served on the electoral committee which upheld the candidature of the imprisoned Raspail. But the break in this uneasy harmony began barely a month later with an incident that reflects not only Proudhon's peculiar individualism, which made it hard for him to accept party discipline, but also the rigidly Jacobinical spirit that reigned on the Mountain.

A Banquet of the Republic had been organised in Montmartre for the 15th October and the organisers had chosen Proudhon as their leading speaker, while the leaders of the Mountain, including Ledru-Rollin and Lamennais, agreed to support it by their presence. Then, on the eve of the celebration, the precarious accord was broken.

Cavaignac had decided to drop Senart from his ministry and to appoint in his place the even more conservative Dufaure-Vivien. The Mountain made this a pretext for an attack on the government, in which Proudhon refused to join. He remembered how Senart had stigmatised him after the June days, while Vivien was the minister who, in 1840, had shown unexpected tolerance by deciding not to proceed against *What is Property?* Accordingly, he abstained from voting, and in retaliation the representatives of the Mountain, except for Pierre Leroux and the faithful Greppo, absented themselves from the Banquet of the Republic.

Despite their defection, it was something of a triumph for Proudhon, who made his one great speech when he proposed the Toast of the Revolution before an audience of two thousand Parisians. This oration has some lasting interest, since it defined Proudhon's ideas on the nature of revolutions. He divided their history into four stages. The Christian revolution proclaimed the equality of man before God. The Renaissance proclaimed equality before reason. The Enlightenment proclaimed equality before the law. The fourth revolution, that of the nineteenth century, was based on the right to work, its motto was equality before fortune, and its goal was fraternity. 'Today work is at the direction of capital. The Revolution tells you to change that order. It is for capital to recognise the preponderance of work, for the instrument to put itself at the disposition of the workers.'

From revolutionary principles, Proudhon proceeded to practice. The Revolution must be built on a foundation of economic change. The people must cling to that truth, and, whatever the government might do or fail to do, must see that it was carried to fruition. 'The people alone, operating on itself without intermediaries, can complete the economic revolution whose foundation was laid in February. The people alone can save civilisation and make humanity advance.' Unfortunately, he was to see in the very near future that even the people were not so anxious as he hoped to play the part that history tried to assign them.

The disagreement with the Mountain was widened into final irreconcilability by the greater dispute which arose over the Presidential elections of the 10th December. Cavaignac was standing as candidate for the right republicans, Ledru-Rollin for the Mountain, while in the background loomed the seedy figure of Louis Napoleon, making a diffuse and ambiguous appeal to the discontent of the most diverse interests, and supported by a sinister combination of Bonapartists, Orleanists, Legitimists, Right Republicans, clericals and reactionaries of all descriptions.

Proudhon denounced the dictatorial ambitions of Louis Napoleon, but he refused to be governed by the Mountain's decision to present Ledru-Rollin as an official candidate, since he regarded him as exemplifying the division of powers between executive and legislative, to which he was opposed. After some hesitation, he eventually gave his support to the socialist nominee, Raspail, still imprisoned at Vincennes. On the 8th November he issued a manifesto in which he and his friends recommended Raspail as 'the democratic socialist . . . the implacable denouncer of political mystifications . . . We accept Raspail as a living protest against the principle of the Presidency, we present him to the suffrage of the people, not because he is or believes himself possible, but because he is impossible, because with him the Presidency, image of royalty, would be impossible.'

Even in these negative terms, Raspail's candidacy enraged the Mountain, who accused Proudhon of playing into the hands of Bonaparte by attempting to split the left Republican vote. Feeling grew so strong that he was forced to fight a duel with Felix Pyat, in which neither of the inexperienced rivals was hurt; shortly afterwards he was challenged by Charles Delescluze, but this time refused to fight on the grounds that he had already proved his courage by fighting Pyat and could now afford to defy the un-civilised prejudice in favour of duelling.

This dispute between Proudhon and his fellows of the left was given an academic flavour by the results of the elections, for Louis Bonaparte was returned on the 20th December with a vote more than double the combined totals of the other candidates. The fears of the peasants and the urban bourgeoisie, the ambitions of the priests, the generals and the industrialists, gave France a leader who was the crystallisation of all these terrors and interests, a vulgarian, a voluptuary, a hypocrite, an authoritarian and, for all his dynastic ambitions and connections, at heart a bourgeois of the first order, a Tartuffe who outdid Tartuffe. Whether the readers of *Le Peuple* had voted for Cavaignac or Ledru-Rollin or Raspail was unimportant, *except as a demonstration*. Only 36,000 out of 7,000,000 voters showed their rejection of the Presidency by calling for Raspail! It was indeed a scanty nucleus, and Proudhon, who on the day of the elections remarked, 'The people have spoken like a drunken man,' consoled himself with the thought that the very discontent which had sent Napoleon into power might force him to take a revolutionary path. On the 15th December he wrote in *Le Peuple*: 'Louis Bonaparte is condemned by universal suffrage to complete the Revolution of 1848. Socialist or traitor—there is no middle way for him.' Three days later he remarked to Antoine Gauthier, 'Soon the five million voices given to Bonaparte will cry: "Down with capital!"' And he added impulsively, summarising his life's creed in one spontaneous sentence: '*Morbleu*, let us revolutionise! It is the only good thing, the only reality in life.'

9

Though the last months of 1848 were filled with excitements and alarms, and the period following the elections was marked by illness,[1] Proudhon was not diverted from his personal schemes for spreading the social revolution by direct economic means, and at the end of January he brought to maturity his long-considered plan for the People's Bank.

His failure to arouse the interest of the Provisional Government in the original scheme for the Bank of Exchange had not discouraged him, and as early as April, 1848, he began to seek support among independent men of public standing. The first he approached was Emile de Girardin, editor of *La Presse*; Girardin was an intellectual dandy with a certain mental daring which appealed to the like quality in Proudhon, and they maintained a lifelong relationship in which antagonism and reluctant admiration mingled. Girardin promised to support the Bank and to publish Proudhon's project in full. By much persuasion Proudhon eventually gained the adherence of a heterogeneous collection of public figures and periodicals. Besides Girardin, who asked to be vice-president of the provisional committee, the sponsors included Considérant and the economist Frédéric Bastiat (the nearest thing France produced to a Manchester liberal), and a number of papers, including *Le National*, *La France Libre*, *L'Organisation du Travail*, *La Commune de Paris* and Baudelaire's *La Tribune Nationale*.

This appeared to represent a fairly broad support for Proudhon's plans, but he had hardly published his project before wide cleavages of opinion emerged. *La Tribune Nationale* published a statement, presumably written by Baudelaire, which showed that its approval was at best conditional; it approved the idea of augmenting credit, but dissociated itself from the wider implications of the scheme as Proudhon saw them; it did not wish to be thought an enemy of property, any more than an enemy of labour. More important, in an immediate sense, was the defection of Girardin, who, after having expressed enthusiastic interest, suddenly announced that he would not co-operate actively in found-

[1] There is no record of the nature of this illness, but Proudhon mentioned it in his letter to the Emperor on the 29th July, 1852, and said that it had forced him to be absent from the assembly. He attributed it to his heart being 'pierced' by the people's choice of Napoleon. Darimon, in constant touch with him at the time, declared that he was 'within two fingers of death.' There is a gap in Proudhon's correspondence between 26th December and 2nd February, while he resumed writing articles in the last week of January, so that it seems as though he was seriously ill during the last few days of 1848 and the first three weeks of 1849.

ing the Bank. Proudhon, in *Le Représentant du Peuple* of the 8th June, reproached him for not giving a direct 'NO,' instead of 'enveloping himself in puns, ambiguities and personalities.' In a way that throws much light on his own ideas of revolutionary action, he went on to analyse the differences between Girardin's conception of the Revolution and his own.

'M. de Girardin is a revolutionary *from above*; he has never been and never will be a revolutionary *from below*. That is to say that M. de Girardin is one of the worst kind of revolutionaries. The Revolution *from above* is the intervention of power in everything; it is the absolutist initiative of the State, the pure governmentalism of Mehemet Ali and Louis Blanc. The Revolution *from above* is the negation of collective activity, of popular spontaneity . . . What serious and lasting Revolution was not made *from below*, by the people? How did the Revolution of 1789 come about? How was that of February made? The Revolution *from above* has never been other than the oppression of the wills of those below; we reject the Revolution as M. de Girardin understands it.'

With differences of this kind among its sponsors, the scheme for the Bank of Exchange soon fell to pieces. But Proudhon did not give up his efforts; he now decided to make a direct call to the workers, and in December, 1848, after the election of Louis Bonaparte had finally convinced him of the folly of expecting anything from political action, he began to devote his time to putting the People's Bank into operation. On the 31st January, 1849, after long discussions with his close friends and associates, he appeared before a notary in Paris and registered the Act of Incorporation of the People's Bank, officially designated 'P. J. Proudhon and Company,' with himself as the sole responsible manager. With the Bank was to be associated a subsidiary organisation known as the 'General Syndicate of Production and Consumption,' for the purpose of encouraging association among workers. It was to be directed by Jules le Chevalier.

On the 15th February, Proudhon told Maurice that the Bank had begun gathering subscriptions at its office in the working-class Saint-Antoine district. With typical provincial caution, Proudhon did not trust Parisian radicals with the more important managerial functions, but sent to Besançon for a trio of his reliable Franc-Comtois friends, Guillemin, Mathey and Prével, men with business experience whom he had known since youth. As assistant managers, they virtually controlled the operations of the Bank, leaving the more colourful public figures, like Jules le Chevalier and Ramon de la Sagra, their positions as figureheads of the organisation.

Once the Bank had been established, Proudhon was occupied from early morning until late at night with one or other of the various concerns in which he saw some hope of improving the conditions of his fellows, and he entered into his many activities with a Gargantuan enthusiasm. 'The three months of January, February and March, 1849, during which the principle of free credit, if not applied and developed, was at least formulated concretely and thrown into the public consciousness by the People's Bank, were the finest time of my life,' he recollected.

Before the Bank's affairs were wound up, the membership had reached 27,000, consisting partly of working men in associations and partly of individual craftsmen. The receipts in cash, slightly less than 18,000 francs, seem hardly commensurate with so many supporters, and, since, according to its statutes, the Bank could not enter upon business until its paid-up capital amounted to 50,000 francs, it was in fact never more than a project in search of finances; apart from the intrinsic interest of the idea, its chief importance lies in the fact that it aroused a fairly numerous support among those very sections of the populace, who, in the hard months after June, had not the means to give it anything approaching an economically sound footing.

10

It seems likely that, like so many other efforts to change the situation of the working class by stimulating its own efforts, the People's Bank would have failed in any case from lack of initial financial support. But its end was hastened by other circumstances in Proudhon's life, incidental to his activities as an opposition journalist.

Towards the end of January, 1849, friction developed between the conservative republicans, who dominated the Assembly, and the President, with his dictatorial ambitions. Proudhon, who had already said on the 22nd December, 'democracy and socialism have no greater enemy than Bonaparte,' entered spiritedly into the struggle, in the hope that the Assembly might be provoked out of its weakness into taking the lead in a national war against dictatorship.

On the 25th January *Le Peuple* published an article entitled *La Guerre*, not written by Proudhon himself, but clearly inspired by him, in which Napoleon, 'personification of all reactionary ideas,' was accused of 'conspiring with all the monarchical cliques, with the Jesuits, with the absolutists, for the enslavement of the people and the return of every abuse.' Napoleon, the article went on, was violating the right of association, the right of meeting, the freedom of the press, the freedom of speech and thought. The article ended by declaring 'the president—that is to say, the monarchy, corruption, lies, privilege, arbitrariness, capitalist exploitation—is impossible.'

On the next day, the 26th January, Proudhon himself published a further article on the same theme, called 'The President of the Republic is Responsible.' After exposing the evidence of Napoleon's imperialist ambitions, he concluded: 'Bonaparte, elected by the reaction, instrument of the reaction, personification of the reaction, Bonaparte at this moment is the whole reaction, to such a point that, if Bonaparte falls, all the doctrinaire, legitimist, Orleanist, imperialist, capitalist and Jesuitical conspiracies will go down with him.'

However much the Assembly and the President may have squabbled among themselves, they were united in detesting Proudhon, and in treating his article as a God-given excuse to suppress him. The legal officers lost no time; on the 28th January the Procurator of the Republic brought charges of sedition, and on the 14th February the National Assembly, with only forty members of the Mountain protesting, passed a resolution withdrawing Proudhon's immunity. Already, on the 2nd February, he had said to Maguet, 'I am in a political duel with Bonaparte.' On the day after the Assembly deserted him, he wrote to Maurice: 'You see my life is a struggle, a terrible struggle. I have a hundred letters threatening to shoot me, to hang me, and I still live.'

On the 28th March he appeared before the Seine Assizes. He assumed responsibility for both the offending articles, pretending that he had merely forgotten to sign that which he had not written, and, in spite of a long speech in his own defence, he was condemned to three years' imprisonment and a fine of three thousand francs. George Duchêne received a year's imprisonment as manager of *Le Peuple*, the first of a series of sentences which became so habitual that, according to Herzen, Duchêne on one occasion turned to the judge after being found guilty and remarked: 'The bill, please!'

Proudhon appealed against the verdict and was left temporarily at liberty. He decided to use the opportunity to seek refuge abroad, and, having written to the President of the Assembly asking a month's leave to prepare his appeal, he boarded a night train for the Belgian frontier. In true conspiratorial style, he replaced his plain spectacles by blue glasses and enveloped the bottom of his face in a voluminous muffler. Otherwise, he wore his usual clothes, and though one of his friends had rigged him out in a wig, he hid it in his pocket, so that, according to Darimon who accompanied him to Lille, 'the least practised eye could have recognised him.' He worried throughout the journey about how foolish he would appear if he were arrested in flight, but the fugitives went unmolested.

In Belgium Proudhon assumed the name of Dupuis, and passed himself off as a magistrate. He went to Brussels and later to Liége, Namur and Mons, 'seeking everywhere an assured retreat.' A few weeks later he described his experiences to Maguet: 'I wandered over the whole of Belgium; I did not know where to stay, realising that everywhere the police had secret instructions and every day hearing myself spoken of in no very flattering way.'

Eventually, having spent between five and six hundred francs of his scanty funds on this fruitless wandering and having gained the impression that the Belgians were hostile to French journalists, he decided to return clandestinely to Paris. He came back on the 9th April, and stayed for three days with Guillemin and Mathey, his assistants at the People's Bank, with whom he arranged the dissolution of that institution. His announcement of the termination of the experiment appeared in *Le Peuple* on the 12th April. The main reason, he said, was that the trend of events had convinced him that the Bank was too slow a means to save the situation, and that it was necessary for those who desired a rapid social improvement to turn their energies immediately towards active propaganda through the Press—'no insurrections, no clubs, no banquets.' He took upon himself the burden of the Bank's liquidation. 'I asked the people for what was necessary to subsidise the first costs as well as the first operations of this enterprise . . . I alone bear the responsibility for the adventure, and make restitution of all that I have received.' Thus he added another few thousand francs to the debts he already owed and made his difficult financial position even worse.

Proudhon has been criticised for the arbitrary manner in which he closed the Bank without consulting his associates, other than Guillemin and Mathey. In his defence it may be said that without his active supervision, which would have been difficult from prison or exile, the Bank might in any case have collapsed from lack of initiative among its other supporters. But this is not certain, and it can also be argued that he should have given it at least a chance to continue. His failure to do so appears to have been due partly to his distrust of some of his collaborators, such as Jules le Chevalier, for he talked to Maguet of 'the clique that surrounded, tormented and spied on me at the People's Bank,' and added, 'I could not rid myself of them in the beginning; I needed this opportunity.'

After the liquidation of the Bank he went into hiding, under the name of Leloir, in the Rue Chabrol, near the Gare du Nord. He thought of travelling up the Rhine to Bâle, to see whether he could find a refuge in Switzerland, but in the meantime he settled down to work, and to write to his friends under assumed names and by devious routes. Even from hiding, he continued to write for *Le Peuple* and to conduct its policy, and he allowed his name to be put forward for the elections to the new Legislative Assembly on the 13th April, 1849. The result was encouraging for, though he was not elected, the vote in his favour was over 100,000, thirty thousand more than he had received on his election to the National Assembly in June, 1848. Despite his condemnation in the courts, his influence with the people was evidently still growing. Nevertheless, a short time afterwards, in July, he refused to take part in a further supplementary election, on the grounds that he preferred 'silence to defeat.'

But as he lurked in his little furnished room, emerging only at dusk to take his exercise in a working-man's blouse and sabots, Proudhon was by no means wholly concerned with business or politics, for at this time Euphrasie Piégard again makes an appearance in the records of his life. He must have seen her frequently during 1848, even though their meetings may have been extremely fleeting, stolen in the scanty intervals when Proudhon was not at the Assembly, at the offices of *Le Peuple*, at the People's Bank, at the revolutionary clubs, or driving frenziedly between these centres of activity; at the same time, there is no reference to her in his diary for the whole year, and in his letters only one very oblique remark which he made in December to Gauthier: 'It would take an eternity for us to agree and understand each other. That arises probably from the fact that you are a triple father and I am a bachelor. I have always been told that I should think otherwise if I had a wife. I would like to test that, but I very much fear that instead of correcting myself I should make my wife worse.' From this it appears that even at the end of 1848 he had still not finally decided to marry.

It was only now, when he was in hiding, that his friends learnt of his secret courtship. Darimon, going one day to visit him in his hotel, met two women descending the stairs. One was middle-aged; her companion was young, blonde and handsome. Proud-hon immediately realised that his friend must be speculating about his visitors, for he burst out laughing and said: 'Come on, I see that I must tell you everything. I want to get married. The presence of a woman at my hearth has become necessary to me. I came back to Paris to see if I can realise this project, which I have been cherishing for the last two years.' To have waited two years before making a decision, and then to do so when, as a fugitive, he had no hearth to grace with a wife, was perhaps an appropriate enough course for a courtship that had begun so extraordinarily.

Meanwhile, Proudhon's friends grew anxious about his continued presence in Paris, and urged him constantly to leave. But the fugitive put up one objection after another. 'I had to be in Paris to supervise the liquidation of the People's Bank.' And when this was completed, he presented other reasons. He had to follow up his policy; he had—man of paradox that he was—to defend the Constitution against which he had voted, since the political struggle had moved so far to the right that the Constitution had now become a bulwark protecting the Revolution; he had to keep the Mountain in check. Darimon objected that if he were to write his articles in Brussels he would do just as good service to the democratic cause, and at the same time he would not be in momentary danger of arrest. Proudhon still refused to depart, and then, one evening when he had extended his stroll a little farther than usual, and was walking in the Place de Lafayette, he was recognised by an acquaintance,[1] who informed the police. His arrest followed immediately, and he was taken to the Prefecture, where the police chief, Carlier, treated him with 'much respect,' as he noted in his diary. The next day, he was transferred to the Prison of Sainte-Pélagie.

[1] Proudhon mentions in his diary the individual whom he suspected of having informed on him; but the note was evidently written in agitation, and I found the name totally indecipherable.

Part Five

THE PRISONER

I

THE long-demolished hostel of Sainte-Pélagie, which lay on the borders of the Jardin des Plantes, was built during the seventeenth century as a place of retreat for repentant whores and for ladies of light conduct against whom their husbands had obtained *lettres de cachet*. During the Revolution of 1789 the ladies departed, and Sainte-Pélagie began its career as a prison; its clientele was distinguished, and included Madame du Barry, Madame Roland and the Vicomte de Beauharnais. During the Empire it was used for political prisoners, and, though it was enlarged under the July monarchy to accommodate common criminals, there was still one part, the Pavilion, which was reserved for critics of the regime, and it was here that Proudhon was installed.

On the day after his arrival he wrote to Maurice, to announce his whereabouts to the friend and to reassure the creditor. 'I am a prisoner, but my spirit is free, as gay and alert as ever. I wish to organise myself to work as much as possible, and so while away the boredoms of prison . . . If I am not mistaken, your interests will be safeguarded just as well, despite the accident which has befallen me, as if I were completely free in Geneva. The freedom of an exile is expensive, his resources are precarious; my new situation changes all that. I alone lose by the misfortune which has overtaken me; I believe that my creditors will gain from it. I do not believe I shall spend in Sainte-Pélagie more than 1½ to 2 francs a day.'

The relative equanimity with which Proudhon accepted his situation is more comprehensible when one remembers that, for the political detainees of a hundred years ago, the disadvantages of imprisonment were generally, except in Russia, far less than in our own day; a few months after his arrival, he described his life in this manner: 'I occupy a square room five metres each way . . . I was not so well lodged in the Rue Mazarin, even when I was a Representative. I eat the prison bread, which is good; I take soup in the morning, twice thick and five times thin each week . . . The rest I supply myself from the restaurant. The administration provides wine at 12 sous a litre, which is better than that of the wine merchants at 1 fr. 50 c. a bottle. I entertain visitors in my room. I have obtained permission to receive pamphlets and newspapers; I have all my books; everything I possess is, like me, behind bars.' Not only was he allowed to work on his books, but he could even continue to edit *Le Peuple*, so long as it observed the limitations of the Press laws.

In one way, indeed, his imprisonment was even positively fortunate, for eight days after his arrest Paris was again engulfed in civil strife, in the responsibility for which, as a fugitive radical, he would almost certainly have been implicated, even if he had remained inactive. On the 13th June, the leaders of the Mountain raised the red flag over a few barricades around the Conservatoire des Arts et Métiers and called upon the Parisians to join them. They were almost a year too late. The vigour of the working class had been sapped in June, 1848, and most of its militants were dead, imprisoned, transported or in exile. The rest had become discouraged by defeat and poverty, and a mere handful came into the streets to support Ledru-Rollin. The revolt was crushed without difficulty, and once again the authorities made it an excuse for reprisals. Heavy sentences were imposed, newspapers were suspended, soldiers who showed socialist sympathies were punished, and it became a crime to shout the slogan of the Mountain —'Long live the democratic and socialist republic!'

Proudhon did not support the rising of the 13th June; he had no sympathy with the government, or the interests it represented, but he felt that the insurgents, who based their stand against Louis Bonaparte on the defence of the constitution, were inconsistent, since their appeal to force was itself a violation of the Constitution. Their action had been 'inopportune, impolitic, ill-conducted.'

But though, thanks to 'my star and M. Carlier,' Proudhon was out of reach of direct reprisals, he nonetheless suffered from the events of the 13th June. Two of the friends he had left in charge of *Le Peuple*, Langlois and Pilhes, were led away by the enthusiasm of the hour to join the insurgents and were sentenced to long terms of imprisonment, while *Le Peuple* was suspended and the National Guards sent to close its offices vented their spite by sacking the establishment, which made it impossible to contemplate an early resumption of publication. Finally, owing to the influx of prisoners, he himself was turned out of his room in Sainte-Pélagie and consigned to the dank mediaeval prison of the Conciergerie.

It was a dismal exchange. A couple of months later—he remained in the Conciergerie until the end of September—he told his brother Charles: 'The room I occupy is like a cathedral in miniature; it receives the daylight only by means of a window placed high and protected by an iron grill. It bears a fair resemblance to a tomb.'

Yet even these conditions did not prevent him from writing, and by the middle of July he had started on a new book. It was to be an analysis of the previous year's revolution and an apology for the part he himself had played.

The regimen of steady work gave his life a calmness and placidity which he had not known since his days as a printer in Besançon, and he remarked to his brother that he felt hardly any privation 'but that of not being able to walk two leagues every evening after dinner.' And, indeed, despite the 'softening' and 'idleness' of which he complained, his speculations and his interest in what was passing in the world beyond the walls remained undiminished.

2

Proudhon's most urgent preoccupation during the summer of 1849 remained the problem of founding a new paper to replace *Le Peuple*. A little money had been retrieved from the latter's collapse, and he thought it possible that, by returning to the tedious process of gathering subscriptions, the editors might soon be able to bring out a weekly publication, and perhaps eventually build up again to a daily. But such slowness was eminently disadvantageous. 'Time is precious, and events happen quickly . . . We know that the surest way to resume the position which *Le Peuple* had conquered in the Press is to return immediately to daily publication.' So he set out to find some person who would provide the means for a regular newspaper. After two months he encountered this sponsor in Alexander Herzen.

Having left his own country in 1847, Herzen had watched the revolutions of 1848–9 with growing disillusionment, and Proudhon's single-minded defiance of the mounting reaction had been one of his few consolations. 'Have you been able to follow Proudhon?' he wrote to Granovsky. 'What a powerful voice! His war with that imbecile Louis Napoleon has been the very poetry of anger and contempt.' Herzen and Proudhon had met in Bakunin's lodgings during 1847, but they had not become intimate, and when the question of journalistic collaboration arose in 1849, the first negotiations were conducted by Charles Edmond and the Russian, Sazonov, both of whom knew Proudhon well. 'I owed a great deal to Proudhon in my intellectual development,' Herzen remarked years later, 'and, after a little consideration, I consented, though I knew the fund would soon be gone.' In August Guillemin went to Geneva, where Herzen was living, to complete the negotiations, and finally, ten days later, Proudhon wrote to his new collaborator defining their respective positions.

'It is understood that, under my general direction, you shall share in editing *La Voix du Peuple*, that your articles shall be accepted without any censorship other than that imposed on the editor of a paper by a respect for his own principles and a fear of the law. You know, Monsieur, that, being in agreement on ideas, we can hardly differ on deductions, and as for the appreciation of foreign events, we shall always be obliged to yield to you. You and we are missionaries of one idea . . . We must raise the democratic and social question to the level of a European league.'

Herzen agreed, and immediately sent the money he had promised, but his active collaboration in *La Voix du Peuple*, as the new paper was called, never became close, though he contributed a few articles on Russia. His share in the editorial responsibility devolved in his intermediaries, Edmond and Sazonov. Edmond remained a loyal collaborator with Proudhon until the end of the latter's journalistic career in 1850, but the more ambitious Sazonov found it, as he remarked to Ogarev, 'difficult to get on with the boss and his Darimon,' and eventually retired to a more remunerative and perhaps more personally satisfying position on *La Réforme*.

Once the future of *La Voix du Peuple* had been assured, Proudhon and his friends went quickly to work on its preparation, the first daily issues appearing at the end of September, 1849. In the interval Proudhon had been moved back to Sainte-Pélagie, where he was given an excellent room with two great windows looking out over the Jardin des Plantes; in authorising this change of prison, the chief of police had asked him to make clear the part he was playing in the new paper. Proudhon complied, at least nominally, by writing a letter in the opening number of the 30th September. 'In your specimen number of the 25th instant,' he told the acting editors, 'you announce that *La Voix du Peuple* counts me among its collaborators. My position as a convicted man, the conventions of every kind which it obliges me to respect, my forced separation from you in these difficult times, and the consequent impossibility of my fulfilling, from evening until next morning, a direction whose consequences may become at any given moment excessively grave, oblige me to recall to your readers and to whomever it may concern that, whatever influence I may exercise by my communications and advice to the editorship of *La Voix du Peuple*, I neither can nor should accept any other responsibility than for the articles signed by me.'

Whether the government was hoodwinked by this statement we do not know, but it is certain that none of Proudhon's friends ever doubted his rôle as effective editor of *La Voix du Peuple*. As Herzen said: 'Proudhon from his prison cell conducted his orchestra in masterly fashion. His articles were full of originality, fire, and that irritability which prison inflames.' According to Herzen, the demand for the new paper was greater than ever; 40,000 copies would normally circulate, but whenever Proudhon wrote a special article, 50,000 to 60,000 were printed, and sold so quickly that 'often on the following day copies were being sold for a franc instead of a sou.' Clearly, imprisonment had only enhanced Proudhon's reputation as a journalistic dissenter.

3

La Voix du Peuple did not interfere materially with Proudhon's other literary activities, and on the 30th October, 1849, he told Maguet: 'My *Confessions* are printed . . . I did them as a kind of surprise to my mind.' This work, which began as a pamphlet, and, on a flood of inspiration, grew into a book during six weeks of hard writing, was regarded by Sainte-Beuve as the best of all Proudhon's books, and while this judgment might be disputed in favour of *De la Justice*, it is true that *Les Confessions d'un Révolutionnaire* is a much more capably written book than anything Proudhon had produced previously. It is also one of the best books written on the events of 1848 by any of the men who took part in them.

The title is misleading; the *Confessions* is actually a study of the revolutionary movement in France from 1789 to 1849, with anticipations of its further development, and interspersed are autobiographical chapters in which Proudhon gives the background to the positions he took up with regard to specific events. It begins with a profession of faith in the form of society promised by the revolutionary tradition. 'The Republic remains the ideal of all societies, and outraged liberty will soon reappear, like the sun after an eclipse.' But the question remains why democracy should have failed so often, and it is to seek an answer that Proudhon sets out.

He begins by examining the trends into which French political movements are inclined to flow—absolutism and socialism at the extremes, and between them the *juste-milieu* or Centre ('the hypocrisy of conservatism') and demagogy or Jacobinism ('the hypocrisy of progress'). Of these only socialism views society by the light of a positive and objective science, but even it, Proudhon admits with an eye to Cabet and Considérant, 'is liable to take its hypotheses for reality and its utopias for institutions.'

Absolutism and socialism represent the poles of past and future between which society moves; the *juste-milieu* and the Jacobins represent the compromise parties of right and left which are brought into existence by the influence of human passions and reasoning on the progress of events. This is the master plan from which Proudhon makes his analysis of the historic situation. And here we come to the touchstone of Proudhonian doctrine against which all the events of the Revolution are judged:

'All men are equal and free: society, by nature and destination, is therefore autonomous and ungovernable. If the sphere of activity of each citizen is determined by the natural division of work and by the choice he makes of a profession, if the social functions are combined in such a way as to produce a harmonious effect, order results from the free activity of all men; there is no government. Whoever puts his hand on me to govern me is an usurper and a tyrant; I declare him my enemy.

'But social physiology does not immediately allow that egalitarian organisation; the idea of Providence, which was one of the first to appear in society, has been in opposition to it. Equality comes to us by a succession of tyrannies and governments, in which liberty is continually at grips with absolutism, like Israel and Jehovah. Thus equality is born continually for us out of inequality; liberty has government for its point of departure . . . Authority was the first social idea of the human race. And the second was to work immediately for the abolition of authority, each wishing to use it as the instrument of his liberty against the liberty of others.'

In other words, Proudhon sees the Revolution as a dynamic progress in which, balancing between the poles of the parties, society proceeds towards the final dynamic equilibrium of anarchy. It is from this point of view that he makes his perceptive criticism of the revolutions of 1789 and 1830 and, in much more detail, that of 1848, calling for a broadening of the Democratic Socialist movement so that it may become the 'party of liberty.' In final peroration, he breaks into a long rhapsody on the idea of Liberty itself:

'The principle of the Revolution, we know it still, is Liberty,' he declares. 'Liberty! That is to say: 1. political enfranchisement, by the organisation of universal suffrage, by the independent centralisation of social functions, by the incessant and perpetual revision of the Constitution; 2. industrial enfranchisement, by the mutual guarantee of credit and sale. In other words: no more government of man by man, by means of the accumulation of powers; no more exploitation of man by man by means of the accumulation of capital.'

And he ends in a curious invocation of the spirit of irony, which he sees as the very vehicle of intellectual liberation: 'Irony, true liberty! It is you who have delivered me from the ambition for power, from the servitude of parties, from the respect for routine, from the pedantry of science, from the admiration of great personages, from the mystifications of politics, from the fanaticism of reformers, from the superstitious view of this great universe, and from the adoration of myself . . . Your smile appeases dissensions and civil strife; you make peace between brothers and cure the fanatic and the sectarian . . . Come, sovereign, spread over my fellow countrymen the rays of your light, ignite in their minds a glimmer of your spirit, so that my Confessions may reconcile them and the inevitable revolution may be accomplished in serenity and joy.'

4

The lyrical termination of his *Confessions* restored Proudhon from the almost frenzied state of inspiration in which he had written to a renewed concern for the more personal sides of his life, and on the 11th October we encounter the first surviving letter to Euphrasie Piégard since the end of 1847.

'Mademoiselle,

I send you an authorisation for M. Micaud. Try to come and see me with him; I shall be gratified. At last my long rhapsody draws to its end. I thought to make a pamphlet; it turns out that I have made a book. You must often have found that care for my party, my ideas, my reputation, absorbs me and diverts me perhaps more than it should from my other duties; it is a fault I am forced to recognise and for which I beg your pardon for the thousandth time. Come and see me alone and bring me your forgiveness. Released from the greatest of my cares, I shall perhaps be less morose and more communicative,

Yours devotedly,

P.-J. Proudhon.'

The formal address should be noted; it suggests that even now Proudhon had not reached a final decision on the thorny question of marriage. It was not, indeed, until the end of November that a decisive intimation of his intentions appeared. On the 22nd of that month he noted laconically in his diary that he had given

Euphrasie a thousand francs to set up a home. It must have been shortly afterwards that he wrote the undated letter in which he treated their forthcoming marriage as definite and, most significant, went so far as to use her Christian name:

'My dear Euphrasie,

You must realise that what I charge you to buy is not destined for anyone but you. I beg you therefore to choose accordingly; since I am a prisoner and am condemned to be modest, you can go as far as 50 or 60 francs. I beg your pardon for charging you with such a strange commission, but necessity has no law. Besides, I was resolved, before occupying myself with that question, to ask you what would give you pleasure. When two people think of becoming united, it is the custom for them to make their acquisitions for the wedding together. I am therefore correct, and I embrace you,

P.-J. Proudhon.

P.S. I forgot to ask you to use the money which you have in hand for all the purposes that may be agreeable to you. I do not want any accounting.'

A few days later he told Guillemin that his 'future' was already gaining a vast pleasure from organising her household. 'Nothing embellishes a woman like happiness.' Euphrasie had been fortunate enough to find an apartment in Rue de la Fontaine; its windows faced Proudhon's room in Sainte-Pélagie, and thus, even when they were not together on Euphrasie's daily visits, or on the weekly days of parole when Pierre-Joseph was now allowed to go out of prison from morning until nightfall, they could still see each other and communicate by signs.

It was on Proudhon's second day of parole, the 31st December, that they were married. He insisted on a civil ceremony and, though Euphrasie was a devout Catholic, she seems to have agreed without demur. Their differences regarding religion continued throughout their married life, and Euphrasie always kept a crucifix in her room, which greatly scandalised the emancipated Mme Ackermann. But Proudhon himself, with his ambivalent attitude towards the sexes, appears to have seen nothing wrong in this. 'The woman who prays is sublime,' he once remarked;

'a man on his knees is as ridiculous as a man who cuts a caper.'

He set great store, however, by his civil marriage, telling Tissot in 1851 that it was 'the beginning of a serious war against the clergy.' At the time of the ceremony he contented himself with noting: 'I have only one regret, and that is not to have made this marriage four years ago.' What Euphrasie thought has not been recorded or remembered.

Later Proudhon was to insist that in his marriage he had not been guided in the least by romantic feelings. 'I made this marriage with premeditation, without passion,' he told Tissot, 'so as to be the father of a family, to live a whole life, and to keep near me in the whirlwind into which I am thrown an image of simplicity and maternal modesty.' And the passion without which he began does not seem to have found its way in with the domestic comforts he enjoyed so sparingly in the first period of his marriage; indeed, he was held back by his ideas of chastity—and perhaps also by a certain fear—from establishing any too demanding physical contact with his wife and, though he was allowed to go out of the prison once every week, he noted early in February: 'In all, during six weeks of marriage, I have slept three times with my wife, a fact I am far from lamenting. It is not good, in my view, always to be together.' Ten days later, when he heard from Euphrasie that she was pregnant and expected a child in October, he was delighted. 'I am captive,' he noted, 'but I am very happy.' And, for all its lack of sentimental motivation, his marriage was destined to be as fruitful as he had hoped.

5

When Proudhon referred to himself in February, 1850, as 'captive,' he meant something more than his ordinary confinement. For in that month, as a result of events which had taken place since his marriage, he found himself again in serious difficulties with the authorities, and the restrictions of his imprisonment were temporarily increased.

The whole winter he had been in a state of mental excitability, and he soon grew impatient with the policy of caution on which he had started *La Voix du Peuple*. The old Proudhon of violent words and gestures was always struggling up for air, and a remark to Micaud on the 17th December gave a hint of a storm to come. 'One must beat on human brains as on an anvil; otherwise they will not listen.' However, at this time he still retained a certain caution, for he also remarked to Herzen: 'As journalists foreseeing the coming catastrophe, it is not for us to present it as something inevitable and just, or we shall be hated and kicked out, and we have to live.'

The incident that precipitated the change in his journalistic policy is recounted by Herzen, who had come to Paris in January, 1850, and called on Proudhon at the same time as two of the editors of *La Voix du Peuple* and Count D'Alton-Shée, a Bohemian dandy who held a somewhat independent position on the foothills of the Mountain. D'Alton-Shée respected Proudhon, whom he called 'the great foreseer,' and he frequently visited him in prison.

'He [D'Alton-Shée] was saying to Proudhon that the last numbers of *La Voix du Peuple* were feeble; Proudhon was looking through them and growing more and more morose. Then, thoroughly incensed, he turned to the editors: "What is the meaning of it? You take advantage of my being in prison, and go to sleep in the office. No, gentlemen, if you go on like this I shall refuse to have anything to do with the paper and shall publish my reasons".'

This verbal reproach was reinforced by a letter to Darimon, in which Proudhon called his friends to order and declared his intention to fight the regime. 'We have discussed long enough. The reaction makes fun of us and prepares to scuttle the Republic. It is time we did a little agitation and threatening once again. . . . Enough of political economy and metaphysics; every week a good article on the State, another on credit, and that is enough. The rest—war. I propose from tomorrow onwards to put you back in that line. We shall, I hope, inoculate the venom of revolt into the whole country. Since we must again pass through the Jacobin orgy, since the reaction forces us to it, since reprisals become each day more a right and a duty, I do not intend to be left behind. I still want to be king of the carnival. Besides, each day irritates me more, and I can no longer maintain this cautious attitude. I prefer Doullens or a dungeon. . . . I must speak or break my pens.'

The results of the new policy were soon forthcoming. The editors combined to put their most scathing criticism of the regime into *La Voix du Peuple*, and in a few days Proudhon was declaring to Darimon, with delighted 'Bravos,' that 'the anti-governmental idea is being unfolded with an irresistible lucidity and power. . . . Another six weeks and the State is finished.'

The State survived, but it was certainly a little disturbed by Proudhon's onslaught, and during the next three weeks *La Voix du Peuple* was seized twice. On the second of these occasions Proudhon had given, in an article entitled *Vive L'Empereur*, a prophetic revelation of Napoleon's ambitions, as well as a call to the people not to neglect their own interests when the ruling class quarrelled among itself. 'It is now an assured fact,' he warned, 'that we shall have a *coup d'état*. . . . At the first signal of the *coup d'état* we should put our bailiffs into the Bank, we should burn the Great Book, throw the registers of mortgages into the river, destroy (to cries of "Long Live the Emperor") the files of the notaries, solicitors and registrars and all the titles of credit and property.'

The *coup d'état* which Proudhon prophesied took place a year and a half later; his augury of a popular rising accompanying it was less exact. But the authorities did not hesitate to proceed against him for a too knowledgeable revelation of the intentions of the head of the state, and on the day following the appearance of his article he was confined to his room and all communication with his wife or his friends was forbidden. He managed nevertheless to inform Euphrasie surreptitiously of his situation, and told her to be 'calm and firm.' 'The wife of citizen Proudhon should not show any weakness.'

On the 13th February he was taken back to the Conciergerie; he bore his transfer stoically, and his thought was more for Euphrasie than for himself. 'Remember, my child,' he wrote to her, 'that in some circumstances misfortune is good. I have the feeling that this little misfortune will be the only sorrow I shall cause you in my life, and that from today onwards we shall be happier than before. Have a little trust in my word, and believe that, while accomplishing what I regard as a sacred duty, I shall find the means to make you happy.'

On the 14th February he was called before the examining magistrate, but remained undisturbed at the prospect of a new trial. 'What is happening to me,' he told Darimon, 'is only an isolated fact in this vast system of provocation and arbitrariness which weighs down upon us.' He was pessimistic about the general political situation. 'The future is ours, no doubt,' he told Darimon on the 20th February, 'but the present belongs to despotism, and this present can be prolonged for many years.' Yet he saw no reason for inertia. 'Despite everything, we must act energetically both against the reaction and against the demagogues; I will never give in to one or the other.'

It will be seen from the letters I have quoted that Proudhon, despite the ban on communications, managed to carry on a considerable correspondence from the Conciergerie, and an idea of the ruses he had to use is given in a letter to a fellow prisoner, Nicolle. 'Would it not be possible,' he asks, 'to get letters to me by a string let down from Bonnard's window, at nine or ten in the evening? It is just above the left window of my room, and the packet would arrive in front of a broken pane, so that I could take it without a light and without opening.' The privilege of correspondence was returned officially on the 22nd February, after 169 members of the Assembly had joined in censuring the ministry for the treatment meted out to him. Shortly afterwards he was allowed to receive his friends and to walk in the rose garden which was maintained in the courtyard by subscription among the detainees; here, on visits to the prison, Victor Hugo would encounter him, tramping solitarily and silently with enormous strides.

It was during the interlude of relative calm which lasted from mid-March to mid-April that he noted in his diary the effect—surprisingly slight in his opinion—that the first ten months of imprisonment had worked upon him. 'The time has seemed short, despite impatience, restlessness and boredom. The men I have seen in captivity with me, the works I have completed, the accidents of my public life, have all filled my days and left me only a feeble sentiment of the trouble I endure. I should add here, and mention particularly among the factors that have sweetened my convict's existence, my marriage with Euphrasie Piégard, the simplest, sweetest, most docile of creatures, and up to her marriage the most innocent. I expect, in five days, a new condemnation. My kind is not forgiven; nevertheless, I am right, despite all the world.' The condemnation he expected so philosophically did not come, for when he appeared before the court on the 10th April the prosecution was annulled on technical grounds.

6

This fortunate escape did not hold him long in check. In the spring of 1850 a series of bye-elections were held, and, despite some misgivings about such a 'phalansterian romancer,' Proudhon supported the candidature of the novelist Eugène Sue, publishing on the 19th April a militant appeal on his behalf to the middle class of Paris. 'Burgesses of Paris,' he declaimed, ' . . . do not disdain the alliance of the people now that it is offered to you; tomorrow it is you who will ask for it and then you will get the same answer as Louis-Philippe and Charles X: "Too late!" Vote with the people, vote with the workers, for I tell you—and I knew it twenty-two months ago when I alone took up their defence—the proletarians are our strength.'

Sue and several other left republicans were returned to the Assembly, and this unexpected increase in the radical minority caused the right-wing factions to pass the iniquitous law of the 31st May, 1850, which deprived three million members of the working class of their franchise.

But the government did not wait for the elections before it punished Proudhon. On the day after the publication of his article supporting Sue, he was sent to the fortress of Doullens, where long-term political detainees were confined. Just before his departure he wrote a hurried note to Euphrasie, telling her, with Panglossian calmness: 'All things considered, what has happened to me now is still for the best; I suffer for the most honourable of motives, for the most just of causes.'

At the fortress he was immediately put into a solitary confinement even more rigorous than he had endured in the Conciergerie. He was allowed no communications, no books or papers, and there was a warder perpetually at his door. Escape, he observed, would be impossible. 'It is just like being in Icaria,' he noted jestingly in his diary.

On the 26th April his wife and brother, who had been waiting for days to see him, were finally allowed into the prison. It was a disastrous visit, for Proudhon surreptitiously handed Charles a letter to the editors of *La Voix du Peuple* which was discovered by the guards. The next day the Governor made a violent scene with Proudhon in Euphrasie's presence, and forbade her to make any visits while the solitary confinement lasted. Accordingly, she departed to Paris where, after several days of persistent effort, she obtained an interview with Baroche, the Minister of the Interior, and persuaded him to put an end to her husband's sequestration. This was done on the 5th May, and she returned to Doullens on the same day. She stayed there throughout his remaining sojourn in the fortress, visiting him daily and assiduously ministering to his needs. 'She knows how to love—she knows nothing but that,' he told Langlois. 'It is enough.'

On the 6th May Proudhon was moved into the section of the prison inhabited by the more distinguished political prisoners. Concerned with his own affairs during the early part of 1848, he had made little contact with these men in the heyday of their celebrity. He belonged to the same club as Barbès, and a tenuous friendliness had existed between him and Blanqui since the Taschereau affair. But with none had he been on anything approaching intimate terms, and the closeness imposed by prison life enabled him to observe them with an interest that was sharpened by unfamiliarity.

He saw, with surprise, that they seemed to detest each other, 'living . . . in isolation'; Raspail carried this tendency to an extreme, remaining 'in retirement like a hermit.' Barbès seemed 'a republican of the other world.' Blanqui, 'the man of black destiny,' he acknowledged to be 'endowed with a rare penetration,' but he added that 'his cold disposition will always betray his great plans.' 'Truly,' Proudhon remarked to Mathey, 'I do not know why I am among these citizens, whom I esteem infinitely but with none of whom, except for Huber, do I find myself in the least sympathy.'

But life at Doullens was by no means confined to observing the habits and characters of professional revolutionaries, for Proudhon had to devote a great deal of anxious thought to the future of *La Voix du Peuple*. 26,000 francs of its funds had been consumed in fines, and he now regarded the paper's career as virtually ended, while his own situation disgusted him so much that he exclaimed in his diary: 'Decidedly, I must quit political life and day-to-day polemics.' But the devotion of his friends kept *La Voix du People* alive even when he had given up hope for it. His pleasure at this fact was mingled with anxiety, and at the end of April, when another issue was seized, he told Euphrasie that the paper should be liquidated. 'Our friends should let things go their own way: they have done enough to serve their convictions and salve their consciences. . . . Every prosecution of *La Voix du Peuple* aggravates my situation; it is absolutely necessary that the paper should cease to appear or that I should withdraw from it.' External circumstances solved his problem, for *La Voix du Peuple* was finally suppressed on the 14th May, and Edmond was expelled from France for his collaboration.

Two weeks later Proudhon went to stand his trial at the Seine Assizes. The charges against him were weighty, including not only the usual accusation of 'excitement to hatred and contempt,' but also such irrelevant and preposterous items as 'provocation of an attempt having for its aim to bring about devastation and pillage in one or more communes.' The accumulated penalties for all these alleged crimes might have totalled fifteen years' confinement; Proudhon himself expected no less than two or three years. But his counsel, Crémieux, made a very persuasive defence, and he was acquitted; it was a singular piece of good fortune, for the mood of 1850 was such that for a democrat to escape conviction once he had been charged was extremely rare.

But once again the almost immediate result of this acquittal on one indictment was the temptation to risk another by trying to resume journalistic activity. Only a few days after the death of *La Voix du Peuple* Proudhon began discussing a new paper with his colleagues; it appeared on the 15th July, under the old title of *Le Peuple*. Fines having eaten the editorial funds almost to nothing, *Le Peuple* was published only irregularly. Moderation seemed now the intended keynote; 'prudence before everything,' Proudhon exhorted his assistants on the eve of its appearance. This did not prevent the first issue from being seized as soon as it was printed.

Furthermore, like most of the surviving minority journals, *Le Peuple* was hard hit by the Press law of the 16th July which imposed a stamp duty on all political literature. Sales fell rapidly, income decreased, and when it was again prosecuted on the 14th October, on charges of 'provocation to civil war,' the editors were unable to meet the fine of 6,000 francs that was imposed. Accordingly, *Le Peuple* ceased to appear, and Proudhon's journalistic career was at an end.

For some months, indeed, he cherished the idea of starting

yet another paper to fight the mounting reaction, and twice in the early part of 1851 he thought himself on the verge of securing a backer. But men like Herzen were not so abundant as he may have hoped, and in each case the negotiations collapsed. By the middle of 1851 he was ready to admit that he no longer hoped for a return to the battlefield of periodical writing.

But his unwilling acceptance of the situation did not imply a mental submission to the authorities, an admission of defeat. 'If we do not pretend to impose our ideas on others,' he told Emile de Girardin at this time, 'we are also decided not to suffer others to impose theirs on us. . . . Our enemies, know it well, are all those who hinder discussion, or who force us without discussion to take their good pleasure for law.' If Proudhon reconciled himself to abandoning journalism, it was only to find another way of putting forward the ideas that had earned him persecution and notoriety.

7

Even apart from the frustration of his journalistic ambitions, the collapse of *Le Peuple* brought a perceptible change in the tenor of Proudhon's life. He was still in prison and still acutely aware of external events, but much of the tempestuousness went out of his existence, and for a considerable period it followed a relatively uneventful course. In July the privilege of paying visits outside the prison was returned to him and, except during Bonaparte's *coup d'état* in December, 1851, he retained it for the rest of his confinement. Deprived of a journalistic outlet, his inventive mind began to project a whole series of ambitious works—on history, biography, revolutionary tactics, political economy, while his correspondence became more discursive and expanded into territories which for long had found expression only in his articles and pamphlets.

One important letter, written in August, 1851, discussed the psychological character of mass movements in a tone that anticipated the viewpoint adopted by Tolstoy in *War and Peace*. Proudhon began by denying that socialism was yet a party in the true sense of the word, and declared that all that had so far emerged was 'a blind and passionate manifestation of the undetermined aspirations of the people.' Using Barbès as an example, he went on to show that the most popular leaders were those who best typified popular myths and ideals, and that such men were in reality the led rather than the leaders. 'It is remarkable on the other hand,' he added in a tone of personal sadness, 'that the more a man gives proof of judgment, of perspicacity, of the progressive spirit and the faculty of understanding, the more he loses his ascendancy over the masses, to whom thought is repugnant and who go only by instinct.'

A theme that becomes significantly consistent in his correspondence at this period is his growing hostility towards the Catholic Church, prompted largely by the rôle of the Papacy as an enemy of democracy in Italy, but partly also by the part the clergy had played in furthering the plans of Louis Bonaparte and destroying the possibilities of the February revolution. When he advocated to Marc Dufraisse the freedom of education, he made a special exception for the clergy, who he thought should not be allowed to teach. 'At this moment Catholicism should be pursued to extinction,' he remarked, 'which does not prevent me from writing *Tolerance* on my banner.' When Chevé, one of the staff of *Le Peuple*, objected to attacks on the Church, Proudhon told him that his protests were too late, since Catholicism had been 'condemned irrevocably' by 'the Revolution, Socialism and the democratic conscience.' And, a month later, he expressed to Darimon a thought which afterwards he expanded to gigantic dimensions in *De la Justice*: 'Religion is authority; authority is the church; the church is Catholicism.'

But his correspondence at this period was by no means wholly that of a polemicist. Often, as well, we encounter the jesting and generous companion, the almost passionate friend, the devoted paterfamilias. There is, for instance, a letter of September, 1850, humorously thanking his old friend Dr. Maguet who, with his neighbour Squire Bessetaux, sent frequent supplies of game and other rural delicacies into Sainte-Pélagie. 'For mercy's sake,' Proudhon exhorts him, 'why send us so many good things at one time? Did you want to regale the whole Piégard family, or all my companions of captivity? Sobriety, moderation, temperance, economy, if you please; these are what a prisoner must have. But whom should I thank for these good and excellent victuals? For you do so little hunting that I cannot suppose you had such a bag in one day. Allow me to believe, without wronging our ancient friendship, that M. Bessetaux and Father Eustache are not strangers to the expedition? Then give them my compliments, my sincere regards, and to Mme Bessetaux all my respects . . .'

In November there is an equally graceful letter to the lawyer Mare Dufraisse, who, in the shared life of the prison, was rapidly becoming one of Proudhon's closer friends.

'My dear Marc,

It is tomorrow, Sunday, at six in the evening, that I count on having you to dine at my house, 9, rue de la Fontaine. I shall probably come to take you from your home at a quarter to six. If something should prevent me, you know the street and the number.

My dear Marc, I am poor—I say it without pride or anger. I have the misfortune not to be able to treat my friends as I would like, and I am forced to withdraw into the narrowest of circles. It is therefore as a token of sincere friendship that I beg you to accept my *pot-au-feu*. Darimon, who is about to leave for Besançon, will be with us—a fellow as poor as I.

Come then, so that our relations, our sympathies, shall not remain enclosed within the walls of the Conciergerie. I shake your hand.

P.-J. P.'

The *pot-au-feu* was not so humble as Proudhon suggested, for a letter instructing Euphrasie in this little feast specified 'a good soup, a roast of veal, escorted by potatoes, a salad, dessert, and coffee for those who like it.'

It was on the 18th October that Proudhon's ambition for paternity was achieved, when his wife gave birth to a daughter. His overt reaction was curiously taciturn; his diary recorded the fact without comment, and Maurice was told of it two days later in a brief sentence which described the event as 'interesting only to me.' Clearly, despite his loudly expressed theories on the excellence of family life, Proudhon was still looking upon his responsibilities with a bachelor's caution. Yet he rapidly became an absorbed and affectionate father, and there seems no doubt that this experience finally reassured him as to the wisdom of the Quixotic series of actions which had culminated in his marriage.

He called this first child Catherine, 'from my mother's name, to whom I owe everything.' By the time Catherine was six months old and beginning to cut her teeth, he wrote to Edmond, whose exile had now led him to Egypt, that she was 'an ideal child.' 'You must see this little slip who has already taken her place in the family under the diminutive of Kathe.'

But, while Proudhon found his family life even more satisfying than he had hoped, its material basis was being steadily undermined by the conditions of his imprisonment, and in the spring of 1851 he complained to Maurice of the evident deterioration of his situation. 'As you know, I have neither revenue nor patrimony. My present means of existence consists solely of the product of my publications. . . . Two years of prison, the need to help my brother, the whole or partial liquidation of various debts, fifteen years of marriage, and a child—you will realise how all that has reduced my fund, without counting that the successive suppressions of *Le Peuple* and *La Voix du Peuple* have cost me 3,000 francs of my own.' The sole relieving circumstance was that even his old books were still selling, and he had been offered 3,000 francs for a work in progress which, despite a number of delays in completion, he expected to publish in June or July.

8

This new work, *Idée Générale de la Révolution au XIXe Siècle*, appeared in the middle of July, 1851. More than any other of Proudhon's books, it represented that positive examination of society which he had long promised as the constructive supplement to *Les Contradictions Économiques*, and it was this aspect that he stressed when he sent a copy to Michelet. 'I dare to believe that you will find in this work an attempt to realise your dearest wishes; the ultimate freedom of man, popular initiative organised in perpetuity, property in land assured to the peasant and freed of all the causes which, by fragmentation, agglomeration, rent, share-cropping, mortgage, abuse, make it an institution which is equivocal to begin with and in time becomes definitely anti-republican and immoral.'

The General Idea of the Revolution begins with an appeal to the bourgeoisie; Proudhon seeks, by recalling to this class its past rôle as a revolutionary force, to bring a reconciliation between it and the workers, and so to precipitate a revolution that would liberate both—not a political revolution, but a basic change in the economic fabric of society.

After this call to unity, he proceeds to a series of studies outlining the shape which the revolution must assume in the nineteenth century. The first, entitled 'Reaction Causes Revolution,' involves an elaborate analysis of the nature of revolution and its inevitability as a factor in social evolution. 'A revolution is a force against which no power, divine or human, can prevail, and whose nature is to grow by the very resistance it encounters' . . . The more you repress it, the more you increase its rebound and render its action irresistible, so that it is precisely the same for the triumph of an idea whether it is persecuted, harassed, beaten down from the start, or whether it grows and develops unobstructed. Like the Nemesis of the ancients, whom neither prayers nor threats could move, the revolution advances, with sombre and predestined tread, over the flowers strewn by its friends, through the blood of its defenders, over the bodies of its enemies.'

A revolution is necessary in the nineteenth century because the movement of 1789 was only half accomplished; its interpreters were concerned with politics only, and paid no attention to the economic organisation called for by the death of feudalism. 'The Republic should have established Society; it thought only of establishing Government. . . . Therefore, while the problem propounded in '89 seemed to be officially solved, fundamentally there was a change only in governmental metaphysics, what Napoleon called *ideology*. . . . In place of this governmental, feudal and military rule, imitated from that of former kings, the new edifice of industrial institutions must be built.'

The means by which this necessary revolution can be brought about is Association, and by this Proudhon makes it clear that he does not mean a rigid Utopian system. Association for its own sake, considered as a dogma, is potentially dangerous to freedom, but as a means to a greater end it is beneficial. 'Working men's associations . . . should be judged, not by the more or less successful results they obtain, but only according to their silent tendency to assert and establish the social republic. . . . The importance of their work lies, not in their petty union interests, but in their denial of the rule of capitalists, usurers and governments, which the first revolution left undisturbed. Afterwards, when they have conquered the political lie . . . the groups of workers should take over the great departments of industry, which are their natural inheritance.'

Here Proudhon goes on to a closer examination of the nature of government. He repeats the criticisms of the idea of authority already made in his earlier works, and against it he places the idea of contract which, he told Michelet, was 'the most formidable part of my work.' 'The idea of contract excludes that of government. . . . Between contracting parties there is necessarily a real personal interest for each; a man bargains with the aim of securing his liberty and his revenue at the same time. Between governing and governed, on the other hand, no matter how the system of representation or delegation of the governmental function is arranged, there is *necessarily* an alienation of part of the liberty and means of the citizen.'

It is in the generalisation of this principle of contract, in the turning of society into a network of mutual undertakings between individuals, that Proudhon sees the new order of economic as distinct from political organisation. When that order is achieved, there will no longer be any need for government, and, returning to his old serialist doctrine, Proudhon concludes that the end of the series beginning in Authority is Anarchy. In more concrete terms, the change of aspect between the old and the new societies is expressed as follows: 'In place of laws, we will put contracts; no more laws voted by the majority, or even unanimously. Each citizen, each town, each industrial union will make its own laws. In place of political powers we will put economic forces . . . in place of standing armies, we will put industrial associations. In place of police we will put identity of interests. In place of political centralisation, we will put economic centralisation.' Law courts will be replaced by arbitration, national bureaucracies will be replaced by decentralised direct administration, and large industrial or transport undertakings will be managed by associations of workers; education will be controlled by parents and teachers, and academic training will be replaced by integrated education, with 'instruction . . . inseparable from apprenticeship, and scientific education . . . inseparable from professional education.' As for such questions connected with authoritarian nationalism as foreign and military affairs, these will have no meaning in a society based on labour and hence on peace, where customs barriers and commercial privileges, colonies, strategic frontiers and fortresses will all have become redundant. In this way a social unity will be attained in comparison with which the so-called order of governmental societies will appear for what it is—'nothing but chaos, serving as a basis for endless tyranny.'

This is the rough plan of the Proudhonian society, deliberately broad in its outlines because the very nature of a free, organic and perpetually growing society is opposed to any elaborate schemes of social organisation; its detailed pattern can only be expected to arise out of the day-to-day experiences of the freely constituted units within the larger mutualist structure.

The General Idea of the Revolution is a book of inextricably mingled faults and virtues. Like everything that Proudhon wrote, it remains strongest on the attack, when it criticises governments and governmental theories, Rousseau and Robespierre, the Utopian socialists and the Jacobins. When Proudhon has finished with them, the rational justifications of authoritarian institutions are torn to shreds. But the positive aspects of his work are less impressive, and this is not wholly due to that vagueness which is inevitable and even desirable in a libertarian social vision. Beyond that, there is a certain naïve optimism, a tendency to see reason as overpowerful, and a faith in man's propensity to detect and choose his own good which is not entirely borne out by experience. The solution of social evils does, indeed, by definition rest on a social level, and will only be reached when political centralisation has been replaced by a much more basic administration of economic affairs than existed in Proudhon's time or exists today. So much has been made increasingly evident by the rake's progress of politically dominated societies—democracies and dictatorships alike—during the century since 1851. But that the solution will be quite as simple a matter of contractual adjustment as Proudhon suggested in his more optimistic flights is something which few would be hardy enough to claim today.

For Proudhon, the period immediately following the publication of *The General Idea of the Revolution* was an interval of tranquillity, threatened by an oncoming storm in French political life of whose approach he himself was uneasily aware. In September he returned to the more congenial confinement of Sainte-Pélagie, where he was given his old room and the family was virtually reunited, dining together every day, either in prison or in the apartment in the Rue de la Fontaine. Back in Sainte-Pélagie, Proudhon also began work on a treatise on 'the philosophy of progress,' and dabbled with 'a crowd of projects, ideas and systems' that haunted his fertile brain. But the latter part of his imprisonment was not wholly dominated by these literary schemes, for a growing number of interesting visitors, and a voluminous correspondence, kept him closely in touch with current events and ideas.

Some of the visitors travelled from his native Franche-Comté, and they ranged from Gustave Courbet to that unnamed but distinguished ecclesiastic of whom he remarked to Euphrasie: 'I do not know why all these priests seek me out; I still do them all the harm I can.'

A much more disconcerting visitor was George Sand, who, in February, 1852, embarrassed Proudhon by calling on him and Marc Dufraisse. He was surprised to realise that this detested personification of feminist romanticism was not lacking in good qualities, and there is a certain compassion in the way he described her in his diary: 'A long, cold, tired face; a woman of great good sense, great good heart and little passion, her speech curt, clear, positive and simple. G. Sand has burnt the candle at both ends, rather, I believe, from fancy than from sensuality or passion. . . . She is too mannish, too poised, too sedate. . . . Nothing in her, nothing, nothing of the feminine!' Yet these impressions seem to have been too fleeting to soften Proudhon's hostile estimate of George Sand's performance and influence, and in *De la Justice* a few years later he was to judge her work with extreme harshness.

For George Sand, on the other hand, it must be said that, like her fellow bluestocking, Madame d'Agoult, she did not allow Proudhon's severe judgments regarding herself to cloud her perception of his good qualities. In 1849 she had seen a hope in the People's Bank and had praised Proudhon as 'a useful and vigorous champion of democracy.' Later, in 1852, when Mazzini was vilifying him, she wrote in protest to the Italian nationalist. Proudhon, she declared, was not only 'very militant, passionate and incisive,' but he was also a 'learned and clever economist.'

The most welcome of all the visitors who came during the latter days of 1851, and the most prized of Proudhon's new friends, was Jules Michelet. If Proudhon never revised his views on George Sand, he profoundly changed his attitude towards

Michelet, whom in 1847 he regarded with distrust, but whose book, *Le Peuple*, later revealed many ideas which he shared. Their relationship began in April, 1851, when Michelet sent him a copy of his *History of the French Revolution*. Proudhon replied with a long letter discussing their points of agreement and difference, and thanking Michelet for giving such a clear account of the Revolution. His tone had an unusual humility. 'The nature of my mind and the mediocrity of my scientific and literary resources do not allow me undertakings of discovery such as your History is and will be, I hope, to its end. I can only analyse and deepen what others have established and brought to light; my speciality, like my method, is the dissection of facts and the isolation of their content.'

The relationship established by this correspondence continued, for Michelet and Proudhon shared not only their conceptions of the autonomy of the popular consciousness (an idea to which Jung has given important support in our day) and their views on the character of the French Revolution, but also their independence of political alliances and their general abstention from the construction of elaborate systems of social or historical dogma.

Towards the end of 1851, indeed, Proudhon showed an admiration for Michelet which it was rare for him to display towards any man. Michelet had tried to visit him in prison, and through some misunderstanding had been unable to obtain access. Proudhon wrote, full of regret: 'It is for me, your disciple of the past eleven or twelve years, to go and see my teacher. Your words of '30 and '40 astounded me; a provincial newcomer, I understood nothing of that way of judging human events; I thought I was listening to a St. John reciting his apocalypse. Since then I have seen that what seemed to me revelation was the true reality of history. The brute fact is nothing; the idea it covers is truly all. Now I follow you. God grant that I remain as wise as you!'

Their friendship lasted through the subsequent vicissitudes of Proudhon's life, and, though the latter's high opinion of Michelet declined in some respects, and the two writers disagreed on such basic subjects as women and love (in 1858 Proudhon dismissed Michelet's *L'Amour* as 'erotic babbling' and later he called *La Femme* 'another piece of obscenity'), their relationship remained cordial to the end.

9

The political crisis which destroyed the Second Republic had long been foreseen by Proudhon. The articles for which he was imprisoned, and for which his newspapers were prosecuted, had revealed the imperialistic ambitions of Louis Bonaparte, and in the months that followed the latter's election, he had watched the deepening antagonism between the President and the Assembly with an uneasy understanding of its implications. As early as January, 1851, he had told Marc Dufraisse: 'The old parties are done for—they are nothing to fear. All the danger is from the side of the Elysée.'

By November the rift between the executive and legislative branches of the government had become wide and evident, and Louis Bonaparte, who had already bullied the Assembly into amending the Constitution to allow him to stand for re-election, was now making a bid for popular favour by demanding the revocation of the discriminatory election law of the 31st May, 1849. By this means he not only annoyed the Right, but also embarrassed the Left, whose representatives were themselves pledged to put an end to this law.

As the conflict developed, Proudhon saw bad faith and intrigue on every side. No party, he thought, was sincerely concerned for the cause it pretended to represent; all acted from reasons of policy. 'The strained situation is the result of the Machiavellianism of the extreme parties,' he noted on the 23rd November, and two days later he added, 'The representatives of the people are no longer mandatories; they are gladiators.'

Though he had long anticipated the Bonapartist coup, Proudhon did not foresee that it would emerge as a result of the dispute over the law of the 31st May. The President struck for power on the 2nd December, and early that morning, before the news of what was happening in Paris had penetrated into Sainte-Pélagie, Proudhon had actually expressed in his diary an opinion that the accord between the Mountain and the President was durable and might be the means of averting conflict. It was not until ten a.m. that he learnt what was afoot in the city; upon hearing the news, he immediately asked leave to go out of the prison, diplomatically giving his wife's indisposition as the reason for his request. 'I . . . walked through the capital and observed the population.

Faces were sad, and all minds were overwhelmed. The fact is that, while not counting in any way on the good faith or prudence of the President, nobody expected that he would risk such a crime.'

In the evening he called on Victor Hugo, who, with a tiny group of members of the Mountain, was planning a tardy resistance to Bonaparte's coup. He saw their plan with a pessimistically realistic eye. 'I have come to warn you as a friend,' he said to Hugo. 'You are creating illusions for yourselves. The people will be taken in, and they will not stir. Bonaparte will win them over. . . . The Republic made the people; he wished to turn them back into the populace. He will succeed, and you will fail. In his favour he has strength, guns, the errors of the people and the stupidity of the Assembly. The few men of the left to whom you belong will not prevail against the *coup d'état*. You are honest, and he has the advantage of being a rascal. Believe me, you must cease to resist. There is no way out of the situation. We must wait, but at this moment a struggle would be mad.'

Hugo rejected this advice, and later remembered it with bitterness, as if it had been a betrayal. Yet Proudhon was right, and those who violently resisted the *coup d'état* merely made a romantic gesture which had no chance of success and no popular support.

But, while Proudhon perceived and took into account the indifference of.the people, he neither shared nor approved of it. On the contrary, the events of the time had just as intense an effect on him as the February Revolution, with the difference that, while in 1848 his feelings were mixed, in 1851-2 he was appalled throughout the period while the *coup d'état* was being consolidated. This is shown clearly in the following passages from his diary.

3rd December. 'Never has such an assault been committed on the good faith of a nation. . . . The insult is too sharp, the nation is lost if it gives in!'

4th December. 'I rise at 5.30 in the morning: I have had a feverish and inflammatory sleep, with intolerable beating of the arteries. . . . If I were free, I would bury myself under the ruins of the Republic with her faithful citizens, or else I would go to live far from a land unworthy of liberty.'

5th December. 'How right I was, in 1843, to cry out against that

absurdity of universal suffrage. No, the masses are not and will not for a long time be capable of a good action for themselves.'
10*th December*. 'Through the defection of the working class, Paris has lost the battle.'
14*th December*. 'She [Mme Suchet confirms the news of the] shooting of citizens taken at the barricades. . . . Thus, he is not content to defend himself; he has not even recoiled before massacre, before crime. France is under oppression. The insolence of the conquerors knows no bounds; indignation is growing.'
15*th December*. 'A sign of Parisian stupidity. Most people go about repeating, with B's newspapers, that without the *coup d'état*, we should have had the revolution, that is to say, pillage, arson, murder, robbery. And they have under their eyes the atrocities, the nameless atrocities of the army!'

By the middle of December his serenity had returned, and on the 19th he told Edmond that, though for a week his nights had been 'like those of a man condemned to death,' he was now calm and 'working like a nigger.' Despite what had happened, he believed that the Revolution in its good time would proceed regardless of the activities of governments. But he had little optimism for the immediate future; he foresaw widespread intellectual purges, resulting in difficulties for himself. 'I still cannot suppress my anxiety,' he told Maurice. 'It is not the authorities, certainly, who fear me; it is the clerical and episcopal party.'

The last remark brings us to a curious ambiguity which at this time began to appear in Proudhon's attitude. For, basing his opinion on evidence which is certainly not available to us now, he came to believe that among the socialists he was the man the Bonapartists regarded most highly. And, while it is hard to imagine that such an attitude existed on their part towards an outspoken critic of Louis Bonaparte, it is at least certain that when Proudhon thought he might use the new ministers for furthering his own social ideals, they received him with a cordiality which at least suggests that the desire to make use may have been mutual.

On the 24th December Proudhon wrote to the Minister of Marine and Colonies suggesting that political prisoners should be given the chance of going to an autonomous colony, outside Europe and the French Empire, which might be subsidised partly by public subscription and partly by funds set aside for the penal colony of Guiana. The proposal was evidently regarded by the ministry as an occasion for sounding out Proudhon's position regarding the *coup d'état*, and a few days later the Comte de Morny invited him to call. At the meeting he put forward some highly controversial theses on the historic function of Louis Bonaparte. The first two, as he reported them to Edmond, were as follows: '1. The government of L. B. is condemned, by the 7,500,000 votes which absolve it, to do great things towards realising, in one way or another, the reforms sought by socialism. 2. L. B. comes, not to close, but to continue the revolutionary series.' These points are important anticipations of Proudhon's later thoughts on the Empire.

Morny, he claimed, admitted both his propositions, and there then ensued an even more curious exchange. 'Replying to various advances from the Minister, I said to him: "I will forgive you the first third of your *coup d'état*, if you will let me make war on the Jesuits." "What Jesuits?" "Montalembert, Veuillot and all the successors of those who attacked Pascal." "That," said the Minister, laughing, "can be arranged."'

Proudhon was clearly suffering from his old illusions that the men of power might somehow be persuaded to help him dig the grave of their own authority. But, however naïve we may regard this assumption, it must be emphasised that, while Proudhon thought the Bonapartists might be forced by circumstances or by his own Machiavellian arts into a policy that would expedite social revolutionary changes, he never regarded Louis Napoleon or his administration as active participants in the Revolution. Bonaparte would only serve the Revolution in spite of himself, because, having destroyed the old parties, he would be unable to create a new society after his own image and would let the country slide into a chaos resulting in the almost imperceptible decay of government and the re-edification of liberty. Anything that might hasten this process Proudhon felt himself justified in attempting.

10

If the outer world has grown more insecure and more puzzling than ever, Proudhon's personal life seemed at this time to become an even stronger source of balance. In January, 1852, Euphrasie gave birth to a second daughter, who was named Marcelle. Proudhon's first reaction was characteristically cautious, and he expressed himself not so well satisfied as he had been with Catherine. 'Käthe has a great, chesty voice, while her little sister has a fluting voice and, if I am not mistaken, her mother's nose. The first is a real Franc-Comtois, the second will be a Parisian.' But a few days later, when Marcelle was barely a week old, the paternal feelings which had been expressed with restraint to his friends became overwhelmingly strong, and in his diary he abandoned himself to an uninhibited expression of delight at the miracle of parenthood. 'I surprise myself each day, each hour, by being as preoccupied with my children as a young man with his mistress. . . . That love of family makes my life normal, clear, easy, free, raised above all apprehensions and above death itself. . . . There was a real understanding of the family in those who made it the basis of the fatherland and extolled brotherhood. Brothers, yes, and fathers, mothers, sons, uncles, aunts, nephews and nieces and cousins, and all those who are connected by all the spiritual, temporal or carnal links that the heart can conceive— that is the Republic!'

His serenity at this time went beyond his happy family life, and his emergence from the emotional storm precipitated by the *coup d'état* seemed to provide a new stability. This was shown when his friends, anxious for his future, pressed him to leave France after his release, in case his freedom should again be jeopardised. Arthur Brisbane offered him journalistic work in New York; he declined the invitation. Charles Edmond urged him to go to Sardinia; 'Who the devil, in Europe, looks for light to Cagliari?' Proudhon retorted.

He felt that all this talk about expatriation showed a disproportionate dread of the future. 'I do not believe in the fall of the heavens because a monomaniac, served by all the old guard of politics, holds us at this moment under his heel.' Besides, he thought there were subjects on which he could write despite the despotism. 'Economics, history, philosophy—these things are far enough above everyday politics for them to pass easily.' And even if he could no longer write, he was still resolved to remain and take whatever living he could find. 'Spinoza was a good lens-grinder in Amsterdam, and St. Paul made tents. Why should I not become a clerk somewhere again, or a lock-keeper?'

This typically Gallic reluctance to leave his country was reinforced by a continued belief that the Bonapartes maintained an almost friendly attitude towards him. 'I have every reason to believe that in the Elysée I am looked on with a favourable eye,' he told Marc Dufraisse. But at the same time he added: 'To indulge in politics is to wash one's hands in dung,' and this Rabelaisian indication that he had no intention of being directly involved in the actions of the government was strengthened when he indignantly rejected a suggestion from Antoine Gauthier that he should obtain state employment; such a step, he held, would hinder his efforts to push the authorities towards a revolutionary path.

Meanwhile, he began to face the problems of his approaching liberation. He realised, as he told Guillemin, that, unless something quite unforeseen happened, there would be nothing for him in the field of politics. Besides, he had 'had enough of the *vile multitude*,' and 'in the midst of a people who can only bleat *Long Live the Emperor*' it would be absurd to cry '*Long Live the Republic*.' He thought instead of a return to the business world, and confided to Guillemin that several friends had approached him to secure his participation in schemes for railways and canals. 'I should not be displeased to prove at least once to the rabble above and the rabble below that I am capable of something else than carrying on a newspaper.'

It was in the same memorable letter to Guillemin that he outlined in stoic terms the mental attitude that had sustained him through his years in prison. 'The more I see people's minds becoming confounded, the more I feel free and at ease. Yes, free, for I am the slave of nothing in the world but natural necessity; I am enslaved neither to priest, nor magistrate, nor man of arms. I am linked to no party, I obey no prejudices, I am above human respect and even above popularity. I wanted to make others free like myself; they concluded from this that I had too much liberty and put me in prison. What have they gained from it? Nothing. What have I lost? If I made the balance with exactitude, I would again say, nothing. I know ten times more than I knew three years ago, and I know it ten times better; I know positively what I have gained, and truly I do not know what I have lost.'

It was in this mood that, on the morning of the 4th June, 1852, he stepped out through the gate of Sainte-Pélagie, free to face a life that would be changed more deeply than he imagined.

Part Six

THE PALADIN OF JUSTICE

I

FOR most men release from prison means a return from a life of inertia to one of relative activity. For Proudhon it was almost the reverse. His three years in as many gaols had been among the most productive in his life; he had written three important books; he had edited three newspapers and contributed to them a large quantity of provocative writing; he had encountered many celebrated men and women in the literary and revolutionary worlds; he had married and founded a family. Circumstances, public and personal alike, were to make the three following years a great deal less full in activity and satisfaction, and Proudhon passed, when he walked out of Sainte-Pélagie, from a world of manifold achievement into one of perpetually frustrated effort.

The pattern of frustration took shape almost immediately. The railway projects which Proudhon had discussed with friends like Charles Beslay were slow to mature, but his concern with them was soon overshadowed by his trouble in connection with the book on Louis Napoleon's *coup d'état* which he had been writing during his last weeks in prison.

This book, *La Révolution Sociale démontrée par le Coup d'Etat du*

Deux Decembre, examined in detail the circumstances that led up to the Bonapartist seizure of power, drew on the record of the first Napoleon as a warning to the third, and again elaborated the Proudhonian doctrine of anarchy as the true end of nineteenth-century social evolution. 'Anarchy, I tell you, or Caesarism,' Proudhon told the people of France. 'You can no longer get away from that. You did not want an honest, moderate, conservative, progressive parliamentary and free Republic; now you are caught between the *Emperor* and the *Social Revolution*!'

On the eve of publication, *La Révolution Sociale* was banned by the Minister of Police. The decision was not unexpected by Proudhon, and he began to consider how to evade what might become a general suppression of his works. He thought that after all he might leave France for some country, Belgium or Switzerland, where he would be among people who spoke his language. Or he might attempt 'clandestine publication under cover of an industry.' But he did not intend to accept either alternative without an effort to regularise his position, and on the 29th July he submitted an appeal directly to the Prince-President. His tone was bold; he declared the purpose of his book quite openly, and asked that it be allowed to appear 'as I made it, with its bitternesses, its boldnesses, its suspicions and its paradoxes.' Responding to the oblique flattery of this direct approach, Louis Napoleon ordered the ban withdrawn. 'The President agrees!' Proudhon exulted. 'A cause won! Censorship defeated!'

La Révolution Sociale appeared at a time of political crisis when it could not fail to arouse interest, and within a month 13,000 copies had been distributed, a result which filled Proudhon with exaggerated optimism; he hoped that the sales would go on rising until he had earned 30,000 francs, liquidated his debts, and stood at the head of the 'revolutionary party.' But the interest shown by these initially large sales did not necessarily imply approval. Few critics were wholly favourable. The conservatives complained that the book had been allowed to appear. The Jacobins exiled in London denounced it and all Proudhon's works. Marx unjustly dismissed it as 'a historical apologia for the hero of the coup.' Lastly, the workers complained of its expensiveness. 'I regret this,' said Proudhon, 'but I can do absolutely nothing about it. . . . Since my imprisonment I have a running account with the Garniers, and I live by what they advance me on the condition of leaving them masters of the commercial side. I have found more help among these business men than in the devotion of the patriots.'

2

Meanwhile, with at least the material success of his most recent book assured, Proudhon started on the tour to the Franche-Comté towards which he had looked with much anticipatory pleasure during his last months of confinement. It was not merely his own inclination that led him to leave Paris. He was also anxious about the health of his children, and particularly Catherine, who had a tendency towards rickets, which the doctors thought might be cured by a stay in the country.

In his childhood haunts beside the Ognon, Proudhon could at last relax. He talked for hours with the peasants, learnt all the news of the district since his last visit before the Revolution, saw his surviving relatives, received the calls of old friends, and resumed the pleasures of his youth, gathering nuts on the hillsides and catching gudgeon and crayfish 'as big as small lobsters.' Late in August he visited Besançon, where he found rural conservatism more rampant than ever, and early in September he went to stay for a short time with his former employers in Lyons. He observed with deep interest the rapid development of the city during his absence, and detected the emergence of a form of capitalist organisation which he defined by the term: Industrial Feudalism. 'France,' he noted, 'will be given up to the monopoly of the companies. That is the feudal regime—textiles, metals, grains, drink, sugar, silks, all are on the way towards monopoly.'

October brought his holiday to an unhappy close, for Marcelle fell sick with chicken pox, and Proudhon himself suffered a severe attack of quinsy, which weakened him so much that, even in November, after he had returned to the capital, he found it hard to resume work. He attributed the severity of the illness to the delayed effects of prison life.

Meanwhile, his removal from Paris did not mean any lessening of his interest in current events. He watched with disgust the increasingly reactionary progress of the Bonapartist regime. 'L. N. goes to the bourgeoisie,' he wrote in his diary on the 8th October. It was steadily becoming clear to him that there was no real likelihood of Bonaparte realising the revolutionary potentialities of the situation produced by the *coup d'état*, and in disillusionment Proudhon's attitude returned rapidly to the bitterness of 1849 and 1850.

At the same time, his distrust of the existing democratic groups was demonstrated in his complicated hesitations over the elections to the legislative assembly during the autumn of 1852. When he was asked by Beslay to stand in the democratic-socialist interest, he first put forward the objection that, now deputies were no longer paid, he could not afford to reduce his remunerative work in order to attend to parliamentary duties. Eventually he agreed to accept nomination only on the condition that he should not stand in the way of a candidate who 'might gather more votes, excite less opposition and give fewer pretexts to the reaction,' and when the banker Goudchaux offered to stand in support of a relatively radical programme, Proudhon withdrew with alacrity.

His evident disinclination to become a deputy was undoubtedly connected with his reinforced distrust of universal suffrage after it had been used with such resounding emphasis to assist the triumph of reaction in the plebiscite confirming Louis Napoleon in power; to be chosen by the voters who had elevated this third-rate Caesar would have been a dubious honour indeed. Proudhon's faith in the people, in fact, fell at this time to its lowest level. 'The vile multitude,' 'the rabble,' no epithet was too severe for the classes in whom he had seen the great hope of humanity. 'Whenever the masses have done anything tolerably good,' he complained, 'they have always been driven or pulled, openly or secretly, by master minds formed from among themselves, and every time the people have been left to themselves they have only been able to make society take a backward step.' Yet even now he had not entirely lost hope that they might be brought back to positive action. 'We affirm the possibility of educating the people,' he noted during October. 'The revolution always advances, making use of each individual, of each interest, of each tongue.'

It was to carry on this education of the people that Proudhon became anxious at this time to re-enter the field of polemical journalism, as the editor of a bi-monthly devoted to a spontaneous and genuinely revolutionary way of thought, and liberated from the narrowness of the socialist sects who, 'excessively jealous of their dogmas and formulae, will only admit, like the theologians, truths which they themselves make and in terms of their own choosing.' The idea had already occurred to him on the eve of his departure from prison, and during the months that followed release his scheme proliferated widely into the fields of economics, philosophy, morals, science, history and literature, until it seemed to him that his review would become a great machine of war against the forces of authority, capital and the Church.

But he was not always optimistic about the possibility of launching these great plans; he did not forget the difficulty with which his last book had been produced, and he was aware that its success had displeased the traditionally reactionary elements among the Bonapartist entourage. 'There is a veritable conspiracy against human knowledge and understanding,' he told Guillemin. Yet he went ahead with his plans, and by mid-December announced that he hoped to publish his first issue ('unless there are unexpected obstacles') on the 15th January, 1853. 'From that day,' he promised Madier-Montjau, 'I shall lead you, as in '48, by unknown paths where the censorship and the prosecutors will not, I hope, be able to reach me.'

It was his gloomier apprehensions that were justified. The regime had grown steadily more severe during 1852, consolidation had brought an end to its need for 'democratic gestures,' and Louis Napoleon's ministers knew enough of Proudhon to see through his naïve Machiavellianism and realise that his pretence of 'pure science' was not likely to be preserved for long. On the 28th December, the application for authority was rejected by de Maupas, the Minister of Police. 'Let M. Proudhon go and make his request to the Emperor,' de Maupas was reported to have said, and Proudhon interpreted this to mean that now there would be no intervention in his favour from above. 'I can only attribute the refusal to the clerical spirit,' he remarked. But he was so anxious to find a means of returning to journalism that a ministerial refusal was not enough to make him abandon his plans; he talked of publishing his review abroad, and he was not entirely without hope that Jerome Bonaparte, the reputedly liberal son of the ex-King of Westphalia, might give him discreet assistance.

His alternating hopes and disappointments continued for more than a year. During this time he pulled such strings as still hung near his hands, he used what meagre backstairs influence he possessed, and eventually, on the 10th January, 1854, there came through various intermediaries at the Tuileries 'the great, incredible news' that the review had been authorised. In a more than usually grandiose moment, Proudhon declared to the Italian federalist, Joseph Ferrari, that the appearance of the *Revue du Peuple* would be 'a still more considerable event than the 2nd December.' But his premature confidence went unjustified. The review was still forbidden.

Yet there is at least a possibility that some serious intention of authorising it may have existed; by the beginning of 1854 the Bonapartist regime had struck a period of crisis and, had not the Crimean War intervened, Louis Napoleon might well have been forced to mitigate the dictatorship. But the war came, and was accepted gratefully by the Emperor, both as an opportunity to revive the military glory of the Bonapartes and as a means of muffling discontent at home. The thought of concessions to democracy was abandoned, for some years at least, and *La Revue du Peuple* went with the rest.

3

This tale of misplaced hopes gives the keynote to Proudhon's whole life during the years following his release from Sainte-Pélagie. From the end of 1852 the political climate of France became steadily more oppressive and fear entered deeply into public life; an increasing ostracism of writers like Proudhon was the result. The atmosphere was not unlike that which pervaded Italy during the earlier and milder years of the Fascist regime, and it was unsafe, above all it was bad for careers and for business, to associate too openly with a man who, in the absence of so many radicals in exile or prison, was one of the few leading men of the Revolution still speaking with an irrepressibly independent voice.

It was during the autumn of 1852 that Proudhon began to realise fully the situation confronting him. On the 18th October he exclaimed bitterly to Edmond: 'For a moment I hoped to find a refuge in some honourably commercial employment; that hope is now destroyed. I am repulsed everywhere as if I had the plague; they would think themselves accursed if they had anything in common with me. I am almost convinced that I would not find a post at 1,200 francs in a commercial house in Paris, Lyons or anywhere else. I am therefore thrown back violently into the trade of man of letters; instead of following great works in the silence of an honest employment, as I should have liked, I must live from the daily product of my pen.'

The prejudice against him penetrated into the most personal aspects of his life. At the end of 1952 he decided to leave the Rue de la Fontaine, in whose airless and sunless atmosphere his children ailed constantly, and in February, 1853, he discovered a suitable apartment, with a good garden, in the Rue St. Jacques. But as soon as the landlord heard his prospective tenant's name, he withdrew immediately from the negotiations. 'Would it not be amusing,' remarked the exasperated Proudhon, 'if the property owners avenged themselves by turning me into the street?'

By April, however, he succeeded in finding an even better dwelling a little farther out of the centre of Paris, on the edge of Montparnasse. It was on the ground floor of No. 83, Rue d'Enfer (now Rue Denfert-Rochereau), near the Observatory, and the windows looked southward, over a large, bushy garden. Proudhon was delighted with the place, where he was to remain for the next five years; it was in its garden that Courbet painted him sitting with his books and papers on the steps of his summerhouse, clad in his worker's blouse and his heavy shoes, the intellectual patriarch surrounded by his sturdy, playing children.

His daughters throve in the more healthy atmosphere. Catherine was 'splendid,' and Proudhon was sure that the change of air and the acquisition of sunshine saved the life of Marcelle, who had been suffering from inflammation of the lungs. But, for all these advantages, the extra rent he had to pay was a severe burden on his unsure resources, strained already by his wife's third pregnancy, which had put him under the necessity of finding a Franc-Comtois maid to assist with the housework and the care of the children.

Indeed, financial anxiety and the fear of discrimination alike became so acute in Proudhon's mind that the earlier part of 1853 was dominated by a frantic search for any kind of employment that might give security to his growing family. He wrote memoirs for the Gauthiers on a proposed packet-boat service to Rio, and advised English capitalists who wished to finance railways in Switzerland. He was in contact with promoters who hoped to form an agricultural credit bank, and with yet others who planned to buy large estates and resell them as small farms.

These ramified interests might give the impression that Proudhon had become converted to the materialistic attitude of the typical business man. But this would be an unfair assumption, since at the back of his mind there was always the hope of somehow inducing his partners or employers to work for the public good, or of himself making enough money to re-start the People's Bank. The Quixoticism of his forays into the business world is illustrated admirably in the history of his connection with the project for the railway from Besançon to Mulhouse, initiated by Huber, the Alsatian veteran of the '48 who had been his neighbour in the prison at Doullens. When Huber first approached him in January, 1853, Proudhon was acutely depressed over his financial situation, and his acceptance of the proposal at that time seems to have been motivated mostly by the desire to improve his position materially. After detailing to Huber the setbacks he had experienced in recent months, he told him that 'all that is left to me, other than dying of hunger, is to re-enter the industrial career in which I won my first spurs.'

Proudhon managed to arouse the interest of Jerome Bonaparte in the projected railway, and in the process he seems to have convinced himself that the plan had its idealistic side, since a decentralised pattern of small railroads would be superior—at least according to his social theories—to a unified system. But the concession eventually went to Pereire, a former Saint-Simonian who became an economic pillar of the Bonapartist regime.

Pereire offered an indemnity of 40,000 francs to be shared between Proudhon and Huber as a compensation for their disappointment. 20,000 francs would have meant a great deal to Proudhon at this time; he could have paid all his debts, and still have kept enough to maintain his family for several months. And he might have accepted it without blame, for the money was offered neither as a bribe, nor as a payment for acting in any way dishonourably. Yet he chose to refuse it on a point of strict principle; he had merely offered an idea for consideration, and therefore no indemnity was due, for 'money and an idea are two incommensurable quantities.'

Such fastidiousness annoyed Prince Jerome, who had exerted his influence to obtain the offer from Pereire, but Proudhon stood his ground stolidly against the Prince's displeasure, and while disclaiming any desire to 'play the part of the virtuous and incorruptible man'—for he did not like 'theatrical virtues'—he declared that he solicited the concession as 'an *economist* and a *democrat*,' and that, since Pereire was 'the representative of the Saint-Simonian principle of industrial feudalism' he felt it would be inconsistent for him to receive money from 'the enemy.'

One can applaud this rigid integrity, but, even in granting Proudhon's personal right to remain poor on grounds of principle, one may legitimately question the deliberate continuation of his family's poverty. Yet that is to venture on the controversial issue of whether a man dedicated to the point of self-sacrifice, as Proudhon was, should become involved at all in domestic responsibilities. He himself regarded the family as a universal necessity, but in effect his domestic needs did not always agree with the demands of his social ideals, and when a conflict arose, it was usually the family that suffered.

In the midst of these cumulative personal setbacks Euphrasie gave birth to a third daughter, Stephanie. 'The triad is victorious,' wrote Proudhon to the ever-thoughtful Maguet, who had sent a present of partridges at the appropriate moment. 'Pierre Leroux wins and your poor philosopher is decidedly confounded.' And to console himself for the steady increase of his family in such materially difficult circumstances, he looked into the hypothetical future. 'In fifteen years I shall have a complete workshop, and, with my career ended and my daughters installed, I shall go into retirement and keep their books.'

4

Towards the end of his imprisonment, Proudhon had been criticised by a philosophical scholar, Romain Cornut, who had indicated certain apparent contradictions in his thought and had demanded the unifying principles in a philosophical attitude that at times seemed so diffuse. Proudhon began to compose a reply for publication in Girardin's *La Presse*, but the two letters he wrote were much too long for this purpose, and he decided to make them into a book. It was not until the middle of 1853 that the completed work was ready for publication; the delay was due to Proudhon's interests having been diverted from the philosophical to the polemical during the period following the *coup d'état*.

In *Philosophie du Progrès*, as the book was called, Proudhon declares that the unifying bond in the many propositions he upholds, the 'something that links them together and forms out of them a body of doctrine,' is the affirmation of Progress and the denial of the Absolute. By Progress, using an almost Heraclitian formula, he means 'the affirmation of universal movement and in consequence the negation of all immutable forms and formulae, of all doctrines of eternity, permanence or impeccability, of all permanent order, not excepting that of the universe, and of every subject or object, spiritual or transcendental, that does not change.'

According to this hypothesis, there can be no completion of evolution; the movement of the universe is perpetual because the universe itself is infinite. Equilibrium, which is the complementary condition to movement, does not tend to uniformity or immobility; on the contrary, by the conservation of forces, it leads to the universal renewal of movement. Thus, for man, as for the universe, there is no final end; progress, though it does not proceed in a regular manner, is constant. 'We are carried along with the universe in an incessant metamorphosis.' In such a world the Absolute has no place, and morality arises spontaneously as a manifestation of Progress; 'morality has no other sanction than itself,' Proudhon declares, anticipating the doctrine of immanence developed later in *De la Justice*.

Though *The Philosophy of Progress* is not primarily a political pamphlet, it contains political undertones; progress is equated with federalism and the direct government of the people, and Proudhon declares that in social relations the notion of progress must replace 'constitutions and catechisms.'

Compared with almost any other of Proudhon's books, this is a mild essay that keeps close to its philosophical subject and avoids those inflammatory outbursts against existing authority or vested institutions which elsewhere occur so regularly in his writing. From the immediate viewpoint of the *status quo* it was probably the most innocuous book he wrote, and it is ironical that, through it, authoritarian prejudice should have struck its first successful blow at his literary career.

The book was set up in type and duly submitted to the police, who declared that they were not opposed to its sale, but at the same time let it be understood that this did not imply a guarantee against prosecution by the legal officers of the government. No printer was inclined to risk production on these terms, and Proudhon resorted to Belgian publication, in the hope that a foreign edition might be imported. But as soon as he tried to bring copies into France, the very police bureau which had registered no objection to internal publication decided to impose a ban on importation.

Even more serious than the actual banning of *The Philosophy of Progress* was the consequent refusal of any French publishers to handle new works by Proudhon and the decision of Garniers, his publishers, not even to continue selling those of his books which were in print. 'I am being attacked by means of unemployment and famine,' he exclaimed in desperation when he heard the last news.

But his situation was at least partly mitigated by the fact that, while Garniers would not accept anything that bore his name, they were loyal enough to help him clandestinely, and shortly after their refusal to publish *The Philosophy of Progress* they commissioned him to prepare what he called 'a hack pamphlet' on the contemporary financial world, for which they agreed to advance 1,500 francs. 'I polished it off,' he said at the time, 'as a cobbler makes a pair of boots.'

The result was the most curious of his works. It was called *The Stock Exchange Speculator's Manual* and consisted of a mass of statistical information, collected with the assistance of George Duchêne, on all the leading companies whose shares were offered for sale at the Bourse, garnished with an introduction, notes and 'final considerations' from Proudhon's own hand. Any genuine speculator who went to the Manual for a hot tip would be disappointed, for not only did the authors condemn speculation itself, but Proudhon also indulged in a lengthy analysis of the growth of the feudal structure in industry which was driving apart the bourgeois and the working class and acting inevitably to the detriment of the latter. He further asserted that in any society founded on inequality of conditions the government was reduced to a 'system of assurance for the class which exploits and possesses against that which is exploited and owns nothing.' He blamed monopolistic industrial developments for the economic crisis that was developing in France. He pointed to associations of workers, based on mutualism, as 'a new principle, a new model, which must replace the present joint stock companies in which one does not know who is the more exploited, the worker or the shareholder.' And he finally declared: 'We believe in a radical transformation of society, in the direction of freedom, personal equality and the confederation of peoples, but we do not want it to be either violent or plundering.'

The Manual sold well, though there is no means of telling whether its buyers were frustrated gamblers or revolutionaries in search of hidden meanings. In March, 1854, a second edition appeared, and there was a third and greatly enlarged edition in 1856, which Proudhon signed, thereby indicating his progressive change in attitude towards the book. At first he had regarded it as 'a repugnant and painful work.' By 1854 he said that it 'established clearly the revolutionary *object*, which has never been done before,' and that it was a 'monstrous bomb thrown on the pavements of Paris.' Still later it became 'the most instructive work of the epoch . . . for the extraordinary light it spreads on the present time.' His esteem had grown with its popularity, but his change of attitude may have been due partly to a feeling of gratitude towards the one piece of writing that had helped to maintain him during these years of adversity.

5

The cycle of personal trouble that marks this period of Proudhon's life reached the level of tragedy during the summer of 1854. Early in August the household in the Rue d'Enfer was stricken with the cholera which was endemic in Paris at this time, and all its members were afflicted. Marcelle died, and it was only on the 1st September that Proudhon himself was well enough to announce the fact to Bergmann.

'Three weeks ago, I was hit by the epidemic, and death visited me. I lost one of my daughters aged nearly three years; she was as if struck by lightning. At the moment when they carried out her corpse, I lay motionless, exhausted by diarrhoea, vomiting, prostration. Finally, homeopathy saved me, but I still have no feeling in my legs . . . I cannot hold the pen and can hardly see it. Goodbye, dear Bergmann; look after your family.'

Later he was to tell how, while he lay in the crisis of his illness, his wife had risen from her own bed to tend him, helped by relays of his friends. It was she who had caused their dead child to be taken to a neighbour's house and had told him the benign falsehood that she was being looked after there. 'It is nothing for an intelligent man to suffer,' he told Suchet, an old companion of the Conciergerie. 'But to watch suffering, the suffering of one's own family, that is a torture. Imagine what my wife must have endured, forced to look after me herself, to be ceaselessly near me—for I was constantly asking for her—to swallow her tears and show me a good face for fear of affecting me by her sadness.'

The loss of Marcelle grieved him profoundly. 'I was attached to that child who, more than her sisters, reproduced the paternal type, and I had promised myself that I should find in her an energetic intelligence and character. It is thus that we are punished in our vanities.' But, bitter as he found this loss, the inroads which the disease had made into his own physical condition were to affect him even more deeply. The doctors warned him that his convalescence would be long, and in a sense he never reached the end of it, for his health, which had been fairly robust until his imprisonment, now became chronically weak. The rest of his life was to be punctuated by long periods of ailing, and the weaknesses that eventually caused his premature death can almost certainly be traced to the cholera of 1854.

Yet, though he was so afflicted by paternal sorrow, weakened by illness, and troubled by the fact that his incapacity had meant many weeks away from the work on which his family urgently depended, there was a warmth in his letter to Suchet which shows a faculty for friendship undulled by misery or misfortune.

'When either of you comes to Paris,' he asked him, 'try to have an hour for No. 83, Rue d'Enfer. We are poor, but we do not take a pride in our poverty; we remain simple and modest, hiding our patches as best we can, living each day according to our resources, and, thanks to work, good conscience and good friendship, ending with perhaps more happiness than those whose luxury insults us in passing. We shall always, I hope, have a leg of lamb or a fowl with a glass of wine to offer a friend. To the devil with pride! I shake your two hands and I believe, when I write to you, that it is a song of my spirit in the centre of your heart.'

6

During these years when his personal anxieties were at their deepest, Proudhon could not remain indifferent to the alarming trends in international affairs. The French participation in the Crimean War angered and humiliated him. He saw it as 'an imperial, conservative, capitalist, Catholic, anti-democratic, anti-nationalist, anti-Greek war,' and declared that Napoleon III was trying to become the head of a new Holy Alliance, not against the Tsar, but against the Revolution. 'The triumph of the allies,' he told Edmond in April, 1855, 'means much less the abasement of Russia than the consolidation of the military regime in France and in all Europe.' He wanted 'no victory . . . no military glory,' and took up the traditional standpoint of revolutionary defeatism when he added: 'If it were necessary that France should be beaten and humiliated so that liberty should be saved, would you hesitate? Personally, I know no such scruples.'

It was while the war was still at its height that he heard once again from Alexander Herzen, who invited collaboration in his first expatriate paper, *The North Star*, then about to start publication. Proudhon was delighted at the renewal of their association. 'Our ideas, I believe, are the same, our causes are in solidarity, all our hopes are mingled.' And he went on to a discussion of their common problems and of the question of Russia which demonstrated forcibly the extent to which he had removed himself from revolutionary as well as from any other orthodoxy.

'While you are preoccupied with governments above all,' he said, 'I for my part see the governed. Before attacking despotism among princes, is it not more often necessary that we should begin by combating it among the soldiers of freedom? Do you know anything that more resembles a tyrant than a popular tribune? And has not the intolerance of the martyrs more than once appeared to you just as odious as the rage of the persecutors? Is it not true that despotism is only so difficult to overcome because it rests on the intimate feelings of its antagonists—I should say its competitors—to such an extent that the sincerely liberal writer, the true friend of the Revolution, very often does not know on what side he should direct his blows, on the coalition of the oppressors or the bad morality of the oppressed?

'Do you believe, for example, that Russian autocracy, is merely a product of brute force and dynastic intrigues? Has it not hidden bases, secret roots, in the heart of the Russian people? Oh, my dear Herzen, most frank of men, have you never been scandalised and desolated by the hypocrisy and machiavellianism of those whom European democracy, whether rightly or wrongly, endures or avows as leaders? No division before the enemy, you will say to me. But, dear Herzen, which is more to be dreaded for liberty—schism or treason?'

He went on to discuss reports that the Tsar Alexander II was proposing to 'grant Poland the most precious part of its liberties.' Could this mean that liberty was paradoxically emerging from the autocracy in the east? 'History is full of these contradictions,' he declared, and he seemed to see the action of the Tsar as setting alight 'a hope for liberty' that might yet shame France, country of the Revolution, and give the moral, if not the military, triumph to Russia.

It would be pedantic to blame Proudhon for being deceived into believing that Alexander was initiating a genuinely progressive policy. The mitigation of autocracy that followed the death of Nicholas I seemed at the time full of promise, and, indeed, there was a certain genuine liberalism in the early part of Alexander's reign. More than once his gestures were to lead radicals into unjustified hopes, and even Herzen was later induced by the emancipation of the serfs to impute libertarian ambitions to this tragic and unstable ruler. At the same time, it is clear from the tone of Proudhon's letter that even now he had not overcome the illusion, which entrapped so many revolutionaries in his time, of finding a ruler who would work, whether willingly or otherwise, for the cause of freedom. Having been disappointed in Louis Napoleon, he transferred his hopes to this Tsar who seemed so enlightened in comparison with his predecessor. But, once again, there was no question of his supporting autocracy; he sought rather to make the autocrat an instrument for destroying his own function, an idea that must have appealed strongly to his paradoxical tastes.

His disgust with the Crimean War continued to the end, and his detestation of the regime that perpetuated it increased rapidly. At the end of July he told Edmond: 'I have regicide in my heart,' and in September he hailed the victory of Sebastopol with a bitter tirade to Maguet: 'The day before yesterday all Paris was spontaneously illuminated to celebrate the great victory of Sebastopol. After the two milliards and the hundred and sixty thousand men that ruin has cost us, we have spent yet another few hundred francs on flags and lights. Today, bread is raised two sous a loaf, from 90 centimes to a franc. Light up, then, swine! As the war continues, we shall probably have a recrudescence of Caesarian absolutism, of clerical hypocrisy, of military brutality, of administrative squandering and stock-jobbers' juggling. I am looking for a corner where there are real savages whom I would like to teach by example to despise and hate the Jingoes, Jacobins, speculators, judges, soldiers and priests. I would gladly exile myself there with my progeny.'

Proudhon's whole-hearted opposition to the Crimean war, his detestation of its barbarity and his realisation of the way in which it fostered the growth of tyranny must be borne well in mind if we are to understand his later writings on the subject of war, on which this experience had a profound influence.

7

During the Crimean War there occurred an incident which, though slight in itself, was to be turned by its consequences into one of the most important single events in Proudhon's life. In the summer of 1854 he met a writer who passed under the pen name of Eugène de Mirecourt (his real name was Jacquot), and who wished to include a pamphlet on Proudhon in a series of 'contemporary biographies' which he was preparing. Proudhon made no initial objection, and the 'biography' appeared in May, 1855. It was nothing more than a mendacious lampoon, which represented its subject as a monster of envy, impiety and inhumanity. Since 'de Mirecourt' posed as a representative of the Catholic interest, it is only fair to the Church to quote the opinion expressed by a modern Jesuit scholar, Father de Lubac.

'His [Proudhon's] indignation against his "biographer" was fully justified,' says de Lubac. 'M. Eugène de Mirecourt's book was an incredibly scurvy production. According to him, Proudhon was devoid of all human feeling. His mother's death had left him indifferent, and he had enjoyed the bloody riots of 1848 as though they had been an entertainment. Gall flowed from his soul. He was a "lying sectarian." His alleged continence was "planned for selfish motives." As for his social ideas, nothing was easier to explain: "Yes, juicy steaks, the belly, gluttony, a fondness for all material things, for eatables, for palpable things, for anything that gives sensual pleasure, the neighbour's dinner, his wine, his bed, his house, his gold, there you have, whatever others may say, the first and only motive of these great reformers." You see the tone of it. The rest is in the same vein. It is a mixture of insults and platitudes, a series of interpretations as stupid as they are spiteful.'

As we have seen, Proudhon was already in a greatly embittered state of mind towards the hierarchy, which he regarded as largely responsible for the present condition of France and also for his own publishing difficulties. De Mirecourt's attack was the last provocation needed to propel him into a full-scale attack on Catholicism. His anger was directed against the Church even more than against de Mirecourt himself, and he had at least one good reason for this attitude. De Mirecourt had requested information concerning him from the Archbishop of Besançon, Cardinal Mathieu. Without troubling to check the antecedents of his correspondent, Mathieu had replied by a personal letter which expatiated on the lack of piety in Proudhon's upbringing and which de Mirecourt printed at the beginning of his 'biography.' As Mathieu never repudiated de Mirecourt, Proudhon naturally assumed that he supported him, and saw the hand of the Church in the whole affair; since he could not let the attack go unanswered, it was to Catholicism, represented in the person of the Cardinal, that he decided to reply.

He proposed to write quickly a short book of a hundred and fifty pages which would 'pose clearly the question of the Church.' It eventually grew into his most massive work, and as it expanded, the date of its completion was constantly postponed. Nearly three years were in fact to elapse before this manifesto of defence and defiance, transfigured into one of the noblest works of social thought of the nineteenth century, finally emerged in the three great volumes of *De La Justice dans la Révolution et dans l'Eglise*.

But replying nobly to an ignoble adversary did not wholly satisfy Proudhon's appetite for activity during 1855. He was still responsive to any opportunity—or imagined opportunity—of putting into practice his economic theories, and in the summer this propensity took a somewhat fantastic turn.

In May the Universal Exhibition opened in Paris, and the idea came to Proudhon that here might be an institution that could be adapted to the purposes of the economic revolution. The exhibition should be continued in perpetuity, with the Palace of Industry turned into a central bazaar where the merchants of Paris could display samples of their products. It might become the place of meeting for consumers and producers; the latter would no longer need to rent expensive shops in the centre of Paris, and so prices would be reduced, while the society running the permanent exhibition could organise exchange between producers and begin the great experiment of dispensing with money.

Only an enthusiast like Proudhon could have seen a Universal Exhibition as a major engine in the social revolution, but he was encouraged in his design by the fact that Jerome Bonaparte had been appointed President of the Exhibition. He wrote a long memoir setting out in detail the basis on which he thought the scheme might be organised, he paid frequent visits to the Palais Royal to press his idea by personal advocacy, he overwhelmed the Prince with letters, he alternately exhilarated himself with extravagant hopes and fumed against the influence which the financiers and the Saint-Simonians exerted over 'Monsieur Isidore,' as he began contemptuously to call the Emperor. But Jerome Bonaparte remained unconvinced, and the plan lay unpublished among Proudhon's papers until after his death.

His enthusiasm had, however, its embarrassing consequences, for his contact over this and other questions with the Prince—that expert political trimmer whom Maximilian of Mexico likened to 'a worn-out *basso* from some obscure Italian opera house'—soon brought him into ill favour with those of the republican expatriates who had remained friendly towards him when he was excommunicated by the dogmatic Jacobins. Early in 1856, Madame Madier-Montjau came to Paris from Belgium and visited Proudhon. The turn of the conversation soon made it evident that she had really called to enquire into the reports that were being circulated regarding his visits to Jerome. So disturbing did he find the implications of her questioning that he wrote to Madier-Montjau explaining his conduct.

'I go to the Palais Royal,' he admitted. 'Yes, sometimes—ten or twelve times in four years. Do I betray that democracy which has devoted its hatred to me, do I compromise or dishonour it? . . . In my eyes, socialism is the revolution. Of that revolution I find myself, as in June, 1848, the first sentinel, and I have no corporal to give me orders. I therefore do what seems good to me; I see whom I wish, from the Prince Napoleon to Ferron.

When I say *I see*, it is necessary to understand one another. I do not draw back from any interview, that is all ... When it happens, which is very rarely, that I meet my former colleague,[1] it is because he himself has asked me to go and see him or because I have need of an audience. And if you wish to know more about this, I will tell you that the object of these visits, when it is not the desire of the Prince, who sometimes likes to listen to me, is a request for a liberation or something similar ... Need I tell you that I have yet to solicit anything for myself? ...

'Those who know me understand well that, in my opinion, Empire, Legitimacy, quasi-Legitimacy, Jacobinism, moderate Republic, Church, University, magistrates and military, are all the same thing. They are always the negation of freedom and justice, they are always the enemy ... I regard myself as the most complete expression of the Revolution, crushed, betrayed, sold, not only by the 2nd December, but by all its rivals and competitors. In order to uphold this revolution, I have sacrificed everything, sometimes even my self-respect; I have accepted calumny itself.'

There is a dignity in these last words which disposes of the possibility that Proudhon was trying to offer a specious justification for equivocal conduct. However mistaken he may have been in imagining that he could use the Bonapartes, Emperor or Prince, to further his radical ideals, it is certain that he calculated to gain no personal advantage. His refusal of Pereire's indemnity is alone proof of this. But, if we cannot question the integrity underlying his conduct towards the members of the ruling dynasty, we are not committed to admitting the wisdom of his relations with them, which sometimes lessened his effectiveness as a writer by making him unnecessarily suspect.

8

1855 had begun, from a financial point of view, so promisingly that Proudhon even imagined the possibility of liquidating his debts before it ended. But as the year continued, his earnings were considerably less than he had hoped, while he was obliged to accept the responsibility for a loan of 2,000 francs which he raised to save his improvident brother Charles from bankruptcy. He complained bitterly to Maurice of the 'double fetters' he had

[1] Jerome Bonaparte sat with Proudhon in the Constituent Assembly of 1848.

to bear; by the end of the year the family was so poor that Euphrasie, who was pregnant again, had been forced to return to her embroidery. The virtues of poverty had long been a theme of Proudhon's eloquence, but now he felt that even virtues should not be allowed to go too far, and he regarded with consternation his own chronic tendency towards impecuniosity. 'I feel that in our century poverty is nothing to an intelligent man,' he told Maurice. 'Nevertheless, it is a level below which one must not descend . . . But unfortunately I am of a race which up to the present has not been able to raise itself above want . . . Am I destined to see myself more indigent, more miserable, more deprived than birth has already made me, than I felt myself up to eighteen? I do not know. But while I despise fortune, fortune takes her revenge for my contempt.'

His situation was made even worse during the spring of 1856, when he fell into a disorder, partly physical and partly psychological, which resulted in an almost complete inability to write or think. It was something more than the usual 'writing block' with which most intellectuals are familiar, for a letter to Dr. Cretin suggests that his condition was an intensification of a long-standing nervous irritability which should be taken into account in considering the sometimes erratic nature of his thoughts and actions.

'For nearly twenty years,' he said, 'I have found that after a sharp emotion my brain is as if paralysed; my pulse becomes slight, my breathing is weak, I have spasms, my head turns, I stumble like a drunken man, etc. I overcome this general stupefaction, which seems to me to have a distinct resemblance to catalepsy, by movement, deep breathing, fresh air, gymnastic exercise, etc. While the crisis lasts, I experience an emptiness of the mind, a general distress, vertigo, inability to sleep, to think, to read, etc.'

But, while previous attacks had been of short duration ('a few hours') and had only followed exceptional stimuli, the present one had already lasted a whole month and seemed to have reached a chronic condition. Proudhon felt not merely 'a complete incapacity to work,' but also 'a real weakening of powers,' and this, in his opinion, without having overworked. He ascribed the disorder to some 'accidental cause' ('I know nothing in my life and habits that could have caused such a condition'), and it is surprising that he did not make the obvious connection with the cholera that had almost killed him little more than half a year before.

His appeal to Cretin was couched in the most agonising terms. 'Not to work, dear friend, is for me worse than typhus or cholera; it is death . . . Can you make me work, make me finish my book, at least?' But, despite the efforts of his physician friends, his condition changed only slowly, and it was not until the beginning of June that he began to feel any measure of relief.

At this time his thoughts often assumed an understandably melancholy tone, and early in May, writing to one of his friends to announce the proximate birth of a fourth child (Charlotte was born a few days later), he listed his anxieties and tried, a little unconvincingly, to give himself encouraging answers. 'Why do I disturb myself? And what do I fear? I live from day to day; what harm is there in that? I am sometimes in difficulties; it is a recall to order and foresight. I shall make my daughters into working girls; have they a right to ask anything more? I admit that my death would make them run great risks, but who today can say he is sure of anything?' Beneath the self-conscious bravado of his concluding statement—'I must suffer a little and feel the goad from time to time'—one feels a hollow insecurity pervading Proudhon's view of his condition.

In mid-summer he decided, on the advice of Cretin, to travel to the Franche-Comté with Charles Beslay, in the hope of recovering his health by a brief return to the country. He took the opportunity to visit many old friends. In Dijon he went to see Tissot; in Besançon he stayed with Guillemin and met Micaud and Maurice, Mathey and various cousins, including old Melchior Proudhon, who caused him a certain anxiety because, in his tenth decade, the aged revolutionary was showing a tendency to slip back towards the Church he had abandoned in 1789.

Dr. Maguet joined him in Besançon, and took him to Dampierre-sur-Salon; there the two friends walked in the hills and bathed in the river, and from the fresh air and exercise Proudhon's vitality began to return. He was so pleased that he even thought for a few days of returning to live in his native province. 'I begin to regret not having in this neighbourhood some property where I could instal myself with you and our dear little girls,' he told Euphrasie. 'If my work is successful, I will tell you of my projects and we will look together . . . What has happened to me is clearly a warning. I am forty-seven years and five months old; I am no longer a young man; I must learn to regulate my life, my work and health, if I wish to accomplish my task and do my duty to the end. I must also think of those three little girls.'

His return to Paris, after almost a month, was irradiated by the ability to observe, with fresh sight, the development of the daughters whose future caused him so much anxiety. 'Catherine begins to use the needle,' he told the Suchets, 'but she refuses to learn to read and has no clear idea of the duty of obedience. However, as she is affectionate and gentle, above all free from self-esteem, we hope, by making use of these sentiments, to inspire in her the feeling of a severe virtue and to teach her that sacrifice without which the human spirit is—and who knows better than you?— like the souls of animals . . . Stephanie is of a stronger temperament and a more generous blood than her elder sister; round as a ball, red as an apple, a republican in petticoats!'

A few months afterwards, for the second time in two years, Proudhon was stricken within that family into which the hostility of the outer world had made him withdraw, and in December his fourth child, Charlotte, died, as he supposed, from complications connected with her teething. 'You know how we feel for these little things,' he lamented to one of his friends, 'with what heartbreak we see them suffer! There was already the look, the smile, love, a beginning of recognition. That child had entered into my soul.'

9

At last, in the spring of 1857, the early part of the long treatise on Justice into which the reply to de Mirecourt had grown began to be composed by the printers, and it seemed to Proudhon that his task was almost completed and that his material fortunes were taking a more encouraging turn. The Garniers had recovered sufficient courage to return his name to their catalogue, and had promised to print a first edition of 6,500 copies. He hoped to earn from 12,000 to 14,000 francs, which would pay his outstanding debts and enable him to put some money aside for the future. He was, however, rather premature in his hopes, since, owing to perpetual delays caused largely by his recurrent attacks of mental debility, the book did not actually appear until a good year later.

A further diversion of his energies occurred during the elections for the legislative corps which took place in the summer of 1857 and which revealed the first significant fissures in the structure of the Second Empire. The republicans, realising the influence Proudhon's name still wielded among the workers, tried to draw him out of his retirement by offering him candidatures in Paris, Lyons and St. Etienne. At first he was hesitant, but a few days of reflection led him to decide that the election was in fact designed by Napoleon to give new blood to the Empire, and he joined the abstentionists, declaring that the essential conflict between the authorities and the people could best be emphasised by the latter refusing to take part in a governmental manoeuvre.

But, despite his stand for abstention, Proudhon noted with satisfaction the setback which the elections brought to the Bonapartists in Paris and the other large cities—the first major shift in public opinion since the *coup d'état*. 'The meaning of the vote in Paris is beyond doubt,' he commented. 'It is a rejection of the imperial rule; all the large towns have spoken in the same way; only the sheep of the country have bleated to the voice of the master . . . In this situation, conflict between the authorities and the country is inevitable; it is a question of time, the time which is needed for public opinion to draw, as I have drawn, the conclusion from the vote.'

Yet, pleased as he was by this sign of dwindling loyalty to the Empire, he was even more delighted by the number of people who had done as he recommended (though it is doubtful whether many of them had the same reasons as he) and had kept away from the polling booths. In Paris alone 190,000 had been absent, and Proudhon found in this a sign of a widespread recognition that the revolutionary issue was being carried out of the field of politics into that of social struggle. Even if he somewhat misinterpreted popular tendencies, his own stand in this matter was historically important, not merely because it established his future attitude towards political action, but also because it made for the first time that clear distinction between social and political struggle, between direct action and governmentalism which later divided the libertarian from the authoritarian socialists, the anarchists from the communists, Bakunin from Marx, Morris from the Fabians.

10

On the 22nd April, 1858, after three years of delays and difficulties, of anxieties and apprehensions, including a police raid on his printers and an Imperial reproof to radical thinkers following on Orsini's attempt to assassinate Napoleon III, Proudhon was able at last to note in his diary: 'Today, Thursday, my book, *De la Justice dans la Révolution et dans l'Eglise*, was put on sale.'

Metternich once described Proudhon as an illegitimate child of the Encyclopaedia. The oblique truth of this quip becomes evident when one reads *Justice in the Revolution and the Church*, that quintessentially Proudhonian book, for in this attempt to give a secular basis to the idea of justice, the influence of the French precursors of the Revolution, Diderot, D'Alembert and Voltaire, is constantly present. Indeed, the link with them is all the more direct since, by rejecting the political elements introduced by the Jacobins, Proudhon returned to the philosophical premises on which the foundations of the revolutionary tradition had been laid. His definition of the aims of philosophy, and by implication of the attitude from which he himself wrote his masterpiece, is one with which none of the Encyclopaedists would have been likely to disagree.

'The object of philosophy is to teach man to think for himself, to reason with method, to create sound ideas of things, to formulate the truth exactly, all with the object of ordering his life, of meriting his own respect and that of his fellows, and of ensuring himself peace of mind, bodily well-being and intellectual confidence.'

In the serene humanity of such an attitude one can detect the lingering influence of the age of reason, of that secure belief in the adequacy of scientific method to solve the most abstruse of personal problems which, stemming from the Encyclopaedists, reached its harsh flowering in that mood of almost religious faith in the powers of science that flourished in the middle of the nineteenth century.

But *Justice* is much more than an expression of the cult of science and reason. The very exuberance of its form, the vast proliferation of facts and ideas, the organic and almost irrational way in which it sometimes burgeons into rhapsodies of enthusiasm or Jeremiads of anger, place it in a totally different category from the grey scholasticism of the scientific materialists. It is a mine of curious erudition, but it is also a furnace of passion, of fantasy and of immense insight. More than any other of Proudhon's works, it represents not only his political opinions and his personal character, but also his broad view of the universe. Like its author, this massive work is paradoxical and contradictory, and like him it expresses the struggle between reason and unreason that underlies the complacent scientism of his time. The inner human conflict, which Dostoevsky expressed openly in *Letters from the Underworld*, Proudhon recognised implicitly and expressed in the vast turbulence of his greatest book. It is this turbulence, this constant movement and mutation within the equilibrium of his idea of justice, and also within the final balance of his literary achievement, that makes *Justice* so important an expression of the dynamic view of human existence, social organisation, and the world in which men and society move.

If *Justice* was born of the Encyclopaedia, it was sired of a long line of inspiration that begins with the Jewish prophets and brings Proudhon into contact at more than one point with the personalist tradition that embraced Kierkegaard and Dostoevsky. If he rebelled against the dogmatism of the Church, he never adopted the closed mind of the materialist, the 'Euclidian mind' as Dostoevsky called it; mysticism, in which he would have included a wider sense of religious feeling than is technically comprehended in that word, was in his opinion 'an indestructible element of the soul.' His view of life took into account those infinities of the spirit and the universe that cannot be plumbed by the intellect; it embraced the mystery that does not deny but goes beyond reason. Even when he was writing *The General Idea of the Revolution* in 1851 he had recognised that 'this old intellectual world, which for so many centuries has exhausted human speculation, is only a facet of the world it is given us to traverse,' and there is nothing in *Justice* to suggest that he had allowed his sense of the immense complexity of existence to dwindle. Again it is necessary to stress the difference between the mere denial of God expressed by the orthodox atheist, and the expression of the insoluble antinomy between God and man in Proudhon's writing. In the last resort, the author of *Justice* had much less in common with Charles Bradlaugh than with Kierkegaard who, as Father de Lubac has pointed out, called God 'the mortal enemy' and declared 'Christianity exists because there is a hatred between God and man.'

But if Proudhon does not deny the ultimate mystery of existence, he insists that it remains impenetrable, and in just the same way he makes a distinction between the Divine as it is and the

Divine as the theologians have portrayed it. 'The absolute is given, as *postulate*, in all knowledge, but it does not follow from this that it can itself become an *object* of knowledge.' The absolute as such is not the enemy of man; it is the idea of God formulated by the theologians as a being outside, above, and opposed to man, that must be attacked, for this idea is the fountain of the concept of authority, and hence the enemy of true justice.

It is here, in discussing the two conceptions of justice, that of the Church and that of the Revolution, that Proudhon defines his theory. Justice as seen by the Church is transcendental; the moral principle is held to originate in God and hence to be superior to man. But, according to Proudhon, true justice is *immanent*; it is innate in the human consciousness.

'An integral part of a collective existence, man feels his dignity at the same time in himself and in others, and thus carries in his heart the principle of a morality superior to himself. This principle does not come to him from outside; it is secreted within him, it is immanent. It constitutes his essence, the essence of society itself. It is the true form of the human spirit, a form which takes shape and grows towards perfection only by the relationship that every day gives birth to social life. Justice, in other words, exists in us like love, like notions of beauty, of utility, of truth, like all our powers and faculties . . . Justice is human, completely human, nothing but human; we wrong it by relating it, closely or distantly, to a principle superior or anterior to humanity.'

On the transcendental theory of Justice, which presupposes absolute and permanent formulae unrelated to the development of the human consciousness or the discoveries of human experience, is based the idea of 'Divine Right, with Authority for its watchword.' Hence proceed all the systems of state administration, of moral regulation, of restrictions on ideas, and of the general disciplining of humanity.

From the theory of immanence, on the other hand, it follows that, 'Justice being the product of conscience, each man is in the last resort the judge of good and evil . . . If I myself do not pronounce that such a thing is just, it is in vain that prince and priest affirm its justice to me and order me to do it; it remains unjust and immoral and the power that claims to compel me is tyrannical . . . Such is Human Right, with Liberty for its watchword; hence arises a whole system of co-ordinations, of reciprocal guarantees, of mutual services, which is the inverse of the system of authority.'

It is towards a realisation of this conception that we should always tend. It is true that we cannot attain it completely; a wholly just society would be perfect, and Proudhon recoils with near-horror from the thought. 'Obeying only a *constant* and depending no longer on *variables*, its movement would be uniform and recti-linear; history would be reduced to that of work and studies, or rather there would be no more history.' But such conditions exist —and we would agree with Proudhon that this is fortunate—only in the minds of chiliasts and Utopians. 'The progress of Justice, both theoretical and practical, is a state from which it is not given us to emerge and see the end. We know how to discern good from evil; we shall never know the destination of Right, because we shall never cease to create new relationships between ourselves. We are born perfectible; we shall never be perfect. Perfection, immobility, would be death.'

Having established the immanence of Justice, Proudhon pro-ceeds, in the remaining eleven sections of his book, to examine the aspects it assumes in our fortunately mobile and imperfect world. It would be impossible to give even a slight idea of the wealth of reference and illustration with which he pursues his investigations and illuminates his discussions; I can only indicate this fact as one of the reasons why the reader should himself study this book, which combines with the merit of being one of the important nineteenth-century works of social theory the more wayward virtue of gathering within its three volumes more odd, abstruse and absorbing scholarship than one is likely to find in any other book of a similar character. Having said as much, I can merely give the bare outline of the arguments embodied in these crammed pages, conscious that my task is as inadequate as that of a man who might attempt to reduce one of the exuberant master-pieces of Bosch or Breughel to the dimensions of a thumbnail sketch.

Proudhon begins by considering the application of Justice to man's personal relations. Here it proceeds from 'the principle of personal dignity,' whose law, 'Respect yourself,' is the foundation of the science of morals. Once this principle is established, its reasonable corollary is that we should respect the dignity of others as much as our own, and this is the essence of Justice, which is distinguished from love because it admits no egoistic elements, but implies a rigorous impartiality. Justice, conceived in this manner, indicates both our right and our duty. Our right is to demand a respect for the human dignity manifest in our own persons; our duty is to respect that dignity in others. Finally, 'from the identity of reason among all men and from the sentiment of respect that leads them to maintain at all costs their mutual dignity, there results Equality before Justice.'

The identification of Equality and Justice leads us out of the realm of personal relationships into the economic field of wealth and poverty. The Church, according to Proudhon, takes no cognisance of economic science and its relationship to Justice; it regards inequality of condition as inevitable, it makes poverty a judgment of God and an effect of original sin, it perpetuates the artificial divisions of society and defends the system of the subordination of work to authority—a system that contains no element of Justice.

The Revolution, on the other hand, has found in equality the point of accord between Justice and economics. Justice demands, not the subordination, but the equality and reciprocity of work. Balance is the economic law, as it is the law of the universe. Men may not be identical, but each has his particular faculty, and it is in the balance of these faculties that Equality is attained. This does not imply that property should be destroyed—Proudhon again insists that he never wished to advocate this—but it must be brought into equilibrium, so that the ancient division between master and servant may at last be eliminated. The means to attain this end are the institutions of economic mutualism described in his earlier writings.

From the economic organisation of society, Proudhon is led to its political organisation. There are three systems on which this has been based. That of *necessity*, presupposing the inevitability of inequality, dominated the societies of antiquity. That of *providence* is maintained by the Church; it sees God as all powerful, man as corrupt, and denies human rights in favour of an irresponsible authority based on an immutable creed. This results in the suspension of morality for the glory of God and the triumph of the Church.

Against these systems Proudhon elevates that of Justice, a positive and realist concept which is expressed in an impersonal, invisible and anonymous social force resulting from the reciprocal action of economic institutions and industrial groups. He clearly envisages an administrative structure, constructed by the people according to their economic interests rather than, as now, by purely territorial or political considerations. The purpose of this administration will not be to *govern* or to impose a central authority but to arrange the mutual co-operation of all interests.

As for external policy, this is simplified by the fact that 'The Revolution . . . takes no cognisance of cities or races . . . Let it be realised in one place, and the world will follow. The power of its economic institutions, the gratuity of its credit, the brilliance of its thought, will suffice to convert the universe.' And, as the finale to this spontaneous spread of Justice, Proudhon foresees a 'universal federation, the supreme guarantee of all liberty and all right which, without soldiers or priests, must replace the society of Christianity and feudalism' and in which 'the life of man will pass in tranquillity of the senses and serenity of the spirit.'

Education is important in any consideration of the destiny of society because it represents the fostering of the whole man, in all his faculties and in all the phases of his life. Like all practical morality, education must rest on the principle, which places the criterion of actions in the individual conscience: 'Sin defiles the spirit; to live with it is worse than to die.' Instead, the Church elevates the authoritarian and terrorist principle: 'Sin offends God, who forbids it, and sooner or later punishes it.' By substituting fear for the free action of the conscience, the Church negates all the principles of morality and thus brings about the degradation of the human character.

More than that, the Church has negated all the vital processes of education which lie outside the maintenance of its own authority. It ignores industry, and is hostile to the sciences, to the arts and letters and to philosophy. Thus it denudes man's inner self, breaks his contact with nature, demoralises him in the face of death, and destroys that mutual respect between men which is the foundation of Justice.

Against the condition of the man whose development has been stultified by religion, Proudhon places that of the man whose education has been integrated through the revolutionary attitude: 'Human life enters its fulness . . . when it has satisfied the following conditions: 1. Love, paternity, family: extension and perpetuation of the being by carnal generation, or reproduction of the subject in body and spirit, in person and will. 2. Work, or industrial generation: extension and perpetuation of the being by his action on nature . . . 3. Social communion or Justice; participation in the collective life and the progress of humanity . . . If these conditions are violated, existence is anxious; man, being able neither *to live nor die*, is dedicated to misery. If, on the contrary, these conditions are fulfilled, existence is full; it is a feast, a song of love, a perpetual enthusiasm, an endless hymn to happiness. At whatever hour the signal may be given, man is ready; for he is always in death, which means that he is in life and in love.'

Work is the keystone of human society, the motive force of Justice, the means by which alone man can eventually reach happiness. At the same time, in an unequal society, work is painful and repugnant, and the worker is inferior, poor and despised. The Church perpetuates this situation, because to conceive of the worker being raised from his situation, to advocate equality, would be to deny the very doctrines of predestination and original sin on which the authority of the Church is based.

Against this attitude Proudhon proposes a revolutionary charter of labour, inspired by the law of Justice, and based on the integration of work not merely in its physical, but also in its mental aspects. In his view, one of the disastrous aspects of modern society is the divorce between ideas and work. Philosophy and the sciences emerge from the working life of man, the idea rises from the action, and the two should not be separated. Philosophy and science must therefore be reintegrated with industry.

As a practical means of bringing about this reintegration Proudhon proposes the application of equality by granting the earth to its cultivator, the craft to the craftsman, capital to whomever makes use of it, the product to the producer, and the profit of collective power to those who contribute towards it, i.e. the whole of society. In this way the fatality of nature may be tamed by the liberty of man.

In order to consolidate this liberation there are two necessary steps: a polytechnic rather than a specialised apprenticeship, which will initiate the learner into the general principles of human industry, and an organisation of the workshop in such a way that the young worker may be introduced to all its operations and eventually be allowed to participate as an associate in its direction. By such integration, work will change from a burden to a source of joy, and the worker's life will become 'a triumphal procession.'

Proceeding from work to 'ideas,' Proudhon repeats the attack on the Absolute already introduced in *The Philosophy of Progress*. What he says here is not markedly new, though it is expressed with a greater variety of illustration and argument. He does not deny the Absolute, but contends that it cannot be known, and seeks to eliminate it from our philosophical arguments and to concentrate our attention on *phenomenal* aspects of the universe, which alone fall within the province of exact knowledge.

Once we have expelled the Absolute from our minds, once we have ceased to refer all ideas to a set and monolithic conception, we shall gain that freedom of thinking which admits the opposition or mutual reaction of ideas and faculties, out of which arise not only the life and dynamism of society, but also its equilibrium and, by implication, its peace. Thus, paradoxically, we can only maintain agreement and harmony within society, and at the same time avoid absolutism of every kind, by sustaining social energies in a state of perpetual struggle.

Priests and philosophers seek a uniform faith; the Revolution thrives on multiplicity and variety. 'Public reason' in a free society would be built on the spontaneous interaction of individual ways of thinking. These would continue their independent existences while taking on extended life within the collective thought, which is made up of them and yet has its own character, different in quality and superior in power. The organ of collective reason is never formalised or institutionalised; it is to be found in any group of men who gather for the discussion of ideas or the search for Justice.

*

Theologians talk in terms of a human conscience, but their absolutism prevents them from recognising its defining characteristic, the faculty of deciding freely between good and evil. Yet the intimate feelings of men and the collective facts of social life prove that such a faculty exists.

The criterion of good that emerges from the action of the human conscience can be summarised in the double maxim, known to wise men in all ages: 'Do not unto others what you would not have them do unto you. Do constantly unto others the good you would like to receive from them.' This is the touch-stone of all human endeavour; as mankind becomes aware of its implications, Justice develops. For morality is linked with the growth of knowledge; it is perpetually emergent, and Justice can only be satisfied by the continual revision of institutions to keep pace with the extension of consciousness. In the last resort, the knowledge of good and evil is nothing less than Equality; Equality is as necessary to the conscience as light to the eye.

Here Proudhon is brought to the ancient controversy between free will and determinism. In his view, determinism, which denies man's power to act as he wishes, when what he wishes is not impossible, is a brutal idea that makes material entities the determinants of our actions and turns the thinking being into the plaything of matter. In reality, the argument has always been seen in false terms, since neither free will nor necessity exists in absolute terms. Neither alone can explain human society, and one can only present a truthful picture by acknowledging an antinomial situation in which Liberty and Necessity both play their parts as extreme terms. The series of Liberty and the series of Necessity are parallel and co-existent. Man owes his liberty to the synthetic union within him of all natural spontaneities; the freedom of social bodies emerges from the harmony of all their varied elements.

Justice is the last word of Liberty, and so the two become identified. In practical terms, the liberty of man advances in relation to his knowledge and practice of social organisation. Liberty, the revolt of man against the law of necessity, is the inspirer of all progress, and gives majesty and power to Justice. Religion itself, art and literature, all stem from the urge to liberty; that urge created in Christianity the revolt against Destiny and now, in the Revolution, it creates the revolt against Providence. It is a power of negation and destruction so far as the old world is concerned, but for the new world it is a power of affirmation and construction.

*

The ninth section of *Justice* concerns 'Progress and Decadence,' and it also is largely a refinement of ideas already discussed in *The Philosophy of Progress*. Progress, the negation of the Absolute, can only be attained through the understanding of Justice. And this can happen only in a rationally constituted society which, without losing any of its fundamental principles, attains constantly new insights into human relationships. It is not the proliferation of written laws that constitutes progress; it is the increase of laws conceived and observed by men in their hearts.

Hence the Church, with its emphasis on transcendence, is the enemy of progress since, by posing the Absolute as the revealer and guarantor of Justice, it has brought about the degeneration of human dignity and spontaneity, has negated equality and has delayed the social regeneration of man by fifteen centuries. The justice which the Church teaches is not real; it is a form of idolatry. 'God is the shadow of the conscience projected on the field of the imagination. While we take that shadow for a sun it is inevitable that we should remain in the twilight.' It is when man sees, not the shadow, but the substance of his conscience, that he begins to be free, and the more he recognises the true Justice within him, the happier he will live and the less he will fear to die. The primitive cycle of ascendance and decadence gives way to progress when man recognises that the gods have departed, that the rôle of the cults is ended, and that Justice is the rule by which human affairs should be regulated and inspired.

The theory of progress, Proudhon claims, applies to the arts as well as to other phases of social life. 'Art, as well as liberty, has for its material men and things; its object is to reproduce them in transcending them, and its final end is Justice.' Those artists who have best interpreted the world of their time and mirrored its aspirations towards Justice are always the most satisfying; it was because they turned away from their own time, because they rejected the Revolution and its implications, that Proudhon found his own contemporaries decadent.

*

The tenth and eleventh parts of *Justice* are devoted to 'Love and Marriage,' and involve an extensive consideration of the status of women; it was these sections, with their attacks on the feminist position, that aroused the greatest misgivings among the liberals and even in such close friends of Proudhon as Michelet and Herzen, who elaborately refuted them in *My Past and Thoughts*.

Proudhon regards marriage as a product not merely of man's

physical nature, having its source in the necessity of generation, but also of an intellectual element which transforms it into a social 'necessity,' a focus of Justice, and a basic unit in society. Christian marriage, however, is a perversion of true marriage. By reserving to God the intimate preferences of the heart, it results in the separation of love from marriage, and thus produces an inevitable upsurge of eroticism and moral degeneration. Only where liberty exists, where the Absolute is dethroned and the innate sense of Justice has become man's rule of conduct, will marriage be reinstated as a source of right and the family as a nucleus of social regeneration.

Thus far Proudhon's reasoning is clear and consistent, but it is when he comes to discuss the position of women that his innate puritanism leads him into paths which, while often ingenious, tend frequently towards absurdity. Particularly strange is the misapplication of mathematics with which he supports the patriarchal attitude of the typical peasant.

The physical inferiority of women, he declares, is uncontested. To man she stands in this respect as 2 to 3. In reasoning and in moral strength, it is clear to Proudhon, she is weaker in the same proportion, and since these faculties multiply each other, we come, by geometrical progression, to the conclusion that the incurable inferiority of woman in the fields of work, knowledge and Justice places her, as compared with man, in the relationship of 8 to 27.

One cannot immediately dismiss Proudhon's statements with the amused contempt which at first sight their odd form seems to deserve. Women are certainly inferior in strength—though they are often superior in endurance, which creates a certain biological balance. It is also true that there has never been a great woman philosopher, and that women in general tend to base their moral judgments on emotional rather than rational criteria. But these criticisms are not universally applicable. Since Proudhon's day many women have become excellent scientific workers; others, like Spiridonova, Louise Michel and Rosa Luxembourg, have shown their devotion to the Revolution and their realisation of the full meaning of Justice as Proudhon saw it. And in considering the mass of women to whom his criticisms still to a large extent apply, one might point to the effects of centuries of subjection, of miseducation, of rearing for a position in life where the powers of moral and intellectual judgment are allowed to atrophy. In a more egalitarian society, women might go far towards upsetting Proudhon's elaborate calculations.

Even he, as a devoted egalitarian, was clearly uneasy about this relegation of the feminine sex to an unequal station, and he extricated himself by declaring that woman has other qualities in which she is superior; in beauty, in intuitive mental grace, in the capacity for love, she scores each time over man by 3 to 2, and so we come again to the geometrical progression of 27 to 8, with woman this time in the lead. The equilibrium is thus established, and the conjugal couple becomes the unit in which Justice, otherwise a mere notion, is made manifest. But this balance of complementary qualities does not establish woman's social equality, or even her equality in family authority, since the economic, philosophical and juridical elements are precisely those in which she is inferior. Socially women are equal in *result*, but not in *principle* or *practice*.

Proudhon ends these sections with some curious reflections on successful marriage, which in his view depends on the rigorous disciplining of love. The best marriage is that in which duty and virtue figure as the principal ingredients, while the amorous element is almost non-existent; paradoxically, the 'secret of escaping the tribulations of love and reaping its happiness is to love with heart and soul all persons of the opposite sex, and conjugally to possess only one of them.'

*

In the last section of *Justice*, Proudhon returns to his general theme with a consideration of the moral sanctions that lead men towards right. In a society dominated by Justice, he declares, the legislator personifies the human conscience, interpreting the moral law, which demands mutual respect, the equilibrium of social forces and the development of the free spirit. But the moral law is expressed in the practice of society as well as within the individual conscience, and its predominance is illustrated by the existence of a series of moral sanctions.

The first and penal sanction is expressed in the fact that men are happy when Justice is observed and suffer when it is violated. This sanction is made concrete within human society; crimes are the result of imperfect social relations, and, since reciprocity reigns here as in other human situations, the duty rests on society to see where it has been at fault towards the delinquent, and to work for its own amendment by the incessant revision of its institutions.

The second sanction lies in the fact that a lack of moral equilibrium produces a corresponding failure of the balance of economic forces, and so our vices and iniquities are punished by poverty. The third sanction is political, since a society without moral equilibrium turns towards violence, expressed in despotism and regicide. When the material and the spiritual are reunited in the reign of Justice, this condition will automatically be amended, and social peace be established. The last sanction is that the violation of Justice engenders metaphysical doubt, leading to moral scepticism, while the Revolution, by restoring Justice, at the same time resolves the problem of certitude and reconstructs philosophy on a sound basis.

Proudhon could not resist ending with a final shot at the Church, and he concluded his third volume with an ironic challenge to Cardinal Mathieu. Let the Church accept the Revolution, and amend itself in such a way that it can take part in the task of establishing true Justice, and he himself will lead his family back into the fold. The Cardinal did not reciprocate.

II

The reception of *Justice* showed a live interest among the Parisian public in the first serious work to appear under Proudhon's signature since 1852. Six thousand copies sold immediately, and Proudhon hoped that, if the public curiosity continued, it would soon run into a second edition. But before this could happen, and less than a week after publication, the police seized the few remaining copies in the possession of the publishers. The grounds for seizure were made known immediately to Proudhon, and the list of charges, as he recorded them in his diary, was formidable: '1. Reproduction in bad faith of false news likely to disturb the public peace. 2. Excitement of hatred between citizens. 3. Attack on the rights of the family. 4. Outrage to public and religious morality. 5. Attack on respect for the laws. 6. Apology for acts defined as crimes or misdemeanours.'

The weight of these accusations showed that the authorities

were not likely to retreat from their position, and it seemed clear to all but Proudhon that whatever the public conscience might decide, his case could not succeed before the courts. 'All the lawyers tell me to expect a sentence of five years in prison,' he noted on the 1st May, and a few days later complained that he received condolences on every side. 'It seems indeed as if they were coming to my burial, as if people would like to see me dead!'

But even in such a grave situation he found reason for satisfaction. Since the seizure of *Justice*, its black-market price had risen to 200 francs, and Proudhon felt sure that, if only they had been available, 30,000 copies might have been sold. A German translation was being printed in Leipzig, while the authorities in Hamburg and Prussia had decided to ban the book. 'I have not failed,' Proudhon exulted. 'Justice exists at last; the Revolution is up and the old society is down. Now they speak of nothing else in Paris, even in the girls' schools!' His very trial had become in his eyes a battle where he was 'fighting for revolutionary justice and human rights,' rather than for his own acquittal.

The process of prosecution went on its ordered course. On the 6th May Proudhon was questioned by the examining magistrate, and on the 11th he presented a petition to the Senate. This appeal was ignored by the senators, and when he published it to bring his case before the public, the police interpreted this as an aggravation of his offence and confiscated copies on the grounds that it was calculated to 'agitate public opinion.' The trial before the Correctional Court on the 6th June was a suspiciously hasty affair. Neither Proudhon nor his friend Gustave Chaudey, who acted as his counsel, was allowed by the President to conduct the case in the way they had planned and, after a hearing that lasted less than a day, Proudhon was sentenced to three years' imprisonment and a fine of 4,000 francs. Garnier, the publisher, received a month in prison and a fine of 1,000 francs, and Bourdier, the printer, 15 days and 1,000 francs. Clearly the case was being used, not merely to attack radical opinions, but also to scare printers and publishers out of giving assistance to the writers who expressed them.

Proudhon accepted his position with an impressive appearance of resignation. 'My health,' he assured Maurice, 'is passable and my tranquillity so great that it astonishes everybody.' Indeed, it is particularly noticeable that all through the tension and activity associated with his trial, the formerly ailing Proudhon complained hardly at all about his condition. Even his financial situation he regarded with philosophic equanimity. He owed four thousand francs in current debts to the Garniers, he had an equal amount to pay for his fine, but when the accounting was all made, he would still have between seven and eight thousand francs to see him through prison. And, he added, 'Prison will not be unfruitful for me: I shall work.'

Having formulated his appeal and engaged Crémieux as his lawyer, Proudhon set about composing a lengthy memoir for publication, in which he intended to discuss in detail the decisions of the Court, hoping thus to have his defence well lodged in the public attention before the hearing took place. The Imperial Procurator would allow him to print only twenty copies of this memoir, but even this number he found it impossible to obtain, since the printers, scared by the sentences already imposed on their colleagues, and by police warnings that *any* publications by M. Proudhon were dangerous, refused unanimously to have anything to do with it. It became evident that many factors were combining against his chance of a fair hearing, and he finally decided to go into exile.

It was a decision he reached only reluctantly. For a month his friends had been urging him to go, but he had opposed their advice and was even liable, on occasion, to interpret it as a sign of lack of confidence. 'They do not cease exhorting me to flee,' he complained to Edmond. 'I carry the flag before the enemy, like Bonaparte on the Bridge of Arcole, and nobody supports me!' Even when he departed, he pretended that he was fleeing less to avoid an imprisonment which he considered unjust than to find the means of publishing the memoir that would be the basis of his appeal. But he had enough realism to admit that once he went into exile there would be no point in returning unless conditions were favourable, and on the eve of his departure he wrote to Mathey: 'A new life is about to begin for me. I have plenty of things to do, and good ones.'

Part Seven

THE EXILE

I

PROUDHON left Paris on the 17th July, and encountered no obstacles on his journey into exile; he noted particularly that he did not see a single policeman, and the ease of his departure suggests that the Imperial authorities may have been pleased to see him go. He was accompanied by a Belgian business man named Bouquié, who saw him across the border to Tournai and then returned to Paris to report the safe crossing of the frontier.

In Brussels Proudhon spent his first night at the home of a sin-obsessed engineer, Bouquié's brother, who made engravings to illustrate the evils of alcohol and on this occasion entertained his guest with 'an incredible quantity of facts regarding corruption, blackmail, swindling, embezzlement, speculation, etc.,' which convinced the easily shocked Proudhon that Belgium was morally as bad as Paris. But, despite this congenial company, Proudhon decided to go in search of a room of his own and next day he found a lodging in the house of a garrulously Anglophobe lady in the suburb of Saint-Josse-ten-Noode, where he assumed the name of Durfort and posed as a professor of mathematics. 'This does not mean that I count on escaping by means of this pseudonym from the searches of the police,' he assured

Euphrasie. 'I only take it temporarily, in order to maintain my *incognito* so far as the public is concerned.'

In fact, he went almost immediately to the Director of the Sûreté Publique in Brussels and informed this official of his situation. He was recommended to make a request for a permit of residence to the Minister of the Interior, which he did in pompous terms, asking 'permission to philosophise among you, as Spinoza formerly philosophised at the Hague, Descartes at Stockholm, Voltaire at Ferney.' He was allowed to remain.

Among the few score French expatriates in the city he was accepted with warmth, for the Brussels *émigrés* were not addicted to the bitter sectarianism of their fellows in London. He was reunited with his friend, Madier-Montjau, who gave prominence to *Justice* in a course of lectures at Antwerp, and one day in the street he met Victor Considérant, whom he had imagined dead, but who had in fact just returned from Texas, where he had tried unsuccessfully to unite the disparate Utopian groups. Finally, he found in Brussels his German friend of twelve years ago, Karl Gruen.

His first reaction to exile was very near despair, and he felt that, if his sentence had not been so long, prison might have been preferable. He was bored by his relatively solitary life in a dull city, the excitement of his flight had renewed his catarrhal afflictions, and he found the climate so damp that in comparison he likened the air of the Rue d'Enfer to that of a mountain peak. He had not been in Brussels more than three days before he was telling Euphrasie that, since he did not intend to return to an enforced silence in France, he must arrange for his family to join him as soon as possible. 'Without that I shall be like the lion in the menagerie whose little dog was taken away from him and who ended by dying of grief.'

His eventual reconciliation with a place of abode that at first had seemed so unsympathetic was due largely to the generous welcome, not only of the exiles, but also of the Belgian liberals. Little more than a week after his arrival he told Pilhes, 'I have already met with precious sympathy,' and his circle of acquaintances among the native writers and scholars increased steadily. From the beginning he avoided becoming too closely involved in the restricted group of expatriates, and by finding his company among the hospitable Belgians he weathered the material and mental hazards of exile a great deal more easily than some of his less adaptable fellows.

2

Meanwhile the course of Bonapartists justice had gone its way. On the day of his flight, Proudhon received a summons to appear before the Court of Appeal on the 28th July. He answered from Belgium that this date did not give him time to prepare his defensive memoir of 200 pages. The court confirmed his sentence by default, but he was allowed to make opposition to the judgment, and the final hearing was adjourned until November.

Proudhon decided to base his future conduct on the way his memoir was treated by the authorities; if they let it circulate freely in France, so that his case became generally known, he would return and face the Court of Appeal. The publication of the memoir was undertaken by a Parisian named Lebègue, who had settled in Brussels and opened a small publishing house. It appeared in mid-September, under the title of *La Justice Poursuivie par l'Eglise*, but, since it adds nothing new to Proudhon's thought, it need detain us little. The author himself described it as 'instructive, interesting, amusing,' and all these things are true; beyond that, it was also an excellent defence of free speech. On the 22nd September, Proudhon sent a copy to the French Minister of the Interior, asking him to decide whether it should be admitted to France. 'If you judge otherwise,' he told him, 'I tell you with sorrow that I shall see myself under the necessity of remaining where I am and renouncing my fatherland.'

This task finished, he departed, clad in his workman's blouse and with a pack on his back, for a walking holiday in the hills of the Ardennes. His companions were Felix Delhasse, a wealthy Belgian man of letters who remained his close and generous friend for the rest of his life, and Thoré, a fellow expatriate. They walked by the rivers of that green country, the Vestre, the Ourthe, the Aublade, stepped over the frontier into Prussian territory at Malmédy, and visited the watering-place of Spa, where Proudhon found the gambling-houses 'ignoble and dreadful.' They made a trip to the industrial town of Verviers, and returned down the Meuse to Maestricht, which Proudhon decided would be a pleasant and quiet place to inhabit if he should ever leave Brussels. They returned to the capital on the 4th October.

In Spa Proudhon had learnt that *Justice Hunted by the Church* was to be excluded from France. 'The expulsion of my memoir is equivalent to the exclusion of my person, unless I decide to enter for three years of prison,' he declared. 'In a word, it is banishment.' He decided to abandon the hope of a decision by the Court of Appeal in his favour and to take the steps necessary to make his residence in Brussels definite. At the end of October, 1858, he obtained permission from the Belgian police for his family to join him, and during the ensuing weeks he wrote his wife a series of urgent letters, crammed with instructions regarding removal and complaints of the difficulty of finding an apartment. 'Nothing is scarcer in Brussels, where for the past ten years they have been building nothing but palaces and barracks, as if they intended to destroy the middle class in Belgium.'

Finally, towards the end of November, he discovered an apartment in the suburb of Ixelles, one of the healthier parts of Brussels. The rent was 372 francs a year, little more than half what he had paid in Paris, and the house, he enthused, was 'extremely tidy' and 'bright as a jewel.' It was only a few steps from the market, and many of his friends, including Gruen, Madier-Montjau and Delhasse, lived in the same quarter.

Assured of a dwelling, he began a busy tour of the furniture dealers, though, since Euphrasie had expressed doubts of his taste, he bought only such things as seemed to him immediately essential. His needs were of the simplest; strong, plain chairs at $3\frac{1}{2}$ francs each were good enough for him, and a table at 10 francs served him as a desk. 'I have warned you that I do not want luxury, but neatness,' he cautioned Euphrasie. 'That is why I buy new things, but of the common kind. It suits our position, and I notice that it is generally approved here, and helps to make me esteemed and accepted. Profit from this caution: no ill-placed vanity, and you, as well as I, will be well-received and well-regarded.'

Finally, on the 1st December, there came an end to the weeks of busy preparation and frantic correspondence, of hurried purchases and multitudinous customs formalities, and promptly at midday the family was reunited in the main station at Brussels.

Euphrasie had lost her voice on the journey, but recovered it with disconcerting rapidity when they moved into the new apartment on the day after her arrival. She expressed the deepest contempt for the 'trashiness' of Pierre-Joseph's taste in furniture; 'Can a man do nothing to please a woman in household affairs?' he complained ruefully, and from his descriptions of the situation one gains the impression that he was not so completely the patriarchal master of the home as his theories might lead one to suppose. Euphrasie, who never read his books or took the least interest in his intellectual life, had evidently attained, during the years of their marriage, a considerable independence in domestic matters.

In other respects her attitude on reaching Brussels was better than he had feared, for she was 'pleased with the town, the district and the apartment.' All in all, Proudhon himself was happier than he had been at any time since he left Paris, and it was almost with glee that he described to his friends the chaos of moving into a new existence. 'All my books in piles, my papers pell mell, *total anarchy!*' His satisfaction was complete when he found, three hundred yards from his house, a school called the Institution of Fathers of Families, to which he could send his children without any fear of the taint of clerical influence.

3

The re-establishment of his household completed Proudhon's reconciliation to Brussels. 'I think no more of leaving,' he assured Maurice comfortably in mid-December. 'I am too old to run about the world, and I stay where I am.' But, though this situation was at first a great stimulus to his plans, the beginning of 1859 brought new misfortunes in the form of a revival of his old nervous ailment. For a fortnight he was unable to sleep; for more than a month he had to spend his nights upright in a chair. 'I am out of luck, and the worst of it is that I am running into debt,' he complained. Only in April could he resume work, and then only very slowly.

Yet even at the height of his illness he was acutely concerned with the questions thrust upon him by the Italian war. He recognised that Napoleon intended to enter the struggle against Austria, not to serve Italian freedom, but to save his own despotism from collapse. War was actually declared between France and Austria at the end of April, 1859, and Proudhon hailed the appearance of Napoleon III as the champion of Italian independence with the bitter remark: 'Napoleon is the counter-revolution. What can he do? Nothing, nothing, nothing.'

He was quick to observe the connection between the war and the progressive diminution of freedom, demonstrated in the arrest of Blanqui, which had immediately preceded hostilities, and in the suspension of civil liberties in Piedmont. He also realised, as so many have done since his day, the futility of war in a modern society, the certainty of loss to victor as well as vanquished. 'Whatever comes in the chances of battle,' he told Gouvernet when the war was barely a month old, 'it is clear that in three months, even if we are victorious, we shall have had three hundred thousand casualties, five hundred millions eaten up, as much borrowed, and for what result? . . . The Austrians, we are told, are worse off. But their dead will not bring ours back to life; their lost money does not enter our coffers, and that is what is so disastrous in this war which leaves the victor without any compensation.'

The course of the war, though it was favourable to France, did not change his views. 'We go from victory to victory,' he said in July, 'but far from that making me withdraw what I have said, I hold my opinion all the more strongly, and I ask continually for what purpose is this abominable mowing down of men.' It was in this way, stirred by the example of a futile conflict, rather than in an academic spirit of cold enquiry, that Proudhon turned from the idea of a pamphlet on nationalities, which he had been contemplating at this time, and began instead to prepare a major work on the problem of war and peace which was to occupy him for many months to come.

4

The news of the treaty of Villafranca was attended by rumours of an amnesty in France to celebrate the 'victory,' and this led Proudhon to consider seriously the possibility of returning home more quickly than he had expected. His attitude was motivated largely by the fact that continuing exile had produced a tension within the family that must have been disturbing to his ideas of patriarchal dignity. After her first favourable reaction to life in Brussels, Euphrasie had begun to pine for Paris and the Piégards; she had told Pierre-Joseph emphatically that, unlike him, she had not 'the resource of ideas,' and her discontent had reached such grave proportions that he even thought of re-establishing his family in Paris, whence they might visit him occasionally.

The need for this drastic step seemed to be removed when, on the 17th August, the Emperor signed the expected decree, granting an amnesty whose terms covered political offences committed under the Press laws. Proudhon asked his friends to regain the apartment in the Rue d'Enfer, and planned to send Euphrasie there in September, and to follow her in October. A day after making this decision he heard that his case was not covered by the amnesty; the Minister of the Interior had announced that it referred to political offences only, and technically he had been convicted on a charge of outrage to public and religious morals. 'Doubtless, if the emperor had made an amnesty for authors of obscene novels, I should be included,' he commented bitterly. But before a month had passed, his usual mental resilience had given him a calmer view. 'If it were not for my wife, a pure Parisian whom exile does not suit, if it were not for my friends, if it were not for the wine of France which costs too much here, I would not give a penny to live in Paris rather than in Brussels, Cologne, Zurich, Geneva or Turin.'

But the wine, though dear, could still be bought, and with his friends he kept in touch through his copious correspondence, besides receiving occasional visits from one or other of them as they passed through Brussels. Euphrasie's longings, on the other hand, were not to be appeased by makeshifts, and it was arranged that she should take the children to Paris for a holiday.

She left on the 29th September, and seems to have been so delighted to rejoin her family that by the 5th October Proudhon had not heard from her and took up the pen of grievance. 'I see, by your silence,' he grumbled, 'that you think a wife can very well receive news from her husband, but that she need not send him any of her own.' The tone of this letter, with its irascible warnings against extravagance, suggests throughout that Euphrasie's departure had taken place in an atmosphere of complicated disagreements, and towards the end there is a paragraph which hints strongly that their marital relationship may have reached at least a minor crisis. 'On my side,' Proudhon remarked, 'I have nothing to tell you. I work at my ease. The house seems much more agreeable since I no longer hear shouts, weeping or grumbling.

Can you not manage on your return, *if you do return*, in such a way that this calm may continue?'

His temper was not improved when he received a letter from his brother-in-law Théodore assuring him that he might return to Paris with impunity. He interpreted this Piégard interference in his affairs as a sign of disloyalty on Euphrasie's part, and, ignoring Théodore, he wrote to her angrily: 'I am vexed by all this tittle-tattle, which can only serve to augment your regrets and to irritate me. No, I tell you, I will not return under such conditions, and if staying in Belgium is painful to you, very well, I have told you that I do not want you to be a martyr. Let us come to an arrangement, and stay where you are. I will see that neither you nor the children lack for anything, and I will follow my destiny alone to the end.'

The suggestion of disloyalty was enough to make Euphrasie abandon immediately her thoughts of remaining in Paris, and she returned on the 10th October, bringing another instalment of the misfortunes that pursued Proudhon so consistently during these years, for the two children had contracted scarlatina, and Euphrasie herself was taken ill a few days afterwards. Proudhon alone escaped, and for six weeks he made beds and cooked and tended the sick. His wife had barely reached convalescence when Stephanie's illness passed into a dangerous dropsical condition. At one time Proudhon had reconciled himself to the untimely loss of a third child, but almost miraculously she passed through the critical hours, and the slow process of recovery began.

Only in December did Proudhon find it possible to resume writing. 'How would you have had me work, with this disorder around me?' he protested to his fellow exile Rolland on the 3rd of that month. 'During the day doctors and visitors, during the night vigils, my wife disabled, the household upside down. Yesterday I renewed my provision of pens, paper and ink. That is all.' By the middle of the month, however, he was again writing vigorously on his study of war and peace. His enthusiasm was renewed, and he told Chaudey that his subject was 'grand, sublime and vast.'

But this work offered no immediate solution to his unusually acute financial situation, and he complained with justification to Mathey that 1859 had been 'an ill-starred year.' 'Apart from the slight difference that there may be between three years in the

Conciergerie and five months of exile in Belgium,' he remarked sardonically, 'the condemnation pronounced against me by the tribunal of the Seine will have dealt its blow and attained its end.' There was a more direct cry of weariness in the letter he wrote to Langlois at the same time. 'It is now that I feel the weight of my poverty, for if I enjoyed only 3,000 francs of clear income, I vow to you that the public would hear hardly anything of me. I would go to live peacefully in Zurich, Geneva, Turin or Nice, and would not even dream of returning to my country on the expiration of my sentence. But I must work, I must carry on! And I have no other trade than that which has cost me so much anger and so much hatred, five trials and two condemnations!'

In his continuing distress his French publishers were the only people he could ask for assistance. 'I do not despair of re-establishing myself,' he told them in a letter of appeal. 'For me it is only a question of time. But time is *money*, say the English.' And he asked modestly for an advance of 250 francs. But this covered only a fraction of his expenses in that season of distress, and shortly he was forced to write to them again, asking in desperate terms for a final loan of a thousand francs. 'I have numerous doctors' visits to pay for, I need a little wine; finally, imagine a household attacked on all sides, and you will see that with an extra thousand we shall not be in luxury. I am ashamed, gentlemen, to express myself in such lamentable terms . . . but I am tired; I begin to find that I have more than my share of suffering.'

Garniers agreed to make the loan, and it was such acts of fellowship that helped to support Proudhon through this unfortunate winter and to give him a surprising renewal of confidence in the future. 'Though I do not hope to convert everybody in the twinkling of an eye,' he told Mathey shortly afterwards, 'I feel more than ever hopeful of emerging from my difficulties and of seriously ameliorating my position.'

On the future of mankind as well he looked at this time with a long view horizoned by eventual optimism, for he told Michelet that the world was entering a new phase of the integral revolution of ideas and hearts which both of them were striving to achieve. The age, from Voltaire to 1848, when France had been the initiator, was past; now the Revolution was becoming internationalised among its devotees in every land.

In March, 1860, Proudhon began to publish the second edition of *Justice*; it appeared in a series of twelve parts, each embellished with an appendix called *News of the Revolution*, which acted as a kind of international review of current affairs. It was a device that allowed him to dilate on the contemporary political situation, which his accurate insight told him was leading, after the long stagnation since June, 1848, to a further period of unrest among the poorer classes. In this way his long-frustrated desire to edit a new radical periodical was partly fulfilled, and he hoped that such a regular survey of current affairs might finally grow into a magazine with international ramifications. Indeed, when the first section appeared he wrote to Herzen, who was then editing *The Bell*, suggesting that they might start a collaboration, and from this slight beginning he saw the possibility of drawing in a whole school of like-minded correspondents in all countries. 'With a little zeal,' he declared, 'we should have Europe in our net within six months.'

Such high hopes went unrealised, yet the reappearance of *Justice* in its new form, and Proudhon's re-emergence as a commentator on current affairs, undoubtedly contributed a great deal towards the increase of his influence which became evident during 1860. Since 1851, he had lived mostly in the shadows, rarely able to publish the books he would have liked to write, and, when he did so, condemned largely to a success of scandal. From 1860 onwards, however, the interest in him became less a matter of sensation, and was increasingly based on a genuine sympathy among people of widely divergent classes and nations. This was due, not merely to the intrinsic value of the ideas he expressed, but also to a general shift in radical circles away from political and towards social conceptions. Proudhon was never to encounter that circle of international correspondence which he had envisaged in his letter to Herzen (though his followers were to build it up a few years later in the International Workingmen's Association), but in an unorganised way the influence of *Justice* was a means of linking him with a steadily widening movement of thought.

By the end of 1859 he was aware of a growing international prestige. 'The more I advance,' he declared, 'the more cosmopolitan I become.' A translation of *Justice* was being prepared in Spain. Two hundred copies were ordered for Italy. He was 'almost naturalised' in Germany. A Tsarist officer brought him felicitations from Tomsk. And in April, 1860, Tolstoy called, and they passed together a great part of the few days which the Russian writer spent in Brussels. They discussed the emancipation of the serfs, and Tolstoy said that not until he had travelled in Western Europe had he been able to understand the emphasis Proudhon placed on attacking Catholicism. Proudhon told Herzen that 'Mr. Tolstoy' stood out with great individuality among the many Russians who had visited him.

In France itself the renewal of his prestige was shown by the number of visitors from that country who made a point of calling on him. In the summer of 1860 there was Etienne Arago, the republican astronomer, and about the same time appeared a representative of the extreme opposing faction, in the person of a legitimist leader whom Proudhon referred to as 'the Viscount XXX.' Early in 1861 his old rival Blanqui called; Proudhon was distressed to find the conspirator 'much aged' by the series of imprisonments that had eaten away half his life. Even Victor Hugo, encountered at the house of a common friend, appeared affable, and offered his hand, which Proudhon accepted. 'But it was limited to that. I remain on my dunghill and he on his. We are not made for each other.'

But what gratified Proudhon most was the evidence that French working-class interest in his ideas was emerging on a much wider scale than at any time since 1848. In August, 1860, he entertained 'a little deputation from a fine society of Rouen workers, who ask me for a revolutionary programme for the day after tomorrow,' and, although he noted ironically that they acted 'as if we were on the eve of February,' he was clearly pleased that they should have chosen to approach him. Later there arrived from Paris the emissaries of other groups of workers anxious for his advice, but Proudhon was careful not to place too high a value on these manifestations of interest. 'I do not want adventures; my age does not permit them,' he had told Bergmann a few years before, and it was with due caution that he viewed the possibility of becoming in some degree an intellectual if not a political leader among the French workers. When Darimon laid too optimistic an interpretation on the visits of workers' representatives, he expressed his doubts at some length.

'As to our concluding from this isolated fact the existence of a *Proudhonian* party, since you use the term, I believe that would be exposing ourselves to a great illusion. The people can be of a Blanquist, Mazzinian or Garibaldian party, that is to say of a party where one *believes*, where one conspires, where one fights; they are never of a party where one reasons and thinks. I have cause to believe, it is true, that since the *coup d'état* the public which from time to time shows me its goodwill has increased rather than diminished; there is hardly a week that does not give me proofs of this. But that *élite* of readers does not form a party; they are people who ask me for books, for ideas, for discussion, for philosophic investigation, and who, for the most part, would abandon me tomorrow with contempt if I spoke to them of creating a party and forming themselves, under my initiative, into a secret society.'

But, even though he was careful not to exaggerate his following, the sense of having a renewed and widened support did much to maintain Proudhon's will during the difficult early days of 1860, and there was a real conviction behind his remark to Michelet: 'I regain strength and resolution. My morale has never been better.'

6

In May, 1860, Proudhon's life was clouded anew by the deaths of his brother Charles and his cousin Melchior. When he heard that Charles was dead, he was overcome with a feeling of guilt because he had not done more for the unfortunate blacksmith. 'I expected his death for several years,' he told Rolland. 'Nevertheless, it afflicts me, or rather renews my regrets when I think that he, my father, my mother, all my family, counted on me, that they expected some little well-being from me, and that, through my socialist impulses, I placed myself outside the conditions of success, outside the communion of fortune. . . . At the moment when I write to you I feel all too strongly that my children will be no better treated by me than my brothers were.'

Yet, loaded with debts though he already was, he raised further loans to provide the money that would apprentice his brother's sons and establish his deaf and witless widow in some place where she would be cared for. A man who would so increase his burdens to help his relatives was little deserving of the reproaches of neglect he heaped upon himself.

On the whole, he surveyed with admiration the way his brother had endured a life whose latter part had been 'condemned to idleness' through constant sickness. 'In all, his last years were the most courageous and the most honourable.' Cousin Melchior's end, however, was bitterly disappointing, for that old Jacobin finally gave in to the priests and died within the Church. 'Is not this to be outraged in my body and soul?' Proudhon lamented, and he drew a comparison between the unworthy end of the late Orator of the Orient Lodge of Besançon and the stoical departure of brother Charles. 'Decrepitude got the better of the old philosopher in the end; he confessed, he communicated; in brief, he died with edification. My poor blacksmith of Burgille was more solid; like my father, he died without fear and without reproach, though not without regret. He regretted leaving nothing to his children.'

7

Through 1860 Proudhon worked 'like a galley slave,' not merely preparing the new edition of *Justice* and completing his treatise on war, but also writing an essay on taxation for a competition which the Swiss canton of Vaud had announced during the summer. The subject, as well as the chance of a prize of 1,200 francs, appealed to him, and in September he submitted a monograph equal to 180 pages. 'It is the first time to my knowledge,' he remarked complacently to the Swiss journalist Delarageaz, 'that a complete and rigorously deduced theory of taxation has been produced.'

The Lausanne jury was slow in considering the forty-four competing works, and by the following January Proudhon had become resigned to failure. It was therefore with surprise and delight that he finally heard, in May, 1861, of the award granting the first prize to his essay. It was the recognition rather than the cash that gave him the greater pleasure. 'M. Proudhon crowned for a work of political economy by the State council of a sovereign state!' he crowed to Delarageaz. 'This moment will one day be notable in the history of the Revolution in the nineteenth century!'

There is something extremely pathetic in this anarchist's delight at being recognised by a government—even the government of a tiny Swiss canton. It was more than a paradoxical urge that prompted him; it was rather the yearning towards the very society against which he rebels that so often attacks the intellectual insurgent. And, indeed, *Théorie de l'Impôt*, as his essay was called, is remarkable among Proudhon's works for its almost complete lack of revolutionary tone. 'The jury,' he told Mathey, 'considered my work eminently conservative.' And the jury was right. In his own writing Proudhon was demonstrating the antinomial tendency he so often saw in society, and, if the new edition of *Justice* was more than ever sharpened into a weapon of revolutionary thought, this essay, which immediately succeeded it, was muffled in a caution that is a gift to Proudhon's critics and an embarrassment to his friends.

An attenuated shadow of anarchism indeed appears in the contention that the State should be restricted to certain purely administrative functions, that its expenditures should be strictly curtailed and its functions submitted to the greatest possible decentralisation. But when Proudhon comes to discuss the practice of taxation at the present time his essay shows its more timid aspects, for, while rejecting a graduated income tax, he retains taxes on consumption goods, customs and stamp duties—the very impositions which weigh most heavily on the poorest class.

The caution and clumsiness that Proudhon here displays in formulating a concrete policy of administration are in part the expression of an incapacity to envisage the details of social reform—an incapacity which contrasts sharply with his brilliant insights into the more generalised aspects of social or historical development. But beyond this there is evident a fear of bold measures that makes this essay unique among Proudhonian writings. The fact, I suggest, must be regarded as of psychological rather than ideological significance. Only his sense of insecurity, his desire to be recognised as the returning prodigal, to expiate his rebellions, even if only to renew them immediately, can explain Proudhon's almost naïve delight when his efforts suceeded in making him a pundit, if not in Paris, at least in Lausanne. Dubiously as we may regard his performance, the joy he experienced in his petty victory was demonstrated with such a candid simplicity that one is reluctant to impute to him any more Machiavellian motive.

8

On the 28th October, Proudhon's manuscript of *La Guerre et la Paix* was completed and sent to Garniers. A month afterwards he still had no news from them, and began to fear that they had submitted his book to the police. When Garniers eventually replied, it was with a blank rejection. Their lawyers had warned them that *War and Peace* was a dangerous book, and not even Proudhon's offer to make alterations would induce them to risk a repetition of the trouble they had experienced through printing *Justice*.

There followed several exasperating months of hunting for a new publisher. One firm agreed to produce the book, but refused to use its name. A 'man of straw' was found, and then withdrew. 'What a bitch of an existence!' Proudhon wailed despairingly. 'I definitely no longer wish to write anything but A.B.C.s and schoolbooks.' Finally, Dentu accepted *War and Peace*, and it appeared on the 21st May, 1861.

The basic argument of this book is that war has in the past played its part as a factor in social evolution, but that the more society advances, the farther war recedes from its original purpose and the more abuses enter its conduct. War has in fact become unreformable; the time has come for it to be superseded, and for the urges that underlie it to be transformed in a positive direction. '*The end of militarism* is the mission of the nineteenth century, under pain of indefinite decadence.'

This simplified account gives only a meagre view of the complex and at times almost perverse arguments of this large and passionate book. There are elements in the phenomenon of war which could not fail to appeal to Proudhon, with his conception of life based on an unending process of change and conflict, and much of the earlier part of *War and Peace* reads like a panegyric in Homeric vein on the glorious past of battles. War, he claims, can bring out the virtues of men; it is an expression of that 'right of strength' which cannot be disregarded among the elements of human progress; in the past it produced the conception of right and engendered society itself out of the need for mutual protection. At times the passion for stating both sides of an argument leads Proudhon into talking like a frenzied devotee of militarism, but even here, as he states the affirmative side of war, there are twists of argument that reassure the perceptive reader. For the war Proudhon praises is only that idealised and chivalrous conflict in which men of equal strength meet in combat with equal weapons. But since such war has taken place only in myth, Proudhon is forced to admit that from the beginning armed conflict has been rendered impure and ignoble by the ferocity, rapine and perfidy that have accompanied it. And thus the antimilitarist who has not grown so impatient as to put aside the book finds the author swinging suddenly to his side. For, despite the noble qualities inherent in the idea of war as an aspect of the eternal conflict, its corrupt elements negate its possible benefits.

The cause of the depravity of war is economic; it is the phenomenon of pauperism. And here Proudhon makes an important distinction between pauperism and poverty. Poverty, the state in which man gains by his work enough for his needs, is the ideal human condition, in which we are most free, in which, being masters of our senses and appetites, we are best able to spiritualise our existence. But the only way to bring this ideal condition to all men is by assuring within the community an equal share in products and services. Equality and sufficiency are inseparable. But this law has been consistently violated, and the lust for wealth has destroyed the equilibrium of freedom. The greed of the powerful has produced pauperism as the accompaniment of their own wealth, and it is to avoid the consequences of this internal disequilibrium without depriving the rich that states indulge in merciless war. Thus, in modern times, war is the consequence of the capitalist regime, which produces economic chaos.

The way to remedy this situation is to renew the economic equilibrium between the members of society. When that has been achieved, there will no longer be need for wars of conquest. But the peace that ensues will not mean the end of antagonism and conflict; it will mean their transformation into forces operating constructively in economic and social development instead of in war. 'Henceforward heroism must give place to industry,' and mankind must embark on an age of indefinite pacification. The paladins may keep their honoured place in legend, but 'I want a plebeian Hercules no more than a governmental Hercules.'

War and Peace was a book made to arouse controversy, and the apparent contradictoriness of its theme was given an almost grotesque emphasis by the way in which it was presented. None of Proudhon's books was so unclearly written, so permeated by conflicting trends of thought, so much affected by feelings of personal bitterness, flowering at times into a peculiar belligerence of expression. Yet basically his position sprang from a positive realisation that the orthodox pacifist attitude of negatively opposing war was fruitless, since war is a social phenomenon whose nature must be understood before one can talk of bringing it to an end.

The reception of *War and Peace*, both among the socialists, who prematurely raised the cry that Proudhon had betrayed the cause, and among the journalists of the rival political sects, who were delighted by another opportunity to attack the age's most uncompromising individualist, brought about in an acute form the return of Proudhon's sense of isolation from his time. He began to brood once again over his situation, and, after six months of largely fruitless arguments with his friends and of unmitigatingly harsh and hostile interpretations on the part of his enemies, he had reached the state of mind when he could write to Gouvernet at the end of 1861: 'More than ever I ask myself whether I am of this world, whether I count in it, or whether I should consider myself a lost spirit who returns to scare the living and to whom the living refuse their prayers.' There was, of course, another side of his character that throve on such isolation, and nothing is more typical of the man than the fact that, in the same letter, he could also declare defiantly: 'We are the Revolution: it is annoying that this sacramental word should have been misused, but it is for us to give it the true meaning.'

9

On the 12th December, 1860, Napoleon III finally issued the pardon which Proudhon had expected a year before. The recipient viewed it with mingled pleasure and suspicion. His immediate impulse was one of acceptance, and on the 19th December he told Chaudey that he would return as soon as his affairs and the convenience of his household made it possible. But within a few days his eagerness was dwindling; an amnesty, he realised, did not mean that he would be able to write freely, and he told Rolland that he would not return until he had published one or two books in Paris and French publishers were reassured about his works. A little later he remarked, with an air of indifference that, so long as his freedom to enter France was acknowledged, it did not matter greatly to him whether he was in Brussels or the Faubourg Montmartre. Now he proposed to remain in Belgium not only the rest of the winter, but also the 'good season' of 1861, and when Garniers refused to print *War and Peace* he remarked bitterly: 'What use would it be to return to my country if my thought remained stricken with ostracism?' Indeed, it was only the thought of his friends that really made him regret Paris. 'It is impossible, after fifty and in a strange country, to make true friends once again.' he told Gouvernet. 'It is like the first love which one never replaces.'

It is to this period, when Proudhon was marking time in the half-world of those who are exiled by financial rather than political necessity, that we owe a group of letters which paint an interesting picture of the more intimate life of this expatriate family. Particularly vivid is the glimpse of its domestic arrangements given in a letter to Buzon, the Bordeaux wine merchant, on New Year's Day, 1861.

'I had the intention of replying on the occasion of the New Year to your joyous letter, but behold the troubles of a philosopher in the home, whose wife is her own cook, chamber maid, etc.! As I receive many letters and am obliged to tie them into packets every now and then, and as, on the other hand, I have neither desk nor drawers, I put your letter by mistake with a mass of others to which I had replied, at the bottom of a great chest among my papers and manuscripts. On these papers my wife laid some apples, as a provision for the winter, and on top of the chest a pile of linen washed the day before, for I must tell you that what is called my *study* is a little room where my wife lays out her laundry. So I work among books, papers, soap, household provisions, and everything connected with them. I live in the most complete promiscuity. It is not very edifying, I know, in a thinker, a reformer, but what would you have? One of my follies has been the desire to have children.'

Within this cramped and frugal household the strains of the previous year had not entirely subsided, and Euphrasie was becoming increasingly discontented with her position as a housewife, showing exasperation when she had to spend her time at the stove and could not take part in the conversations between Proudhon and his friends. 'This is what comes of marrying a revolutionary,' Proudhon confided to Victor Pilhes. 'My wife rebels in her own manner, and in the things that interest her you will one day see that my paternal and conjugal authority has been demolished. Ah, how quickly I would be consoled if I saw the good people of Paris animated by such sentiments!'

But while her mother revolted against the kitchen, Catherine was becoming more useful and willing in the household, and was relieving Euphrasie of some of the many tasks that fell on her now she had to spend much of her time in embroidery to pay for the children's school fees. 'Catherine . . . sees to the lamp, lights the fire when her mother is detained, warms my soup, hems handkerchiefs, knits, but does not know how to protect herself from the greengrocers, who rob her unmercifully.'

Proudhon was anxious to give his children an early sense of the practical knowledge which his poor health made him fear might become necessary in the event of their being left without provision. Accordingly, he made an elaborate financial arrangement by which he paid them for any good points they gained at school and for any services they performed in the house. These earnings they were encouraged to save against the time when they would become independent, and Catherine, who was old enough to think about such things, was promised 'a drapery, needlework and repairing establishment.' Whatever one may say in criticism of Proudhon's patriarchal view of household administration, there was good sense in the way he refrained from bringing up his daughters as ladies, and encouraged in them the realisation that almost certainly they would have to live by their own abilities. 'I set less store by fashionable talents,' he declared, 'than by good feelings and the work of one's hands.'

10

By the summer of 1861 Proudhon had accepted the need for an indefinite prolongation of his stay in Brussels and had returned to work on his literary projects with as much application as if he had a life to spend in exile. Having, in *War and Peace*, stated his basic views of international relations, he now turned to the specific problems of contemporary nationalism. He was one of the few liberals who realised the danger of reaction implicit in the general nationalist tradition inherited from 1848, and also in the particular instances of Italy and Poland, whose unification into large states was one of the cherished hopes of the Jacobins in France and their counterparts in other countries. These questions had been touched on in *War and Peace*; now Proudhon was anxious to deal with them intensively, and he began an epistolary campaign against the nationalists which immediately involved a series of disputes with some of his most valued friends, and brought an estrangement from his old colleague, Charles Edmond, who was offended by his attitude on the Polish question, and from Herzen, whom he reproached for lending himself 'to all these intrigues, which represent neither political liberty nor economic right nor social reform.'

During the late summer of 1861 his interest in the nationalist question led him to make extensive journeys in Belgium and the German Rhineland, a region which seemed to provide excellent material for his researches into one aspect of his problem, i.e., the existence or otherwise of so-called 'natural frontiers.' Early in June he went to Ostend, Ghent and Antwerp, and later to Namur, and in August he travelled along the Rhine to study the significance of that disputed river in the general context of the national question. Accompanied by Delhasse, he journeyed through Aachen to Cologne, and thence by way of Bonn, Coblenz and Mainz to Frankfurt, from which he returned by steamboat down the Rhine. As a result of these travels he reached the conclusion that the real culture of the area was largely homogenous, that 'all the towns are alike, all the shops offer the same goods, all the men have the same features, and all the women wear crinolines,' and that the celebrated 'natural frontier' of the Rhine formed no barrier to the interpenetration of social influences.

Like most Frenchmen, he did not take well to travel; had it not been for the gathering of facts useful to his future writing, he would greatly have preferred to remain among 'the shades, the restfulness, the fresh milk of Spa,' rather than 'tiring myself out on the railways, and sleeping in great hotels, which make me regret the old inns of my country.' In his discomfort and vexation, however, he did not forget his family, and exhorted Euphrasie to 'see that the children work, that they are occupied, that they sometimes indulge in recreation, but that they are *never idle*. Idleness is an abominable vice.'

It was a vice from which he himself did not suffer, for as soon as he returned to Brussels, he resumed writing with redoubled energy. Some articles on Poland by Elias Regnault in *La Presse* decided him to begin work on a book intended to expose finally the reactionary character of Polish nationalism and to wean the French democrats from their prejudices. But, though it was completed during 1862, this work was never printed. Proudhon was more sensitive than he liked to appear to the demands of revolutionary comradeship, and when the Poles rebelled in 1863 he decided not to publish his book lest he should seem to attack them in their adversity. He was also worried about the effect it might have on many of his old friends, particularly Herzen, Edmond and Bakunin who, having escaped from Siberia in 1861, had embarked on an abortive expedition to aid the Polish insurrectionaries. For these reasons he decided to abandon the result of so much work and to leave his treatise unpublished. The manuscript is still in possession of his family, a monument to the seriousness with which he took the obligations of friendship.

By a somewhat involved path, this work on the Polish question led Proudhon back to a reconsideration of the basic ideas on property with which he had made his first appearance as a writer. The conclusions derived from this return to his intellectual past are embodied in the posthumous *Théorie de la Propriété*. Much has been made of this essay in an attempt to show that it represents a retreat from Proudhon's original radicalism. Fundamentally, it does not, though its expression is certainly much more temperate than that of, say, *The Warning to Proprietors*. What Proudhon does is to change his definition of property; when he now justifies it as the safeguard of liberty, he is thinking, not of the usurial property he condemned in his earlier works, but of the property that guarantees the independence of the peasant and the artisan. He raises a new antinomy—property versus the State. Property represents individualism, the State is the extreme negation of individual liberty, and Proudhon therefore seeks an adjustment of property which will help men to control their own destinies independently of the State.

This, he hopes, can be accomplished by a series of social checks designed to prevent abuses in either direction. The mutualist institutions of free credit and association will prevent abuses of property; decentralisation and federal organisation will save men from the impositions of the State. Property without principle is evil; property governed by principle can become the support of society 'against the assaults of an unbridled industrialism.'

Because of his changes in definition, Proudhon appears more conservative, but the alterations are not radical, since he continues to uphold the basic right of the producer to control his land or his workshop. He agrees for the present to retain property in a mitigated form because he can see no other protection for the freedom of ordinary men in a world where the sense of justice is not so well developed as he would wish. But, against any suspicion that he was ageing into complacency, we need only read the final paragraphs of the essay, in which he declares his personal feelings towards the idea of property.

'I have developed the considerations that make property intelligible, rational, legitimate, and outside of which it remains usurpatory and odious. Yet even in these conditions, it retains something egotistical which is still antipathetic to me. My egalitarian and anti-governmental reason, inimical to rancour and to the abuse of force, can admit and support property as a shield, a point of security for the weak; my heart can never cleave to it . . .

'*Private Property!* I sometimes read these words written in great letters at the beginning of an open way, like a sentinel forbidding one to pass. I swear that my human dignity bristles with disgust. Ah, in such matters I have remained of the religion of Christ, which recommends detachment, preaches modesty, simplicity of spirit, and poverty of heart. Away with the old patrician, greedy and pitiless, away with the insolent baron, the grasping bourgeois and the hard peasant! Such people are odious to me; I can neither love nor see them.'

II

The end of 1861 found Proudhon in a better position financially than he had enjoyed for several years. *War and Peace* and *The Theory of Taxation* had done a great deal towards re-establishing his solvency, and he began to hope that he would soon be free of debt. It was the mirage he had been seeing habitually for the past two decades, and once again it was to fail him, for the early part of 1862 brought renewed attacks of nervous exhaustion, accompanied by the most alarming symptoms. 'I stagger in the street; I have terrible nightmares; I see spectres besetting me in the shadows . . . There are moments when I cannot move a foot or a hand.'

His doctor told him to do nothing for six months, but such sustained idleness was impossible for Proudhon, and he worked obstinately whenever his health would permit him. Nevertheless, there were long and unavoidable periods of inaction, during which he suffered from the most melancholy reflections on his condition. He was conscious of his age, of the possibility that he might spend the rest of his life in chronic invalidism, and of the almost total lack of improvement in the world since he had first become conscious of its deficiencies. He complained that the enthusiasms of youth had died down in him, that all his chivalrous generosity had gone and he felt 'nothing but an ardour for merciless justice.'

When his friends insisted that he should return to Paris, he showed himself almost morbidly reluctant to do so. A number of incidents had made him doubt the sincerity of the Imperial intentions. Blanqui had been imprisoned again, and Greppo, returning in all innocence to take advantage of the amnesty for political offenders, had been arrested and kept for three months in Mazas Prison. Moreover, the French police still showed an undue interest in his own activities. One friend who visited him was questioned on his return to France. Letters from other friends had been opened clumsily in the mail. Finally, he recognised that once in France he would find it hard to keep his pen out of dangerous polemical squabbles. 'I would very much like to grapple with the gentlemen of *Le Siècle* and *Les Débats*,' he told Rolland, 'but at the first word I can see the Imperial prosecutor making an *auto-da-fe* of my person.'

When Jerome Bonaparte took a hand by remarking to Darimon that he thought it high time the exile returned, and that his difficulties in getting work published in Paris were largely due to his staying away so long, Proudhon burst into indignant protest at Plonplon's unimaginative failure to appreciate his position. 'It is easy for the Prince Napoleon to reproach me for delaying my return so long. Does he know that my removal here cost me 1,500 francs, that my re-removal will cost no less; that in the meantime I have experienced some grave difficulties and that I have only begun to get my head above water during the last few months? And besides, for what reason should I be in such a hurry to run back? Is it perchance the agreeableness of life under Imperial discipline?'

One begins to suspect that by this time the demands of necessity were supported by a certain perverse obstinacy, and that the very fact that the Bonapartes seemed anxious for his return, so that they could point to it as evidence of their new democratic policy, may have seemed an excellent additional reason for staying in exile, despite his own continued sickness and his wife's rheumatism in the damp Brussels climate. He was even reluctant to make a short visit to France, which he could have afforded without great difficulty, and the summer saw him travelling, not with Euphrasie to Paris, but with Delhasse to Spa, there to watch with delighted horror the antics of the *haut monde*. 'All those who come to Spa are either aristocrats or exploiters, swindlers or courtesans,' he told Euphrasie when she expressed a desire to join him. 'It is a brazen luxury beside which a modest household would be out of place. As for me, with my flat hat, my thick shoes and my turned-down collar, I pass everywhere because I am 53 and I am M. Proudhon. But a woman and two misses are different.'

He returned during the third week of August, feeling renewed in health and able to resume his writing. But he was not left long in peace, for within a month his outspoken pen had again involved him in trouble. During the summer of 1862 he was disturbed by a number of trends in the international situation, and particularly by the issue of Italian unity. Mazzini, Garibaldi and the majority of Italian revolutionaries wished to construct a centralised national state out of the freedom that at last seemed within their grasp. They were supported by most of the French democrats, but, in Proudhon's view, this policy was suicidal; with an eye that events have since proved prophetic, he saw that a strong Italian state would not only lead to the oppression of the people by internal Caesarism, but would also form a new disruptive element in international politics. His own solution was federalism, favoured in Italy by the existing pattern of small principalities; this would prevent either the rise of Italian chauvinism or the appearance of a central government hostile to social progress.

On the 13th July, 1862, he published in Lebègue's paper, *L'Office de la Publicité*, an article entitled "Mazzini and Italian Unity," in which he criticised sharply the policy of the Italian leader and his French supporters. His essay aroused the anger of Jacobins throughout Europe, but the criticism he provoked made him even more convinced of the necessity of proceeding to an extended examination of the question of nationalities. He felt the danger was acute. 'Once United Italy is constituted,' he told Buzon in August, 'the reaction will make itself felt throughout Europe, and the social question, the real question of emancipation, will be adjourned for several generations.' Accordingly, he returned to the subject in a second article, on "Garibaldi and Italian Unity," which appeared on the 7th September.

This time the uproar was greater than ever, for the Italian nationalists were joined by the aggrieved chorus of Belgian patriots. In order to illustrate the dangers of the unionist principle, Proudhon pointed out that the corollary of an Italian unification might be an expansion of France to embrace the outlying fragments of Charlemagne's empire, including Belgium. This argument was embodied in an ironic exhortation to Napoleon III: 'Dare, Sire, as Mazzini said to Victor Emmanuel, dare, and the Rhine, Luxembourg, Belgium, Holland, all that Teutonic France, the ancient patrimony of Charlemagne, is yours.' What Proudhon meant was that the annexation of the Low Countries by France was no more absurd than the unification of Italy as a single state. But the Belgians chose to regard it as a direct incitement to invade their country, and the Press burst into a chorus of denunciation, not only in Brussels, but also in every little town in Belgium and Luxembourg that supported a newspaper. Pamphlets attacking Proudhon were published, and notes passed busily between government officials as to whether he should be asked to explain his statements. Such a mass misunderstanding is difficult to comprehend, and it seems all the more ironical since Proudhon was in fact one of the few French democrats unreservedly opposed to annexation.

This formidable Press campaign robbed Proudhon's position in Belgium of all semblance of security, and his danger was dramatically confirmed when a group of Belgian nationalists demonstrated outside his house on the evening of the 16th September, beating drums, singing the Brabançonne, and shouting 'Down with the annexationists!' A couple of policemen dispersed the crowd and put three of its leaders in the cells for a few hours. Next evening the demonstrators returned, but they found the street barred, police on duty and their quarry gone.

During the previous weeks Proudhon had been thinking of

visiting Paris to deal with the publication of his books, and the demonstration on the 16th decided him to leave immediately, so that he would be able to answer his critics in a less disturbed environment. On the morning of the 17th September he departed and, with a rather unimaginative disregard for their mental tranquillity, left Euphrasie and his children at Ixelles.

Part Eight

THE STRICKEN YEARS

I

'THE enormous grandeur of Paris always strikes anyone who, after having left it, returns again from a large town like Lyons, Brussels, etc. It is like Notre Dame compared to a village church.' So Proudhon expressed the effect of returning out of exile, and in a long letter to Euphrasie he dilated on the improvements of French living since 1858 and extolled the Bois de Boulogne and the walks at Passy, where he had gone to visit Antoine Gauthier, now a resident of Paris. There had also been gratifying reunions with other friends—Rolland and Beslay, Darimon and Cretin and Chaudey, and Proudhon was already suggesting that the family's removal from Brussels might take place sooner than he had anticipated.

Any indecision he may have had on this point was resolved by the actions of Lebèque, who was scared by the continued Press campaigns against Proudhon in Belgium, and published a note in *L'Office de la Publicité* renouncing any further collaboration between them. Upon hearing of this, Proudhon resolved to remain in France. 'It is useless to turn back,' he told Euphrasie. 'Even though I do not believe there will be any further outrage, I do not wish to remain longer in Belgium. Either they would continue to regard me as a French agent, or they would be humiliated by my presence. When two people have mutually hurt each other, they can no longer live together; it is the same between the inhabitants of a country and the stranger who lives in their midst.'

Early in October Proudhon was able to take to the printers a volume entitled *La Fédération et 'Unité en Italie*, which formed his reply to the Belgian Press. Though primarily polemical, aimed at showing the flaws in the actions of the Italian nationalists, it also put forward a positive vision of a 'confederation of free cities' in which men would be able to live more fully and happily than in the unity of 'empires of forty million men.' 'In a little state, there is nothing for the bourgeoisie to profit from . . . Civilisation progresses, and services are rendered to the world, in inverse proportion to the immensity of empires . . . Any agglomeration of men, comprised within a clearly circumscribed territory and able to live an independent life in that spot, is meant for autonomy. The principle of federation, corollary to that of the separation of powers, is opposed to the disastrous principles of the agglomeration of peoples and of administrative centralisation.'

The most controversial passage was that in which Proudhon denounced Mazzini's form of anti-papalism. Proudhon's critics tried to make this an excuse to represent the author of *Justice in the Revolution and the Church* as a supporter of the Papacy. The injustice of this accusation is evident from a careful reading of the following crucial passage: 'Whatever may be the opinion of a statesman in matters of faith, unless he serves a government of the revolution, armed for revolutionary propaganda, it is not permissable for him to act against religious thought and institutions. . . . The idea which the Pope represents, says Mazzini, is exhausted; it must be sacrificed with the rest. Capital! But at the same time something must be put in the place of that idea, and for that we need . . . something more than the motto *Dio e popolo*, adopted by Mazzini.'

Clearly, what Proudhon argues is that it was unjustifiable to destroy the traditional ways of thought of the Italian people in the name of some nebulous liberal creed, or to suppress the States of the Church merely to incorporate them in an Italian kingdom. The Papacy, he suggests, can only be overthrown with profit in the name of a revolutionary conception of Justice such as he himself had already advocated in 1858.

Proudhon had hoped that *Federation and Unity in Italy* might, with luck, pay for the costs of his journey to Paris, but it attained a quite unexpected popularity, and in February had sold more than twelve thousand copies. Materially it was an auspicious beginning for his return from exile, and it brought him back to the very centre of public discussion. The Liberal press attacked him in strength, and he suspected it was instigated by the Piedmontese embassy. The dynastic and clerical journalists, on the other hand, sought to turn to their own purposes his exposure of the fallacy of Italian unity, and he complained that the true spirit of his federalist idea was being ignored. It was because of this confusion about his theory that he accepted the suggestion of Dentu to write a further book to expound in detail his general federal principles.

But before he could begin this work he had to arrange for his family's return. With the help of Madame Gauthier, he had discovered a suitable set of rooms at No. 10, Grande Rue, Passy. 'It is very pretty, but dear—800 francs,' he told Euphrasie on the 10th October, and a few days later he left for Brussels. Finally, on the 25th October, the Proudhon family departed from Belgium, arriving in the evening at the Hôtel du Saxe in the Boulevard Magenta. Here they stayed for three days, 'more concerned with medication than with business,' since Catherine and Stephanie were both unwell, Euphrasie was completely exhausted by the efforts of removal and travel, and Proudhon's own affliction of the head had returned with great intensity. By the 27th, however, the whole family was sufficiently recovered to move into the apartment at Passy.

The constant upheavals which his life had involved since the Revolution were beginning to tell on Proudhon. His chronic illness, whose periodical returns made him feel certain that no final cure was possible and that his health must worsen progressively as he grew older, rendered the complications of his present life all the more unendurable, even though his restless character made them hard to avoid. It was not until November that he was able to start work again, and even at this time the appearance of returning health was deceptive, for by January, 1863, before he had been able to finish his treatise on federalism, his old symptoms came back with distressing intensity. 'I am frightfully exhausted,' he told Darimon. 'My head feels as big as a barrel; I have reached such a state of debilitation that walking gives me sea sickness and I can no longer direct my steps.'

It was the beginning of a final period of physical decay that was to continue in an alarming progression for the remaining two years of his life. But, no matter how his body might decline, his mind remained as acute, his will as strong as ever, and during these final two years, despite interruptions through sickness, despite those perpetual discouragements which are the lot of any man who sets himself apart from the current of the time, his literary production was considerable both in quantity and importance, and he still played an important part in the shaping of events during these critical years in the disintegration of the Napoleonic regime.

2

Proudhon's study of federalism was not merely an exercise in social theory; he also saw it as a means of presenting a practical policy around which could be grouped the forces opposed to the current democratic trend towards nationalism and centralisation. When he introduced it to his publisher, he remarked: 'Here is a powerful, fertile idea which comes at the right time, which, rising up against great errors . . . will carry with it a great part of the masses and, in that way, operate a revolution in ideas.'

The book was not completed without a vast mental travail. 'For three months,' Proudhon told Buzon at the end of January, 'I have been sweating blood and water to give birth to a wretched pamphlet which I fear very much you will judge unworthy to see the light of day.' As had happened so often in the composition of his earlier books, his ideas proliferated alarmingly as soon as he came to write them down, and he began to see that the brisk, argumentative essay he had originally proposed represented a wrong approach to the problem. Again, in the proofs, he totally reconstructed his book, and then, when the printing had actually started, he stopped production to alter and enlarge, until finally a volume of 300 pages emerged, of whose faults the author was well aware 'It is a book and not a book . . . I tell myself that the contents will perhaps save the form . . . But my brain is on fire and my head is like a ripe pear.'

Proudhon's doubts were largely justified. For all his efforts, *The Federal Principal* remained an awkward compromise between a constructive political treatise and a collection of topical wrangles. Its form was diffuse, and of the three parts into which it was divided only the first is permanently important. The second regurgitates the Italian question, the third replies at length to 'the unitary press,' and even the first is more capable than original, since it consists of a systematic recapitulation of the ideas on anarchy and federalism which had already appeared elsewhere in various tentative forms. Perhaps, indeed, Proudhon himself made his own best summary of the social conception he was aiming at in a letter written to his old workmate Milliet while the book was still being constructed.

'If in 1840 I began with anarchy, the conclusion of my critique of the governmental idea, I had to finish with federation, the necessary basis of the rights of European peoples and, later, of the organisation of all states . . . Public order resting directly on the liberty and conscience of the citizen, *anarchy*, the absence of all constraint, police, authority, magistrature, regimentation, etc., will be the correlative of the highest social virtue—and, beyond that, the ideal of human government. Of course we are not there, and centuries will pass before that ideal may be attained, but our *law* is to go in that direction, to grow unceasingly nearer to that end, and it is thus that I uphold the principle of federation.'

It must be emphasised that by federation Proudhon does not mean a world government or a confederation of states. For him the principle of confederation begins from the simplest level of society. The organs of administration are local and lie as near the direct control of the people as possible. Above that primary level the confederal organisation becomes progressively less an organ of administration than of co-ordination among local units. Thus the nation itself will be a confederation of regions, and Europe a confederation of confederations in which the interest of the smallest province will have as much expression as that of the largest, since all affairs will be settled by mutual agreement, contract and arbitration.

The Federal Principle finally appeared on the 14th February, 1863, and was immediately successful; less than three weeks after publication six thousand copies had been bought, and new impressions were being made. Proudhon, however, was not content that

his message should be confided only to the relatively static form
of a book. He wanted to support it with a periodical in which it
could be kept alive by constant adaptation to the changing shape
of events. Accordingly, almost immediately after his return to
Paris, he revived the project of a review of which he would be
controlling editor, and in February, 1863, he wrote to the Minister
of the Interior asking permission to produce a weekly entitled
Federation. But if the Bonapartists were willing to allow Proudhon
to return to Paris and even to publish his books again, as a sign
of their own tolerance, they regarded without favour the possibility of his regaining an influence such as he had wielded through
his journalism in the revolutionary era of 1848–50, and his
application was rejected. Proudhon could not regard this refusal
as final, and for months he continued to make abortive plans for
a journal at some time in the future, but the authorities remained
adamant, and he was never allowed to resume that profession of
journalism which he often regarded as having been the glory of
his career.

3

While Proudhon was thus prevented from returning to journalism, he was not hindered from entering actively into the field
of political affairs. A parliamentary election was due to take place
in May, 1863, and even before he had finished work on *The
Federal Principle* Proudhon began once again to advocate a complete abstention from voting. Such a tactic, he contended, had
not merely temporary value; it might lead to the emergence of a
new movement devoted to the genuine reconstruction of society
in the direction of federalism and anarchy. 'This time,' he declared, 'I mean to raise boldly the flag of schism, to break with
that coterie of intriguers and begin a movement of purgation, as
Robespierre said, which might well end in a regeneration of
democratic reason and consciousness.'

Early in February Proudhon and his immediate friends, among
whom Beslay, Massol, Cretin, Langlois and Chaudey were the
most active, began their campaign for the foundation of a party
of 'Young Democracy,' which would seek to use abstention from
parliamentary activity as a positive means of weakening the Bonapartist regime and precipitating a movement towards federalism.
Committees of Abstention were set up in Paris and Bordeaux,

where Buzon took the initiative. Though the active core of these committees consisted of old Proudhonians or working-class militants with whom Proudhon had made contact during the past three years, these were by no means the only elements who joined in the campaign. Among the Republicans there were a number of men, distant from Proudhon in most respects, who were impressed by the arguments he had put forward for abstention as a means of fighting against the despotism. The most prominent was Jules Bastide, who had been Minister of Foreign Affairs in the Provisional Government of 1848, and whom Proudhon had then described as 'one of most honourable men of the party.' With such support Proudhon (who admitted at this time: 'For more than thirty years I have got into the habit of upholding lost causes') began to feel that there was a chance of giving his views a much greater impact than he had first anticipated.

Proudhon's first contribution to the abstentionist campaign was a detailed exposition of his arguments for presentation to the general public. It appeared in April, 1863, under the title of *Les Démocrates Assermentés et les Réfractaires* (*Oath-taking Democrats and Non-Jurors*).

As the title suggests, Proudhon's main object was to mark clearly the line between those willing to co-operate in a limited degree with the Empire by becoming candidates for the legislative corps and those, like himself, content only with complete opposition to the State as constituted. He described it as 'a little philosophy of universal suffrage, in which I show that this great principle of democracy is a corollary of the federal principle or nothing.' But he went beyond this objective by exposing the falseness of a pretended democracy where the Press was not free, where executive power remained firmly in the hands of the dynast, where the representatives of the people could not discuss and criticise the actions of the government, and where the alleged sovereignty of universal suffrage was belied by the oath of allegiance to an emperor He contended that in such circumstances only the people's refusal to participate in the mockery of the elections would shake the power of the dynasty and prepare a revival of the revolutionary way.

Les Démocrates Assermentés was a well-argued pamphlet, concise and brisk, and it was read with much attention. But it did not stimulate any great uprising of public opinion, and the active mass following from which Proudhon had expected to mould his new revolutionary party seems as yet to have been almost non-existent. On the other hand, if the circumstances in favour of the abstentionists were slight, the difficulties they had to endure were considerable. The authorities wisely decided not to interfere directly with Proudhon's activities, for any action on their part that remotely savoured of martyrdom would have increased his influence at this time of delicate balance between social forces. But the newspapers of the parliamentary opposition attacked him bitterly. Girardin was particularly insulting in *La Presse*, but when Proudhon sent a reply he refused to print it, sheltering under the excuse that some of its arguments constituted offences against the Press laws. This policy of suppressing the propaganda of the abstentionists by turning against them their own method of boycott was not restricted to the newspapers. When the Committee published a manifesto prepared by Buzon, not only did the bookshops refuse it, but the newsvendors in the streets were warned by the police against selling it.

Proudhon gained some consolation from the results of the elections, which he hailed as a moral victory for abstention, although in fact the number of non-voters was much lower than in 1857. In Paris, out of 317,000 electors, 85,000 abstained, while 150,000 voted against the Bonapartist candidates. The proportion of abstentions had been high in Bordeaux, Lyons and Rouen, the three other areas in which the propaganda of the Committee had been effectively carried out. The result, Proudhon thought, augured well for the future. 'Do not let us ask too much,' he told Bastide. 'Now it is a question of not allowing that victory to vanish like a show of fireworks.'

But the component elements of the Committee of Abstention were too disparate to agree on any wide or sustained programme, and once the electoral campaign had passed, it disintegrated rapidly. Yet it bequeathed to the movements that followed it, and particularly to anarchism and syndicalism, at least two important elements—the rejection of expediency as a dominant element in political behaviour, and the rejection of the democratic myth of the vote as a universal political panacea.

4

The schematic pattern of a biography often gives the impression that the interests which may dominate certain periods of men's lives are more all-embracing than is in fact the case. With a man of restless and perpetually enquiring mentality, like Proudhon, this kind of false emphasis must particularly be guarded against, and if the preceding chapters have given the idea that sickness as a negative force and federalism and abstention as motives for action completely ruled the months after his return to Paris, it must be emphasised that these were only the leading themes of a time when his return to a familiar environment had stimulated his thoughts in many directions. Glancing through the record of these months, one can detect not only the emergence of many new ideas, but also the resurrection of old ones which had been put aside in the past.

His book on Poland still haunted him; he worked at revising his views on property, and sketched out an attack on the feminists and a study of the relationship between Caesarism and Christianity. He collected some essays on literary copyright which he had written in Belgium into a book, *Les Majorats Littéraires*, which appeared in the spring of 1863. It was an ably written work, full of literary knowledge and persuasive arguments against restrictions on publication, but its success was slight; clearly it was on the burning questions of contemporary political urgency that Proudhon could command most attention.

There was a certain fragmentariness about Proudhon's work at this time, a difficulty in maintaining concentration over long periods, and this fact, which explains why so many of his later writings were only published posthumously and incompletely, must certainly be attributed to the state of his health, which made any sustained effort increasingly difficult. 'I do not lack work,' he said in July, 1863, 'and if I could listen to it alone, I should labour ten hours a day and never leave the house ... But I am in such a state of fatigue and disgust that reading, writing and correspondence are all horrifying to me. I have only enough strength to drag myself to the Bois de Boulogne, where I lie in the shade on the dry grass and sleep whole hours away.'

As for his mental state, he presented to Defontaine in September a sad spectacle of depression. 'I become gloomy and morose and, except for old and tried friends, I receive nobody with true pleasure. The spectacle of our epoch saddens me; I lose confidence in my nation; I feel myself growing older, and I see my health giving way and my strength declining.' A few weeks later he complained to Buzon, in a near-agony of frustration: 'This middle way which is neither rest nor work annoys me more than anything else. Either death, or work and production, I cry endlessly to myself. And neither strength, death nor the devil comes.' He had the feeling that shadows were moving in his head, and at times seemed to feel a friendly and very gentle hand resting on his shoulder and a voice saying to him: 'Enough!'

It was perhaps the feeling that he was approaching the final reckoning with time and death that filled Proudhon's letters during this unhappy year of 1863 with passages of reflection that often show a revealing insight into some of the more puzzling aspects of his own thought and character. He returned, for instance, to the question of contradiction of ideas, and told one friend: 'The truth is one, but it appears to us in fragments and from very different angles. Our duty is to express it as we see it, no matter whether we contradict ourselves in reality or in appearance.' And to another friend he defined the character of his thinking very clearly in the following sentence: 'The nature of my mind could be characterised in one phrase; mobility itself, but always returning to equilibrium.'

The idea of mobility is linked with Proudhon's conception of life as a conflict, never terminated but sometimes stabilised by an equilibrium between opposing forces, and in this symbolic war it was not surprising that he should see himself as a perpetual warrior.

'The life of man, in all professions, is ever the same,' he told Maurice. 'It is a real war; one must exterminate the adversary or resign oneself to being devoured . . . Since it is impossible to escape from it, I do it well, and the more I advance in age and experience, the more decided I am.'

Often Proudhon's feeling of being in the midst of perpetual conflict led him to behave with preposterous arrogance. But beneath this pasteboard armour of bombast was concealed an essential modesty, which emerged in his more intimate friendships and which was displayed in a letter he wrote to Buzon after his Bordelais friend had praised him more than he felt he deserved.

'Frankly, you make me ashamed of myself,' he protested, 'and if you wish us to understand one another, never lose sight, in writing to me, of the fact that you are addressing an old countryman, endowed with an ingenious mind, who has studied a little, who has fairly well rid himself of silliness, but in whom study has only increased the faults of his nature and rendered his rusticity all the more prominent.'

Such an admission of his failings reminds one that Proudhon's apparent pride was largely due to a perpetual inner recognition of his deficiencies. The boy who had rebuffed Weiss in Besançon, the mature man who had so rudely put aside the advances of Madame d'Agoult and who in later life looked so sourly on the elegances of Paris and Spa, are all acknowledged in this letter to Buzon; the only compromise he makes is to attribute entirely to a rustic upbringing the blemishes which were as much the result of privations that roughened his arrogance into a forbidding defence for an amiable, generous and even gentle nature.

For, though he felt his own misfortunes sharply, Proudhon was not oblivious to the predicaments of others, even outside his family circle. Towards the end of 1863, when he was burdened by sickness and financial anxiety and harassed by a continuing governmental hostility (the ministry had just intimated to the scholastic profession that he was 'a dangerous writer') he still found time to raise a subscription for his rival Pierre Leroux, to provide for him in a helpless old age.

Nor was he oblivious to the moral difficulties of his friends, and when Penet gave way to despair, Proudhon wrote him a reproachful letter in which he revealed the philosophy that, despite ill fortune, kept him working and fighting with the same devotion, if not the same vigour, as had inspired him from the day when, as a young man, he first began his struggle for Justice.

'It is now, however little you may realise it,' he exhorted Penet, 'that you must begin to live the true life of a man and speak to yourself in the language of one who sums up his last wishes and writes his testament. Would you be one of those people for whom the existence of man has only one end: to produce, acquire and enjoy? Neither one nor the other. We must work because that is our law, because it is on that condition that we learn, that we fortify and discipline ourselves and assure our existence and that of our dependants. But that is not our end; I do not refer to our transcendental, religious or supernatural end—I mean our earthly, temporal and entirely human end. To be men, to raise ourselves above earthly fatalities, to reproduce in ourselves the image of God, as the Bible has it, and finally to realise on this earth the reign of the spirit; that is our end. But it is neither in youth nor in manhood, it is neither in great works of production nor in the struggles of affairs that we can attain it; it is, I repeat, in complete maturity, when the passions begin to grow quiet, and when the spirit, more and more disengaged, spreads its wings towards the infinite.'

In this passage the mystical under-current of Proudhon's thought comes very near the surface. He saw man advancing beyond religion as they would advance beyond metaphysics, but the condition at which he saw them arriving, after they had cast away all the childish trappings of the past, would by no means be the arid desert of the dogmatic materialist; rather, the spiritual life would burgeon into new and purer forms in man's realisation of his own direct contact with that vast and final equilibrium of all the struggling forces of the universe which is called eternity.

5

Proudhon's view of life, indeed, was always many-sided and never uncolourful. He wished to see a world where the rational organisation of economic and social problems would free the dynamic impulses for a more productive function in man's existence. The raising of the struggle of the opposites on to a higher plane would lead to an intensification of intellectual activity, and so, while Proudhon concentrated his main effort on enunciating the primary principles of Justice and determining the means by which they could be applied in social life, he also directed his attention into those fields of literature and the arts through which man's existence could be enlarged in scope and his understanding of himself and his environment illuminated. His early flirtation with drama had shown a leaning in this direction, and later, in *Les Majorats Littéraires* and in many pages of *Justice*, he had discussed various aspects of the relationship between literature and society. Now, in 1863, he turned, at Courbet's suggestion, towards the consideration of the visual arts within their social context.

It would be hard to imagine an artist more sympathetic to Proudhon than Courbet. Both were of Comtois peasant stock, and their friendship was of long standing. From 1848 onwards, Courbet was a constant companion of Proudhon, and painted portraits of him, alone and *en famille*, as well as a frank, coarse portrait of Euphrasie which she is said to have regarded with displeasure. Courbet delighted in Proudhon's conversation and writings, shared his love for the common people, and accepted his theories. In his painting, in so far as he chose to transmit a message, it was the Proudhonian one of the dignity of labour and the degeneracy of those who prey upon it, while his style, breaking with the conventions of the academicians as well as those of the romantics and the classicists, had a robust and direct quality not unlike that of Proudhon's own prose. Proudhon saw his friend as a true representative in art of the best aspects of the age, and defined him as a 'critical, analytical, synthetic and humanitarian painter' whose work displayed other aspects of what he himself had expressed in his theory of 'immanent justice;' as an artist who belonged to the movement that would bring 'the end of capitalism and the sovereignty of the producers.'

Courbet's painting, *La Retour de la Conférence*, which represented the clergy very unfavourably, had been refused by the Salon for this reason, and the artist, who was intending to hold an exhibition in London, asked Proudhon to write a brief essay to expound the theoretical basis of this picture. The original suggestion was for a mere note of four pages but, as usual, the essay grew vastly as the process of writing stimulated in Proudhon a whole flow of new ideas on the general function of art. By August all thought of anything brief had vanished as, egged on by the painter ('Courbet is in anguish,' he told Bergmann. 'He assassinates me with letters of eight pages—you know how he writes, how he wrangles!'), Proudhon enlarged his essay by rapid stages from a leaflet to a book.

Courbet continued to bombard the writer with his wordy, ill-spelt and ill-written letters, and in June Proudhon complained to Chaudey: 'I have received an enormous letter from Courbet. I believe he went looking in the oldest grocer's shop in Ornans for the dirtiest, yellowest, coarsest schoolboy's exercise book in order to write to me. One would believe that letter belonged to the century of Gutenberg. Ink to match. Courbet does not write often, but when he sets himself to it, beware! This time he covered no less than fourteen pages with the dregs of wine. It will be a business to answer all that!' But even such Gargantuan prodding could not urge the tired Proudhon into completing the book, and on his death-bed he sent Courbet a message, by way of the Comtois novelist Max Buchon, regretting that he had not been able to finish his task. It was finally made ready for publication after his death by Courbet himself, with the help of Chaudey.

Du Principe de l'Art, as this posthumous book was called, has some importance in the history of art criticism, since it was one of the first studies devoted exclusively to considering the social relevance of art. Proudhon's approach was as frankly didactic as Ruskin's; art must have a moral purpose, or it is devoid of meaning. At the same time, it would be wrong to rank him among the direct forebears of such doctrines as social realism, which see art as a form of partisan propaganda. Proudhon's view of art as a stimulant to man's intellectual and moral development was a good deal more subtle, though he claimed that it should be strictly contemporary and should respond to the aspirations of men in the society where it is produced.

Just as he had once seen the germ of poetry in all men, so he now sees the aesthetic faculty as a common human attribute which some are able to express more ably than others. It is the faculty of 'perceiving or discovering the beautiful and the ugly, the agreeable and the ungraceful, the sublime and the trivial, in oneself and in things, and of making out of this perception a new means of delight.' In practice, the object of this aesthetic faculty is 'what is generally known as the ideal,' and this is what makes the work of art superior to the purely naturalistic reproduction of actuality. 'Art is nothing except through the ideal. The greatest artist will therefore be the greatest idealist.' Proudhon means idealism in the Platonic sense; the ideal is what conforms to the idea, and 'the idea is the typical, specific, generic notion which the intellect forms of a thing, setting aside all materiality.' Such a conception rules out implicitly strict realism ('Physical reality is only valuable because of the spirit and the ideal which breathe in it'), and at the same time rejects explicitly the doctrine of 'art for art's sake' which, 'resting on nothing, is nothing.' Art can only be justified if it exists within its social context, as art for man's sake. It 'has for its object to lead us to the knowledge of ourselves, through the revelation of all our thoughts—even the most secret of them, of all our tendencies, all our virtues, vices and follies, and thence to contribute to the development of our dignity, to the perfection of our being.' Proudhon saw Courbet and his school as the painters who in his time were most faithfully carrying out this aim, and in the historical perspective he was right, for Courbet represented a necessary revolution from the moribund art forms of the past. *The Principle of Art* should therefore be regarded as a healthy protest against the unrealities of the academicians, and a necessary recalling of artists to the fecund and inspiring actualities of the life around them.

If Proudhon saw art drawing its inspiration from life, he also saw life in its turn irradiated by art. In *Les Majorats Littéraires* he had anticipated William Morris and modern industrial designers by suggesting that industry and work could be ennobled by their contact with art; in machinery, precision instruments, textiles and books he saw the beginning of a collective art in which all people could share. He also envisaged this beneficent influence spreading beyond industry into wide new domains of human living. 'Our whole life, our words, our actions, even the most common of them, all that we do, all that we are, call to art and ask to be raised up by it.' Proudhon saw the possibility of art asserting a dominant influence in the rebuilding of French cities, and a new style emerging that would be adaptable to the age and would respect the needs of each regional environment, for, in art as in everything else, he was a great opponent of centralisation, uniformity and metropolitanism. In such a society the artist would cease to be a man apart; reintegrated into the daily life of his time, he would enter the world of labour as an equal, sharing its rights and its common dignity.

6

The projects that spawned in Proudhon's mind and lay half-written on his desk were abruptly thrust aside in the beginning of 1864 by an event whose implications were to dominate his thought and work for the remaining months of his life. In *L'Opinion Nationale* on the 17th February there appeared a letter, signed by a group of working men, which became known as The Manifesto of the Sixty and which was to constitute a historic document in the development of the French socialist movement.

As we have seen already, the early sixties was a time of rising activity among the French workers, who had been relatively quiescent since the June days of 1848, and the influence of Proudhon's mutualist and federalist ideas penetrated so widely into the nascent movement that French historians are agreed that he, even more than Blanqui, and certainly far more than Marx, was the most influential socialist theoretician of the decade. During 1863 the revival began to assume concrete forms; productive co-operatives appeared in considerable numbers, and parallel with them emerged Societies of Credit which acted as savings banks and, in a modified way, utilised some of the Proudhonian theories of mutual banking.

Apart from these manifestations of social mutualism, the new movement also began to express itself in a political direction, through the desire of the workers to be represented in the legislature, not by the old bourgeois parties, but by spokesmen who would enter parliament from the bench or the factory and return to labour among their fellows when their term was done.

This recognition of differing class interests, of the 'two nations' within an industrial world which Disraeli had observed many years before in England, was an extension of the distinction between bourgeois and proletarian approaches which Proudhon himself had made in his speech to the National Assembly in July, 1848, and the fraction of the workers who put forward these claims were in many ways influenced by his ideas. They were federalist and mutualist, they looked to a reconciliation of social differences in a final classless anarchy, but they differed from Proudhon in rejecting abstention from parliamentary action, and in the elections of 1863 three candidates stood in the working-class interest and gained minuscule votes.

They were not deterred by this slight success, and it was before the supplementary elections of 1864 that this small group prepared and circulated The Manifesto of the Sixty. With the exception of a schoolmaster named Bibal, they were all working men; some had taken part in the commission of workers' delegates sent to the Universal Exhibition in London two years before, and others became members of the International Workingmen's Association —The First International—which arose as a long-term product of the meeting at that time with English and German workers. Only three left any mark on the history of their time—Henri Tolain and Charles Limousin, most active of the French founders of the International, and Camélinat, who played a minor rôle in the Commune seven years later and survived incongruously into the 1940's as an aged mascot of the French Communist Party.

The Manifesto, which was written mostly by Tolain, was remarkable for the restrained dignity of its manner. Its essence can be found in this paragraph:

'Universal suffrage has made us politically adult, but it still remains for us to emancipate ourselves socially. The liberty which the Third Estate conquered with so much vigour and tenacity should extend in the democratic country of France to all citizens. An equal political right necessarily implies an equal social right. It has been repeated to satiety that there are no longer any classes; since 1789, all Frenchmen are equal before the law. But we who have no other property than our hands, we who suffer every day from the legal or arbitrary conditions of capitalism, we who live under exceptional laws, such as the law on coalitions, which offend our interests at the same time as our dignity, find it very difficult to believe that affirmation.'

After enlarging on this point to show the ways in which existing society militates against the interests of the workers, the Manifesto goes on to sketch the aims of its signatories. 'The law should be broad enough to allow each man, whether in isolation or collectively, the development of his faculties, the employment of his powers, savings and intelligence without any limit being imposed but the liberty—though not the interests—of another.... Freedom of work, credit, solidarity—these are our dreams. The day on which they are realised, for the glory and prosperity of our country, there will no longer be either bourgeois or proletariat, employers or workers. All citizens will be equal in their rights.'

The Manifesto examines the current parliamentary situation, and shows that, though the present deputies claim to speak for all their constituents, in fact they represent only the limited interests in which they themselves are intimately concerned; from this the manifestants deduce the need for representatives who will formulate 'with moderation, but with firmness, our hopes, desires and rights.'

Proudhon immediately recognised the importance of the

Manifesto. He discussed it closely with his friends Langlois, Beslay and Duchêne, and with some of the signatories, including Camélinat. 'It may become something of an event,' he told Chaudey, and he decided that he would write a book about it. It was on the preparation of this book that most of his remaining energy was to be expended.

It is possible that his decision to make The Manifesto of the Sixty the pretext, rather than the subject, of his last book was due largely to the fact that this document started off a whole chain of reactions among French working men and resulted in several groups writing to ask his opinion of working-men's representation. To one of them, in Rouen, he wrote on the 8th March a letter of sixteen manuscript pages which laid the foundation of his thoughts on the political function of the working class.

The points emphasised are, firstly, the reawakening of the socialist idea, secondly, the fact that the workers are not represented and that this situation must be changed, and, thirdly, the affirmation of the class nature of contemporary society. 'French society is divided fundamentally into two classes: one that lives exclusively from its work and whose wages are generally below 1,250 francs per year and per family of four persons, and another that lives from the revenue of its capital.' This division of society is contrary to justice, and should be changed 'by a better application of the laws of justice and economy.'

But since existing parties and governmental institutions are designed to serve the propertied classes, any workers who find themselves involved in such machinery will be ineffective; they will become frustrated nonentities or political prostitutes. The only solution, Proudhon concludes, is to recognise and act in accordance with this division within society, and here he shows himself an unwilling forerunner of the bitter conflict between workers and rulers that dominated France during the later nineteenth century. 'I say to you with all the energy and sadness of my spirit: Separate yourselves from those who have cut themselves off from you, separate yourselves as in the past the Roman people separated themselves from the aristocrats . . . It is by separation that you will win; no representatives, no candidates.'

Soon the steadily widening reaction in working-class circles to the Manifesto of the Sixty was strengthening Proudhon's hopes. 'The social republic approaches more quickly than is apparent,' he exclaimed in April. But sickness impeded his own efforts to foster the ideological development of this new movement. At the beginning of June he succumbed to erysipelas, and it was not until early in July that the doctors pronounced him convalescent. He was still extremely weak, and told Delhasse that never since the cholera of 1854 had he been so prostrated. 'My eyes see the letters dancing on the books I read, my hand trembles in writing, and I can collect my thoughts only with difficulty.'

His sickness had again set him back financially, but he was saved from immediate anxiety by his friend's considerateness, for Delhasse promptly sent him 2,000 francs. 'It is a real ransom to me,' he wrote in gratitude; now he could, 'without agitation or fever, set myself to work again in all the fulness of my powers and the calmness of my reason.' He confided to Delhasse the thought that he was probably entering the last, but also 'the most important and decisive' phase of his career. He still hoped to enjoy ten or twelve years of active work. 'I ask no more—I have so many things in my head and my heart.'

Convalescence was painfully slow, but he did not let weakness dim his resolution to sustain the main work he had planned. His body was clearly decaying more rapidly than ever, but the inner drive was undiminished. 'Alas, here I am coming back like an old athlete,' he jested grimly to Buzon in mid-July. 'I weep as I look at my wasted limbs, my softened muscles, my exhausted nerves. There only remains my heart, whose fire is inextinguishable. I shall fight to the end . . . I do not want to die without having developed my ideas to the last degree.'

7

Through the summer of 1864 Proudhon's condition improved little, and at last, in the hope of re-establishing his health by a change of scene, he decided to revisit the Franche-Comté. He set off in August, accompanied by his most constant medical adviser, the homoeopath Cretin. Despite his weak condition, this last journey to the Jura was more arduous than any trip he had made before. He seemed eager to cram in every experience, to visit every place, to see every friend, and there is a kind of doomed poignancy in the series of letters in which he described to Euphrasie this voyage after a lost health and a departed youth.

The first of them was sent on the 21st August, from St. Hippolyte, a little town among precipitous mountain slopes which formed 'an immense funnel where one breathes the best air in France.' The holiday was beginning propitiously. 'I hope a great deal for my health from this journey,' he said on his first day in the mountains, and two days later he reported that his breathing was much improved. The mountaineers went out of their way to entertain him. He dined with the magistrate, and an open-air fishing party in his honour was attended by 150 people, who ate and drank and danced until twilight. He was taken for drives in the region, saw 'the most beautiful precipices in· the world' and looked vertiginously into great caverns with underground rivers.

But soon a note of doubt entered his letters. His optimism had been premature; during the day he felt well, but at night the misty dampness oppressed him, and he had to sleep upright in a chair. At such times he would forget the charming hospitality of St. Hippolyte and the 'mad gaiety' of Cretin, and long to be back with his family and above all with his wife. 'I have need of you then, and nobody, you understand, can replace you near me. You will doubtless say that it is egoism that makes me speak thus. Good God! dear wife, there is always a little egoism in our actions. What at least is certain is that, ill or not, I hold above all to my nest, and that I love you more than ever.'

At the end of August he returned to Besançon, and called on Weiss, who was now 86. Weiss wept as he embraced him, partly from joy and partly because of the almost unrecognisably changed appearance of the man who walked heavily into the room, supported on a cane. The two friends spent a morning discussing their ideas and the writers of their time, and Proudhon acknowledged his debt to Weiss for the benevolence he had repulsed so proudly as a child. 'You are my spiritual father,' he told the old scholar. 'In my eyes you are the last incarnation of the eighteenth century. May you understand one day that I, for my part, am one of the incarnations of the nineteenth.'

He spent the rest of his vacation at Dampierre, in the care of Dr. Maguet, and on the way there he stopped at Fraisans to see yet another old friend, Guillemin, whom he found, despite his 62 years, enviably healthy. 'If his beard and hair were not completely white, one would believe that he did not grow old at all. He is capable of hunting sixteen hours a day, taking only a crust and a glass of wine in the morning.' Proudhon himself showed no such evidences of indestructibility. From Dampierre he told Euphrasie that his hair was falling, as a result of the erysipelas, and that his beard, which had been blond when he set out on his travels, had turned decidedly grey in a few days. These signs seemed to belie his efforts to convince himself that his health might really be improving, and it was with a rather desperate bravado that he wrote to Delhasse from Dampierre, prophesying 'a universal European bankruptcy, political, economic, social and moral,' which would precipitate the social revolution. 'Feeble as I am,' he added, 'I shall live long enough to see that downfall.'

In mid-September he returned to Passy, having gained a vast pleasure from the kindness of the friends among whom he had travelled; he even thought of a final return to the Franche-Comté, where he might end his days in the congenial company and pleasant air of some village of the Jura. But he was still anxious about his condition. He jested to Beslay that, instead of being cured, he was more likely to become accustomed to his illness, but he wrote to Delhasse in a more gloomy tone, as if he were already conscious of the proximity of his end. 'I live in resignation, so passionately does man cling to life, but if I were called from this earth, I should not be at all surprised; I should only regret not having been able to put my hand to my testament. My testament —if I can say this without seeming to ape Jesus and Moses—is the complete exposition of my thoughts on Justice.' By October he was complaining to Cretin of the alarming asthmatic symptoms which appeared with increasing regularity, and he declared that he was weaker than ever before, with no sign of a halt to the frightening regression. 'I do not think I can continue in this way for another year, and I believe that if, after next summer— supposing I get so far—I do not triumph over my illness, which despite you has become chronic, I must make up my mind and set my last wishes in order.'

Now, with the desperation of a man who knows he has little time, he forced himself to work in spite of his sickness. 'Every day,' he told Buzon at the end of October, 'from seven to noon, I work at my task; a repugnant labour, inspired by sorrow, anger, disgust, the desire for death, which I have not yet been able to finish . . . Despite the gods, despite everything, I will have the last word.' And as he laboured, fighting often for breath, battling with the certainty that his death could not be long postponed, he was sustained by the enthusiasm he saw around him. He heard with delight of the formation of the International, partly through the initiative of French workers who adhered to his own ideas, and told Delhasse that this was a proof that 'democracy everywhere is becoming aware of itself; it recognises its solidarity.' 'There are formidable indignations in the air,' he told Buzon.

It was to serve this awakening of rebellious thought, to give expression to these formidable indignations, that Proudhon devoted his last fragments of strength, and by early November he was trying to persuade the Garniers to abandon their terror of political subjects and accept his book. On the 23rd November he was still working with determination, and told Delhasse that the book would be finished in another week. It would be the last effort of its kind, he added wearily. 'Books overpower me, and I have decided to write only articles in future.' But even this limited ambition was beyond him, for a few days later his illness took an alarmingly acute turn, and he had to abandon writing altogether. The attacks of asthma had become so severe and so weakening that he was no longer able to hold his pen, and even had difficulty in reading. When he wrote to Maurice on the 30th November, Catherine, now fifteen years old, had to act as his secretary. Except for painfully signing letters, he did not write again.

It was in the early days of this final illness that his friend of twenty years ago, and his most formidable disciple, Michael Bakunin, visited him for the last time. Bakunin and Proudhon had disagreed over the Polish question, but they had met during 1862, when the latter confessed his feeling that, wanting to write like Voltaire, he always seemed to end up writing like Rousseau. Bakunin had come to Passy again at the end of 1863, and now, in November, 1864, he broke a journey to Florence in order to call on Proudhon for their final meeting. As of old in the Rue de Bourgogne, they argued long and good-humouredly, and Bakunin, with considerable insight, accused Proudhon of being swayed at one moment by the Bible and the next by Roman law, and of being an incorrigible idealist. What Proudhon replied is not recorded, but we can well imagine that the enthusiasm Bakunin displayed at this time for the rising workers' movement helped to sustain the flickering flame of his activity.

During December it became evident that Proudhon's heart was gravely affected, while his limbs swelled, and he found it almost impossible to sleep. Yet, despite this progressive physical decay, his mental faculties remained as acute as ever, and on his bed of sickness he dictated to Gustave Chaudey the final passages of his last book, which he called *De la Capacité Politique des Classes ouvrières*.

Once again, his friends rallied to give him what help they could. The generous Delhasse, hearing of his extremity, sent a further 1,000 francs, and there survives a pathetic letter of thanks in Catherine's childish hand. 'Your friendship, which already we knew so well, has moved my father to tears. He alone is capable, when he returns to health, of depicting the sentiments he feels.'

The ten doctors—all of them friends—who had attended Proudhon, not to mention such amateur physicians as Bergmann and Squire Bessetaux, united in asserting that he could still be cured, but Proudhon became increasingly sceptical. Already, asking Cretin in October to be frank about his condition, he had said: 'Do not let us die like fools or cowards; let us die worthily and like brave men.' And now, following the example of his father and brother, he looked with stoical resignation to his approaching end, and in a courageous letter which Catherine wrote to Maguet at his dictation on the 4th January, 1865, he told the reasons why he felt that death was near.

'The sickness has made progress with an unheard-of rapidity . . . A fortnight ago the sick man still had the strength to eat a meal; now he refuses to eat because mastication tires and suffocates him. A fortnight ago, he did not stay in bed during the day; now, if it depended on him, he would not rise at all. A fortnight ago, as I told you, his crises were hardly one or two a week; now he lives in a continuous crisis, and in a fortnight, if this progress is not halted, my father claims that he will be able to rise no more . . . With all that he maintains a healthy reason, and all his liberty of thought, which is exactly why the more the doctors examine him, the more hopes they conceive—and the more they are deceived. The divorce between body and spirit is pronounced. What is called *life* has become an incompatibility.'

It was Proudhon who was right, and on the 12th January he took his formidable pen for the last time to scrawl his initials to a letter thanking Buzon for a present of fruit, and saying: 'At the moment I am more overwhelmed than ever; more than ever I doubt my resurrection, and I sweat blood and water to put my signature to this missive, which I would not like to swear will not be my last to you.'

The sickness continued a few days longer in its fearful progress, until, at 2 o'clock on the morning of the 19th January, 1865, Pierre-Joseph Proudhon died in the arms of his wife and of his friend, Amadée Langlois. He remained faithful to his principles; on being asked if he wished for a priest, he refused and, turning to Euphrasie, said: 'I shall confess to you.'

8

The news of Proudhon's death brought a shock to the whole democratic world of Paris, and the day of his funeral, the 23rd January, was, as Gustave Lefrançais remembered, 'at once a sad and a good day for the socialist revolutionaries.' It manifested a public grief which Proudhon himself would not have expected, but it also became a spontaneous expression of the rising spirit of revolt. Old friends and old rivals from the struggles of three decades gathered by the hundred in the courtyard of the house or in the street outside, and comrades of the '48 who had not met for many years exchanged their reminiscences of prison and exile. But, though the tried revolutionaries and the liberal journalists were numerous, it was the anonymous working men of Paris who made the bulk of the great crowd of six thousand that waited in the Grande Rue to accompany Proudhon to his grave.

Just before the cortège was due to leave for the cemetery of Passy, a curious incident happened, whose authenticity is attested, not merely by legend, but also by Proudhon's family and by memoirists like Lefrançais.

'Suddenly a drum resounded,' Lefrançais recalls. 'The sound increased and grew near, and soon we saw a contingent of soldiers approaching, with their colonel at the head. The same thought invaded us all: the troops had been sent to disperse us and prevent us from following the cortège. Immediately, with a spontaneous movement, we closed our ranks and barred the way. Our looks were anxious but resolved. The troops would have to retire or march over our bodies. A terrible silence replaced the noise of our conversations.

'Langlois and Duchêne went up to the colonel, who was hardly fifty paces from our first ranks. Langlois explained that Proudhon was dead and that the crowd before him had come to accompany the body to the cemetery. The colonel knew nothing: he was returning from a march to the barracks of La Pépinière. As he could not change his itinerary, he asked Langlois to open the ranks so that his men could continue on their way.

'We understood. The crowd opened, and the troops passed between two living hedges. Suddenly a voice cried: "Beat the salute!" The colonel instinctively raised his sword, the drums beat out the funeral march, all our heads were uncovered, and the regiment passed before the house of the dead presenting arms.'

Paradox followed Proudhon to the end, and one can imagine that he would have relished the irony of this fortuitous tribute by the forces of the State to the first of the Anarchists. Afterwards the great procession moved peacefully through the streets to the cemetery where, over the open grave, Proudhon's companions in the struggles of a quarter of a century, Langlois, Chaudey and Massol, delivered their tributes to the inspired fighter for liberty and the man with a genius for friendship.

Part Nine

EPILOGUE

M ANY writers have sought for the phrase that would arrest-
ingly define Proudhon and the philosophy that emerged
from his impact on the world of ideas and action. Marx dismissed
him as a 'petty bourgeois,' and several French writers have classed
him as a representative of peasant radicalism. The latter definition
has the greater proportion of truth, for much that is puzzling in
Proudhon becomes clearer when one remembers that in character
he was nearer to the solid French countryman than any of his
socialist contemporaries.

The combination of stubbornness and impetuosity that marked
his actions, his suspicion of strangers and his abounding affection
for those who proved themselves friends, his often disastrous
attempts to combine craftiness in tactics with probity in principles, and his perpetual efforts to reconcile the individualism of
the typical farmer with the tendency to mutual aid imposed by
their environment on agricultural populations—all these characteristics have their evident roots in that peasant world where he
was born and reared. To the same source we may also trace the
regionalism that made him perpetually conscious of being a good
Franc-Comtois, and the distrust of the engulfing State that in-

spired his hostility to political centralisation. His consciousness of tradition, which was combined with a desire to establish justice by radical social changes, reflects the oscillation between conservative living patterns and the anarchic passions of Jacquerie which is a recurrent phenomenon of peasant societies. His wit was earthy and vigorous, resembling that of another countryman of paradoxically mingled conservatism and radicalism, William Cobbett, and he never wrote more eloquently than in describing his childhood as a mountain herdboy or celebrating his rural forebears. Even his domestic pattern was that of a peasant. His sense of family solidarity was immense, embracing not merely his wife and children, but also his parents and his brothers. He liked to rule the household in the manner of a Judaic patriarch, and few French farmers would disagree with his view of the functions of women. Lastly, he had that sense of the importance of the earth in the moral as well as the material life of society which is rarely experienced intensely except by those whose contact with the land has been deep and endearing.

Yet not every aspect of Proudhon's personality is explicable in these terms of a rural background. It was his individual qualities that brought him out of the peasant mass, and they were not always admirable. His arrogance and his exaggerated *amour propre*, however we may explain them by the misfortunes of his early life, remain unpleasing But they are counterbalanced by more positive traits. He had both moral and physical courage, and he was tenacious in enduring the most adverse circumstances. His friendship was boundless, and his generosity went to and sometimes beyond the limit of his scanty and badly managed means. The heat of polemical battle might lead him into verbal injustice towards his opponents, but it was moral indignation, not personal hatred, that inspired his wildest denunciations. In private he was as mild and jovial as he appeared ferocious in print, and towards rivals he respected, like Blanqui and Leroux, he knew how to be generous. On fundamental points of conduct he was scrupulous; even in his greatest need he declined to earn money in ways that he thought dishonourable, and he was always ready to defend an unpopular cause if justice seemed to demand it.

In some moods, indeed, Proudhon presented the aspect of a stern puritan; he proclaimed—and practised—the virtues of an austere poverty, he extolled the discipline of work, he preached chastity, and rejected with suspicious violence the enticements of carnal love. Yet he did not affect the narrow existence of the ascetic, and in its own way his life was full and rich. His letters were illuminated by humour and magnanimity, he delighted in good conversation, he loved wine in moderation and appreciated good food, he was responsive to natural beauty. His scholarship was vast, and his knowledge of French and classical literature was almost encyclopaedic. He applauded and understood the most vital painting of his time, he liked music and (though he distrusted actresses) enjoyed the theatre, and he combined an appreciation of good craftsmanship with an unostentatious plainness in his daily living. If one adds to these facts the bold and arresting nature of his thought, the penetrating and often prophetic insight he displayed into the world of his time, and the strong and subtle prose in which he expressed his ideas, the finished picture of Proudhon, even taking into account the defects which his very largeness of nature made the more apparent, is that of a man whose vitality, integrity and humanity were unusual in his or any age.

I began this chapter by remarking that the identification of Proudhon as a peasant radical seemed nearer to the truth than most of the other generalisations that have sought to explain his career. Today, when the unsatisfied demands of the world's peasants have taken on an imperative urgency, such a rôle seems more relevant than it may have appeared to Proudhon's immediate successors, but it would be wrong to regard him as nothing more than a prophet of the Jacquerie. Experience soon gave him a much broader view of the life of the poor than could be found within the village, and it is illuminating to recall the stages of development which his thought underwent as his knowledge of the various sections of the working class became progressively more comprehensive.

What is Property?, written in 1840, presented a vision of social reorganisation that seemed to take into account only the farmer and the handicraftsman. By 1848, however, contact with the Lyons weavers had made Proudhon conscious of the need for co-operation, and his vision of the People's Bank was based on the idea of association for the exchange of products between peasants and small workshop groups. Later, the spread of industrialism and of the railroads revealed to him that the larger projects of the industrial era demanded the creation of closely knit productive associations of workers in certain trades. Finally, the revival of working-class activity in the 1860's led him to write, in *The Political Capacity of the Working Classes*, a book which called as much to the factory workers of France as to the country people and the Parisian artisans, and which was to be more influential than any of his earlier and better books in shaping the radical movements of the later nineteenth century.

In *The Political Capacity of the Working Classes* Proudhon signalised the entry of the workers as an independent force in the field of politics. 'To possess political capacity,' he explained, 'is to have the *consciousness* of oneself as a member of a collectivity, to affirm the *idea* that results from this consciousness, and to pursue its *realisation*. Whoever unites these three conditions is capable.' The Manifesto of the Sixty, he declared, had shown that the French proletariat was in fact beginning to fulfil the three conditions. Like all other classes that had become significant in the community, it was conscious that its life and needs made it a separate group with its own place in society and its own mission in social evolution. The *idea* resulting from this dawning self-consciousness was that of Mutuality. The possession and development of this idea distinguished the working class (including the peasants) from the bourgeoisie, and conferred on it a progressive character, since by developing mutuality the workers could at last bring justice into the economic life of society and organise it on an egalitarian basis, which the anti-mutualist spirit of the bourgeois class had prevented them from doing.

Politically, mutualism was expressed in *federalism*, which would guarantee the true sovereignty of the people, since in the federal republic power would rise up from below, and would rest on the 'natural groups' which, by means of a series of delegations, would coalesce in co-ordinating committees to implement the general will of the people Its complete sensitivity could be assured by the immediate revocability of any delegation. Since the 'natural groups' would be identical with the working units of society, the nature of the State would change from political to economic and social, and Saint-Simon's vision of the government of men being replaced by the administration of things would be finally achieved.

If Proudhon realised that it was impossible to achieve reconciliation with the *grande bourgeoisie*, he did not abandon hope of gaining the allegiance of that larger section of the middle class whose independence was threatened by the spread of industrial feudalism. He realised that nothing would be gained by dragging the middle class down to the level of the poorest wage-earners; the progression of society should be upwards rather than downwards, and the revolutionary's aim should be, not to enslave all men by pauperism, but to make all men free by guaranteeing their economic independence. Thus, while the workers alone, by their recognition of the mutualist idea, could initiate that fundamental social change which Proudhon described by the ambiguous title of 'social liquidation,' they should seek the alliance of the harassed middle class, so that the whole community might move towards liberation without that violence of civil war which Proudhon always regarded as inimical to the healthy growth of freedom. Indeed, while recognising the divided structure of society in his day, and realising that a real class struggle existed, he also believed that out of the fluidity of this struggle might emerge the equilibrium of mutualism, and for this reason he sought to avoid any measures that, by institutionalising the class struggle, might tend to make the division permanent.

At the same time, he believed that the workers must be clear in their rejection of bourgeois ideas of government, which perpetuated a system in which the people had no direct voice, in which freedom of the Press and sound education were impossible, in which neither credit nor exchange could be guaranteed. They must seek to convert the majority to their ideas, and afterwards establish real popular sovereignty by the power of numbers and justice. Just how this triumph was to be established, Proudhon did not say, and it seems almost as though he looked, like Godwin, to the day when the powers of truth and reason would impose themselves and almost unaided bring about the flight of error and the consequent defeat of the forces of reaction.

Proudhon's teachings entered the movement of the 1860's partly through *The Political Capacity of the Working Classes* and partly through his friends (particularly Beslay and Chaudey, Langlois and Duchêne) and his worker disciples, such as the first secretaries of the International, Tolain, Limousin and Fribourg. This first manifestation of Proudhonism within the socialist movement was also its purest, for the French section of the International followed in almost every detail the policy laid down in *The Political Capacity of the Working Classes*. Its members opposed without compromise the political activity advocated by Marx, who had installed himself strategically in the London General Council and was already seeking to turn the organisation into an instrument for furthering his own policy. Instead, the French Internationalists sought to create credit unions, popular banks, co-operatives and industrial associations. They looked to a decentralist, federal society in which the State would vanish and freedom of credit would allow every man the means of producing independently or co-operatively. They held much more strongly than the Marxists that the emancipation of the workers is the task of the workers themselves, and carried this idea so far as to propose the exclusion of all non-workers from the International. They even proved that Proudhon's anti-feminist ideas were in no way repugnant to Latin working men by calling for the exclusion of women as well.

For the first four years of its life, the International was dominated by the French mutualists, who consistently defeated Marx and his policy of collectivism and political action. 'Proudhon has done enormous harm,' he complained angrily to Kugelmann in October, 1866. 'His appearance of criticism and his appearance of opposition to the Utopians have corrupted first the young people, the students, and then the workers.' At the Brussels Congress of 1868 the dominance of the mutualists was finally broken, but they were never eliminated from the International, and Marx overcame them only to clash with the adapted Proudhonism of Michael Bakunin and his Swiss, Spanish and Italian followers.

Bakunin's anarchism differed from Proudhon's on a number of important points. He taught the resolute pursuit of the class struggle and the use of violence in certain circumstances, he denied the possibility of reconciliation between workers and bourgeoisie, he was a collectivist (though he never went so far as to call himself a communist). Finally, while he did not set out to form a political party in the strict sense, he had a romantic hankering after that conspiratorial activity which Proudhon eschewed. On the other hand, he retained many of the basic Proudhonian ideas; he rejected the State and wished to replace it by a federal structure of economic and social organisations; he denounced political activity and joined Proudhon in rejecting the dictatorship of the proletariat—an idea borrowed by the Marxists from Blanqui—and in welcoming the peasantry as a potentially revolutionary group.

This heretical disciple was the man who most effectively transmitted Proudhon's seminal ideas to the main stream of nineteenth-century radicalism, for the struggle between him and Marx split the International into the irreconcilable factions of authoritarian and libertarian socialists and thus completed the breach that began in the exchange of letters between Marx and Proudhon in 1846. The power of the anarchists in this conflict should not be minimised, for, though the First International has often been remembered as a Marxist organisation, there was in fact no time when the combined forces of the mutualists and the Bakuninists was not as powerful as that of the Marxists; often it was more powerful.

If the Marxists have often claimed the International for their own, there has never been any disputing the fact that in the Paris Commune of 1871 the influence of Proudhon was immeasurably greater than that of Marx; the men of the International, Courbet and Beslay, Longuet and Camélinat, Theisz and Debock and Duchêne, devoted themselves to its public administration, and the very title of Federals by which the Communards are often known is a tribute to the influence of Proudhon's decentralist doctrines. In *Federation and Unity in Italy* he had raised the cry of 'Paris for the Parisians!' and the implications of that slogan stirred the imaginations of the Communards, who found themselves, like their fathers in 1848, members of a revolutionary city threatened by the domination of a reactionary country. Federalism seemed a solution made to fit their predicament, and, among all the divergences of their opinions, the one point on which they seemed to agree was in wishing to replace the unitary State that had been the dream of the Jacobins by the loose union of free communes and regions preached by the mutualists. There are demands in the Commune's Manifesto to the French People of the 19th April, 1871, that might have been written by Proudhon himself:

'The absolute autonomy of the Commune extended to all the localities of France, assuring to each its integral rights and to every Frenchman the full exercise of his aptitudes, as a man, a citizen and a labourer. The autonomy of the Commune will have for its limits only the equal autonomy of all other communes adhering to the contract; their associations must assure the liberty of France.'

The movement which had grown under Proudhon's influence came to an end with the defeat of the Commune and the subsequent suppression of the International, and in its pure form mutualism rarely appears in subsequent social history. Proudhonism, however, is almost by definition a fluid doctrine. Proudhon himself constantly altered the expression of his ideas to suit changing circumstances or to take into account what seemed to him a more accurate view of the truth. 'I distrust an author who pretends to be consistent with himself after an interval of twenty-five years,' he declared, and, though he clung always to his main general doctrines, he almost certainly would not have expected his ideas to survive him unchanged. The rather static attitude which his immediate followers adopted was perhaps less true to his own progressive spirit than the tendency towards a developing body of thought shown by his later heirs.

After the Commune, his ideas emerged through the transforming media of Bakuninism and Kropotkinist anarchism. This is not the place to tell the chequered story of the anarchist movement from Proudhon's death down to our own day. It is a long and complex history, sometimes almost incredibly fantastic, sometimes disturbing, sometimes pathetic, and often inspiring in the idealism of its thinkers and the dedication of its saints. It is sufficient perhaps to say that, though in many respects the anarchists departed—often with tragic results—from Proudhon's teachings, they always preserved his essential doctrines and fought for the destruction of the State and the reunion of humanity in a great federation of federations in which the rights and freedom of every region and every man would be guaranteed by mutual accord. For many years they were the most active working-class movement in France and Italy, while in Spain, through all the vicissitudes of civil war and repression, they have remained the most tenacious and most numerous of the radical groups.

Through anarchism, the Proudhonian influence was transmitted to the movement of revolutionary syndicalism which dominated French trade unionism well into the present century. Syndicalism assumed its militant form through the extreme disillusionment of

French working men with the corrupt political life of the early Third Republic, and it was inspired largely by the tradition of the First International, particularly as it had been expressed by the federalist wing.

Like Bakunin, the syndicalists believed in the violent prosecution of the class struggle, and their favourite weapon was the general strike, by which they hoped one day to usher in the revolutionary millennium. But, on the whole, they showed more parallels with than divergences from Proudhon. Like him, they saw the condition of social struggle as incessant and hailed it as a creative force. They declared economic groupings to be 'the most fundamental and the most permanent' of human organisations, and sought to build future society as a network of syndicates and other workers' associations which would administer economic affairs and, by dispensing with the State (which they dismissed as the political organisation of the capitalist class), enable men to manage their affairs in freedom. They denounced the deceptions of democratic government, based on what they regarded as 'the fiction of the general will,' and declared, in almost the same terms as Proudhon had used, that the liberation of the workers was their own task and that this very fact precluded them from taking part in political action, which merely served to perpetuate the rule of authority.

Outside the Latin countries, Proudhon's influence was probably strongest in Russia. Herzen and the Narodniks adopted his distrust of the State, his decentralism, and his recognition of the importance of the peasantry. Tolstoy was impressed by his writings, and absorbed the Proudhonian criticisms of property and government into his non-violent anarchism, while his *War and Peace* owed not only its title but also a great deal of its theory of war and of the nature of leadership to Proudhon's book of the same name. The two other great Russians who were profoundly influenced by Proudhon—Kropotkin and Bakunin—have already been mentioned. Their teachings were most effective in Western Europe, and the anarchist movement that arose in Russia under their influence was the least of the major revolutionary groupings of Tsarist days; significantly, it was most influential among the peasants of the Ukraine. In America, Proudhonian echoes can be found in the financial reform ideas of the Populists and in the homebred anarchism of the Wobblies, and, beyond the Rio Grande, in Mexican agrarianism. In England, apart from the small anarchist movement, the mutualist influence seems to have been strongest among the Guild Socialists.

Seminal social ideas and the movements they produce are seldom coterminous, and thus we often find that potent theories disappear from sight and re-emerge at some later point in history like an underground river coming to the surface. Something of this kind has happened to Proudhon's teachings. The large anarchist and syndicalist movements that stemmed from his influence were shaken by the rise of the Comintern, and reduced by the destruction of the Spanish republic to mere skeleton groups of devoted militants, idealistic literati and ageing sentimentalists.

But his ideas, divorced—as he doubtless would have preferred them to be—from organisational trappings, are still alive in the world. The absolute sacro-sanctity of property, which he attacked so resoundingly, can almost be regarded as a thing of the past, so few and so guilty supporters does it now find. His ideas of mutual banking have found expression in thousands of credit unions all over the world, and his theory of an abundant system of credit based, not on gold, but on total productivity, has been reproduced, not only in the somewhat fantastic visions of Social Credit, but also in the ideas of more orthodox economists who have moved away from the gold standard towards more rational bases for currency. The emergence of totalitarianism and the experience in many countries of authoritarian socialist administrations have led men to a new distrust of the centralised State, while the events of the present century have more than underlined Proudhon's warnings of the dangers of nationalism and have given a new appeal to the federalist solution.

Proudhon, indeed, dealt with problems that are perennial, and, while he expressed his ideas in a manner that was often chaotic and sometimes appeared contradictory, while his positive vision was not always so well developed as his critical insight, there are many passages in his works which retain exceptional durability and which at times offer a stimulating viewpoint that has not lost in validity. Neither his writings nor his career can give any total solution to our own difficulties, since they were inevitably conditioned by the age in which he lived, but they contain so many pertinent warnings and open so many vistas of constructive thought that he remains among the small group of nineteenth-century social thinkers whose work still has meaning and relevance in our own age, when we are reaping the evil harvest of the very centralisation and nationalism against which he made his loudest protests.

BIBLIOGRAPHY

This bibliography is frankly selective. Faced by a mass of French material on Proudhon, ranging from pamphlets and doctoral theses to biographies and specialised monographs, and with an even larger quantity of secondary material, particularly in the periodical press of Proudhon's day, in the public archives of Paris, Brussels and Besançon, and in the memoirs of his contemporaries, I have decided to restrict my list to his own writings and to works directly concerning him. For the reader who wishes to place Proudhon more securely in his period and in the socialist tradition, I would, however, recommend the following general books, all of which deal copiously with his significance—from points of view that range from the admiring to the condemnatory: G. Weill, *Histoire du mouvement social en France, 1852–1902* (1904); Sir Alexander Gray, *The Socialist Tradition: Moses to Lenin* (1946); E. Dolléans, *Histoire du mouvement ouvrier*, vol. 1 (1936); Benoît Malon, *Histoire du socialisme*, vol. 2 (1883); Max Nettlau, *Die Forfrühlung der Anarchie* (1925); G. D. H. Cole, *History of Socialist Thought*, vols. 1 and 2 (1953–4).

In listing Proudhon's own works, I have omitted only those pamphlets of 1848–9 which were merely reprints of newspaper articles later collected in the three volumes of *Mélanges*. In listing the works concerning him, I have included all the serious studies; of the many controversial pamphlets which his career occasioned, I have mentioned only those which play a decisive part in his life.

One important primary source is not mentioned in the bibliography. I am referring to the invaluable Diary of Proudhon, lasting from 1843 to 1864, and covering eleven manuscript volumes, in the possession of his descendants. This Diary, which I was allowed to consult, has never been published as a whole, though scanty extracts appeared in *La Grande Revue* during 1908.

I. WORKS OF PROUDHON

Essai de Grammaire générale (an anonymous study forming the epilogue to Bergier's *Eléments primitifs des langues*). Besançon, 1837.
De l'Utilité de la Célébration du Dimanche. Besançon, 1839.

BIBLIOGRAPHY

Qu'est-ce que la Propriété? ou Recherche sur le principe du Droit et du Gouvernement. Paris, 1840.

Lettre à M. Blanqui sur la Propriété. Paris, 1841.

Avertissement aux Propriétaires, or *Lettre à M. Considérant.* Besançon and Paris, 1842.

Explications présentées au Ministère Public sur le Droit de Propriété. (Proudhon's defence before the Court of Assizes of the Doubs, 3rd February, 1842.) Besançon, 1842.

De la Création de l'Ordre dans l'Humanité, ou Principes d'Organisation politique. Besançon and Paris, 1843.

Le Miserere ou La Pénitence d'un Roi (a letter to R. P. Lacordaire on his Lenten sermons of 1845). Paris, 1845.

De la Concurrence entre les Chemins de Fer et les Voies navigables. Paris, 1845.

Système des Contradictions économiques ou Philosophie de la Misère. 2 vols, Paris, 1846.

Solution du Problème social. Paris, 1848.

Proposition relative à l'Impôt sur le Revenu. (Proudhon's speech to the. National Assembly, 31st July, 1848.) Paris, 1848.

Le Droit au Travail et le Droit à la Propriété. Paris, 1848.

Résumé de la Question Sociale. Banque d'Echange. Paris, 1848.

Banque du Peuple (documents). Paris, 1849.

Les Confessions d'un Révolutionnaire. Paris, 1849.

Intérêt et Principal. Discussion entre M. Proudhon et M. Bastiat sur l'Intérêt des Capitaux. Paris, 1850.

Idée Générale de la Révolution au XIXᵉ Siècle. Paris, 1851.

La Révolution sociale démontrée par le Coup d'Etat du 2 Décembre. Paris, 1852.

Philosophie du Progrès. Brussels, 1853.

Manuel du Spéculateur à la Bourse. Paris, 1852.

(This edition was published anonymously; it was not until the enlarged third edition of 1857 that Proudhon's signature was added.)

Des Réformes à opérer dans l'Exploitation des Chemins de Fer. Paris, 1855.

De la Justice dans la Révolution et dans l'Eglise. 3 vols, Paris, 1858.

La Justice Poursuivie par l'Eglise. Brussels, 1858.

La Guerre et la Paix. Recherches sur le Principe et la Constitution du Droit des Gens. 2 vols, Paris, 1861.

Théorie de l'Impôt. Paris, 1861.

Les Majorats Littéraires. Brussels, 1862.

La Fédération et l'Unité en Italie. Paris, 1862.

Du Principe Fédératif et de la Nécessité de reconstituer le Parti de la Révolution. Paris, 1863.

BIBLIOGRAPHY

Les Démocrates assermentés et les Réfractaires. Paris, 1863.

Si les Traités de 1815 ont cessé d'exister? Paris, 1863.

Nouvelles Observations sur l'Unité Italienne. Paris, 1865.

De la Capacité Politique des Classes ouvrières. Paris, 1865.

Du Principe de l'Art et de sa Destination Sociale. Paris, 1865.

Théorie de la Propriété. Paris, 1865.

La Bible annotée. 2 vols, Paris, 1866.

France et Rhin. Ed. Gustave Chaudey. Paris, 1867.

Contradictions Politiques: Théorie du Mouvement Constitutionnel au XIXe Siècle. Paris, 1870.

La Pornocratie ou Les Femmes dans les Temps Modernes. Paris, 1875.

Césarisme et Christianisme. Ed J.-A. Langlois. 2 vols. Paris, 1883.

Jésus et les Origines du Christianisme. Ed. Clément Rochel. Paris, 1896.

Napoléon Ier. Ed. Clément Rochel. Paris, 1898.

Commentaires sur les Mémoires de Fouché. Ed. Clément Rochel. Paris, 1900.

Napoléon III. Ed. Clément Rochel. Paris, 1900.

2. ENGLISH TRANSLATIONS OF PROUDHON'S WORKS

What is Property? Tr. Benjamin Tucker. Princeton, 1876.

(This includes *Qu'est-ce que la Propriété* and *Lettre à M. Blanqui.*)

System of Economic Contradictions: or the Philosophy of Poverty. Tr. Benjamin Tucker, Boston, 1888.

(This covers only Volume 1 of *Système des Contradictions économiques;* Tucker's translation of the second volume has never been published.)

General Idea of the Revolution in the Nineteenth Century. Tr. John Beverley Robinson. London, 1923.

Proudhon's Solution of the Social Problem. New York, 1927.

(This volume consists of a selection of Proudhon's articles and pamphlets on mutual banking, together with essays by Henry Cohen, Charles Dana and William B. Greene.)

3. COLLECTIONS, SELECTIONS AND CORRESPONDENCE

Oeuvres Complètes. 26 vols. Paris, 1867–70.

(Volumes 17, 18 and 19 of this collection are entitled *Mélanges*, and consist of selections of Proudhon's most important articles published between 1848 and 1850 in *Le Représentant du Peuple, La Voix du Peuple*, and the two series of *Le Peuple.*)

Correspondance. 14 vols. Paris, 1874–5.

Abrégé des Oeuvres de Proudhon. Ed. Hector Merlin. 2 vols. Paris, 1896.

Lettres à Chaudey et à divers Comtois, 1839–64. Ed. E. Droz, Besançon, 1911.

Oeuvres Complètes. Paris, 1920–1939.
(This collection of Proudhon's works, published by Marcel Rivière under the general editorship of C. Bouglè and H. Moysset, is the most reliable edition. Unfortunately, it was interrupted by the outbreak of war in 1939, and has not been resumed, but it contains definitive and well-annotated texts of almost all of Proudhon's important works.)

Lettres de Pierre-Joseph Proudhon, selected by Daniel Halévy and Louis Guilloux. Paris, 1929.

Proudhon. Ed. C. Bouglé. Paris, 1930.

Proudhon. Ed. Armand Cuvillier. Paris, 1937.

La Pensée Vivante de Proudhon. Ed. Lucien Maury. 2 vols. Paris, 1945.

Proudhon. Ed. Alexandre Marc. Paris, 1945.

Lettres au Citoyen Rolland, 1858–1862. Ed. Jacques Bompard. Paris, 1946.

Lettres de Proudhon à sa Femme. Ed. Suzanne Henneguy. Paris, 1950.

Portrait de Jésus. Ed. Robert Aron. Paris, 1951.

4. WORKS ON PROUDHON

Amoudruz, Madeleine. *Proudhon et l'Europe.* Paris, 1945.

Berthod, Aimé. *P.-J. Proudhon et la Propriété; un Socialisme pour les Paysans.* Paris, 1910.

Bertrand, A. *P.-J. Proudhon et les Lyonnais.* Paris, 1904.

Boniface, Joseph. *La Belgique Calomniée, réponse à M. Proudhon.* Brussels, 1867.

Bouglé, C. *La Sociologie de Proudhon.* Paris, 1911.

Bourgeat, Jacques. *Proudhon, Père du Socialisme Français.* Paris, 1943.

Bourgeois, Nicholas. *Les Théories du Droit International Chez Proudhon.* Paris, 1926.

Bourguin, Hubert. *Proudhon.* Paris, 1901.

Bourguin, Hubert. *Les Rapports entre Proudhon et Karl Marx.* Lille, 1892.

Brogan, D. W. *Proudhon.* London, 1936.

Desjardins, Arthur. *P.-J. Proudhon, Sa Vie, Ses Oeuvres, Sa Doctrine.* 2 vols. Paris, 1896.

Diehl, Karl. *P.-J. Proudhon, Seine Lehre und Sein Leben.* 3 vols. Jena, 1888–96.

Dolléans, Edouard. *Proudhon.* Paris, 1948.

Dolléans, Edouard, and J.-L. Puech. *Proudhon et la Révolution de 1848.* Paris, 1948.

Droz, Edouard. *P.-J. Proudhon.* Paris, 1909.

Duprat, Jeanne. *Proudhon, Sociologue et Moraliste.* Paris, 1929.